Jonathan Edwards

Perry Miller

The University of Massachusetts Press
Amherst, 1981

Copyright © 1949 by
William Sloane Associates, Inc.
Reprinted by permission of
William Morrow & Company, Inc.
New introduction by Donald Weber
Copyright © 1981 by
The University of Massachusetts Press
All rights reserved
Printed in the United States of America

Library of Congress Cataloging in Publication Data
Miller, Perry, 1905–1963.
Jonathan Edwards.
(New England writers series)
Reprint. Originally published: New York :
W. Sloane Associates, 1949. (The American men of
letters series) With new introd.
Bibliography: p.
Includes index.
1. Edwards, Jonathan, 1703–1758.   I. Title.
II. Series.   III. Series: American men of letters
series.
BX7260.E3M5   1981   285.8′092′4   81–4496
ISBN 0–87023–328–9   AACR2

Contents

INTRODUCTION

PERRY MILLER AND THE RECOVERY
OF JONATHAN EDWARDS

DONALD WEBER

WRITING IN 1915 to Carl Van Doren, Stuart Pratt Sherman offered the following evaluation of Paul Elmer More's essay on Jonathan Edwards for the newly conceived *Cambridge History of American Literature*:

> I am returning to-day the Edwards manuscript. I have studied reasonably hard to determine mainly what sort of comment you expected to get from me upon it. You ask two questions. First whether I think P.E.M. has treated Edwards with injustice and in the manner of Beecher. To which I answer in the negative. It seems to me that he has brought out with force and clearness the intellectual vigor and integrity of the man and also the mystical and poetical elements in him. . . . The second would be valuable. I should think it would. In the present treatment he has a little too much the air perhaps of a wreck on the remote sands of time. The addition of a few sentences showing his connection with the current of subsequent thought and indeed with the moral consciousness of New England would make him more of a *figure* in the literary history.[1]

Along with Van Wyck Brooks and other early twentieth-century critics of American culture, the editors of the *Cambridge History* wished to stimulate interest in the national past;[2] to create, in Brooks's famous phrase, a "usable past" for modern

America. The figure of Jonathan Edwards, however, still appeared too remote, too inaccessible to be included in the pantheon of American writers who could speak of the needs of an America at the end of innocence. He was still perceived, however sympathetically portrayed by the humanist critic More, as a discarded wreck—an image that looks back to Oliver Wendell Holmes's "The Deacon's Masterpiece," where the "one-hoss shay" of the ramshackle New England theology simply falls apart, and forward to the progressivist condemnation of Edwards as an "anachronism."

In 1949, a generation after the *Cambridge History*, Perry Miller overturned 200 years of (as he called it) "deciding against Edwards," declaring him the "spokesman, almost the first, for the deep, the most rooted, the really native tradition." Indeed, Miller went on to assert that "no American succeeded better . . . in generalizing his experience into the meaning of America." [3] The cryptic "meaning of America" was a key phrase for Miller; his absorption with the "idea" of America, following his famous jungle epiphany, has become part of the legend—Miller himself is now a *figure* in the history of American studies, his explorations into the Puritan psyche the subject of meta-historical inquiry. His *Jonathan Edwards* has been termed, in this respect, "strikingly personal," a touchstone of Miller's historiographic art.[4] According to Alan Heimert, Miller's " 'approach' to history can never be understood without considerable attention to his study of the mind of Edwards." [5] Thus *Jonathan Edwards* leads us to the heart of Miller's vision of America. It also marks a turning point in the history of Edwards criticism: here was an Edwards shaken loose from the weight of revival brimstone; no longer rebuked as the misanthropic author of "Sinners in the Hands of an Angry God," but presented as a "modern," better understood in the twentieth century than in his own time. "At last," R. W. B. Lewis wrote of Miller's restoration, "a Jonathan Edwards fully realized." And a grateful Reinhold Niebuhr, perhaps recognizing a kinship with this "backwoods genius," pronounced that "it was very important for the understanding of our culture that someone should give a fuller appreciation of the significance of Edwards" for our time.[6]

There was also a wary cry of disbelief voiced by some critics who were not convinced by Miller's provocative thesis. Although Edwards was a vital figure in the culture, he was surely not, they insisted, a contemporary. Moreover, Miller's notion that the bulk of Edwards' writings was an immense cryptogram that only a modern mind could penetrate irked many commentators (Joseph Haroutunian, for example) who could not dissociate Edwards from his orthodox Christian context.[7] Interesting in this respect is Miller's reversal at the end of "The Marrow of Puritan Divinity" (1935), where he had originally concluded that Edwards was "the first consistent and authentic Calvinist in New England." Reprinting the "Marrow" essay in *Errand into the Wilderness* (1956), Miller called that sentence "a total miscomprehension," and, referring to his later view, formed by his recognition of the impact of Newton and Locke on Edwards' thought, along with (in my view) the influence of the "critical realism" of neo-orthodoxy, he now explained that what he had meant to say was that "Edwards brushed aside the (by his day) rusty mechanism of the covenant to forge a fresh statement of the central Protestant definition of man's plight in a universe which God created." [8] This new appreciation, with its Niebuhrian overtones, suggests the cultural context within which *Edwards* may be placed. For Miller's Edwards is a figure fashioned by and in many ways a response to the religious and intellectual climate of post–World War II America. In order to understand the achievement of *Jonathan Edwards* we need to review the image of Edwards in American cultural history, from Sherman's "wreck on the remote sands of time" to Miller's controversial recovery of "our" Edwards.

I

The modern revaluation of the American literary tradition was not kind in its estimate of Jonathan Edwards. A rising generation of literary historians in search of a usable past discovered that much of the cultural sterility of contemporary life could be traced to the baneful influence of colonial Puritanism. To Van Wyck Brooks, for example, Edwards represented "the infinite inflexibility of the upper levels of the American mind" in contrast to the "flexibility" of Ben Franklin. But Brooks did not invoke Franklin as exemplum, for he was the source for that negative "current of catchpenny opportunism" which, in Brooks's view, had come to mark "the atmosphere of our contemporary business life." [9] In a recent biography James Hoopes has shown that Brooks was not original in his use of Edwards and Franklin as symbolic of the split in the American psyche.[10] Brooks appropriated the example from his Harvard mentor, Barrett Wendell, whose *Literary History of America* (1900) summarized:

> In Jonathan Edwards we found theoretical Puritanism, divorced from life, proclaiming more uncompromisingly than ever that human nature is damnable. . . . Franklin, by living as well and as sensibly as he could, was demonstrating that, at least in America, unaided human nature could develop in an earthly shape which looked quite as far from damnable as that of any Puritan parson.[11]

Although in 1891 Wendell had published a sympathetic biography of Cotton Mather (the first Harvard effort at recovering the Puritan tradition), his stance was prophetic of the evaluation Edwards would receive in the 1920s.

In 1915 Carl Van Doren was concerned that Edwards be faithfully portrayed, not in the manner of older stereotypes, but rather with a new justice befitting a revised literary history of the country. Yet his introduction to an edition of the selected writings of Edwards and Franklin (1920) belied that earlier request. Van Doren's Edwards and Franklin, in the tradition of Brooks and Wendell, were symbols of warring establishments striving for "the mastery of their age." While Brooks found little to admire in either figure, Van Doren's sympathies were clearly reserved for the leader of the American Enlightenment: Edwards was a "dim figure" from a remote past, while Franklin was "contemporaneous, fresh, full of vitality." Indeed, Van Doren's Edwards continued the nineteenth-century stereotype. His theology removed him from "the humaner concerns" and locked him into a "mighty, and appalling . . . defense of High Calvinism"; as a result, Edwards was shackled by a theology so outworn that its conclusions forced him to challenge "the march of reason . . . and the march of democracy." A thorough-going Calvinist, Edwards could only perceive in the burgeoning rationalism of the eighteenth century "insurrection and error." [12]

Of course Van Doren did not inveigh against Edwards (as Parrington later would) for battling the forces of reason and democracy. Van Doren realized that the founders' dream of a "high crystal-walled city" had "melted away," only to be replaced by the "grayer . . . towns" planted by their sons. The only tribute Van Doren could offer, though, was that Edwards "was tragically born out of his true century" into a culture swiftly moving away from all that his theology represented. Concluding his cultural comparison, Van Doren identified his own time, not with an "Edwards defeated," but as "we . . . [,] the sons of Franklin." [13]

Another of the sons of Ben was V. L. Parrington, whose *Main Currents in American Thought* answered Brooks's call for a usable past.[14] Published in 1927, *Main Currents* was overwhelmingly acclaimed as the first comprehensive analysis of the American mind, the most convincing account of the development of the national literature yet produced by an American scholar. Though later scholars, notably Lionel Trilling, have dismissed Parrington's three-volume opus, emphasizing its simplistic, doctrinaire assumptions, *Main Currents* was, in Howard Mumford Jones's words, a "brilliant publishing success." Even Perry Miller, whose first published article attacked Parrington's categories, confirmed what Jones recalled as the "tingling sense of discovery" upon reading Parrington: "Anyone alive in 1926 who was responding to the fresh interest in things American which blew like a gale across the country will remember the excitement of Parrington." [15] *Main Currents* filled a vacuum in literary/cultural criticism by defining what was then deemed the American tradition—namely, the Jeffersonian mind in politics, morality, and art.

Edwards, of course, was not a hero of that tradition. He represented, along with the Mather dynasty, a dam against the onrushing waters of eighteenth-century liberalism. In Parrington's scenario, Edwards found himself with the impossible task of defending his theology to a people on the threshold of revolution. The "rugged virtues" which "animated the life of the average New Englander" could not be reconciled with a harsh, unforgiving theology of damnation. As a result, Edwards became "a rigid disciplinarian," defending the old theology "against the developing experience of his generation." Therein lay the tragedy of his life. As a youth his almost mystical turn of mind was warped by an obsession with religious dogma and theological controversy. Instead of embracing the revolutionary spirit of the future, Edwards followed "a path that led back to an absolutist past." [16]

Parrington did not bemoan that reactionary choice, however. Edwards' decision to defend a dying theology was indeed fortunate, for his unrelenting defense hastened the demise of Calvinism. Once its "horrors . . . were disclosed to common view," Parrington recounted, "the system was doomed." [17] Thus the Edwardsean tradition, inherently anti-democratic, provoked the masses to rebel; Edwards' dismissal and defeat, then, not only proved a turning point in the history of American culture, but symbolized the death of the Mather dynasty and marked the triumph of Jeffersonian ideology.

Perhaps the most strident attack upon Edwards from the progressivist stance was issued by Henry B. Parkes, whose 1930 biography, *The Fiery Puritan* stated emphatically in the epilogue (fittingly titled "The Blight upon Posterity"): "If Edwards had never lived, there would be to-day no blue laws, no societies for the suppression of vice, no Volstead Act [the law enacting Prohibition]." For Parkes, Edwards survived as a "living and baneful influence," his legacy a "dark stream" that continued to pollute the country's liberal tributaries.[18] In retrospect, Parkes's attack was the last gasp of a cultural reflex that sought to trace America's ills to the Puritans.

II

In the decade between 1930 and 1940 three studies of Edwards appeared. Parkes's shrill analysis, the first of these, reinforced older stereotypes; by 1940, however, in a landmark of Edwards scholarship, Ola Winslow had rehabilitated the figure of Edwards.[19] Why did Jonathan Edwards so interest the 1930s? Why was Edwards and the Puritan legacy in general beginning to be viewed as vital to the American tradition? An answer may be found in the often-noted shift in literary and religious sensibility during the decade. The figures who enraged Parrington (the Mathers and Edwards) or those who left him virtually silent (Melville, to cite the most famous example) were rediscovered by a generation responsive to the aesthetics of paradox and ambiguity as well as to the doctrines of original sin and the necessity of transforming grace. The generation who embraced Hawthorne, Melville, and Henry James located an alternate American imagination distinct from that embodied in Parrington's democratic heroes.[20] They also discovered that the writings of Jonathan Edwards and his Puritan forebears expressed a metaphysics uniquely applicable to the condition of an America in a state of economic and psychic depression.

In a well-known essay Henry F. May has stated that the "recovery of American religious history really began in the 1930s." [21] The recovery was effected by historians who challenged the progressive tradition in historiography and by religious thinkers who rejected the cosmic optimism attendant with its ideology. Scholars have pointed, in this respect, to the career of Reinhold Niebuhr—from his disillusionment with the Social Gospel to his formulation of a revitalized Protestantism —as paradigmatic of the shift in historical perspective. The neo-orthodox stance, according to this account, influenced literary and historical assumptions by highlighting man's "natural" limitations yet reminding him of his potential for aggressive social reform with the aid of visionary faith.[22]

The neo-orthodox movement drew heavily on contemporary European thinkers, notably Karl Barth and Paul Tillich. But a major source for its perspective came from the American Puritan heritage. The call for "realism" in social and ethical discourse, the effort to reveal man as hereditary sinner yet capable of true Christian virtue, recalls the doctrines of Jonathan Edwards. It is not surprising, therefore, as Sydney Ahlstrom has noted, that the restoration of Edwards' reputation began in the 1930s.[23] The mood of neo-orthodoxy was one of "paradox and the contradictions of history." [24] Edwards, too, was confronted with paradox and ambiguity. His attempt to reconcile the providential meaning of the Great Awakening with the reality of a backsliding New England (or, say, the implications of his Uncle Hawley's suicide), his burden to defend the principles of Christian orthodoxy, and his exhortations to a complacent Northampton congregation to reform spoke powerfully to the neo-orthodox Jeremiahs of the 1930s. Edwards' message and career thus attained a new relevance.

The figure of Edwards also furnished an example of the prophetic mode often ascribed to the spokesmen for neo-orthodoxy. Their desire for a church that could be continuous with and fulfill that of the New Testament community found an important analogue in Edwards' writings,[25] especially his treatises penned on the eve of and during the Great Awakening, *The History of the Work of Redemption* and *Some Thoughts on the Revival*. For example, H. Richard Niebuhr's *The Kingdom of God in America* (1937), one of the most influential books of neo-orthodoxy, consciously invoked Edwards as a model. In the preface, Niebuhr confessed that his "greatest hope" was that *The Kingdom* might "serve even as a stepping stone to the work of some American Augustine who will write a *City of God* that will trace the story of the eternal city in its relations to modern civilization instead of to ancient Rome, or of Jonathan Edwards *redivivus* who will bring down to our own time the *History of the Work of Redemption.*" *The Kingdom* was Niebuhr's contribution to the history of redemption in the mode of Jonathan Edwards—a chronicle of America's revival tradition, from "our national conversion" during the Awakening (our "awakening into national self-consciousness") through the revivalism of Charles G. Finney. A jeremiad directed at a nation in sore need of a revival of religion, *The Kingdom* invoked Edwards in order "to rouse to new life the party of the kingdom of God." [26]

This shift in literary/theological perspective was the subject of Austin Warren's 1932 essay review of Parkes's *Fiery Puritan*, and *Jonathan Edwards* (1932) by A. C. McGiffert, Jr. Noting the effort then underway "to reveal and acclaim the true Edwards," Warren made an apparently astute observation about McGiffert: his "principal admiration for Edwards," Warren remarked, "reflects the neo-Calvinistic 'Crisis Theology' of Karl Barth which is currently fashionable amongst younger Protestant thinkers." [27] McGiffert, however, would have denied the neo-orthodox label. In writing his *Jonathan Edwards* he "had no desire to promote orthodoxy"; in fact, he was totally unaware of any "ground swell toward orthodoxy" in the early 1930s.[28] Nevertheless, McGiffert's study contributed to the ground swell of Edwards scholarship. It contained a severe critique of the liberal wing of contemporary Protestantism: Edwards, McGiffert wrote, "found himself in a situation similar to ours"—a religious "depression" evidenced by the "saccharrine sentimentality" of a liberal Protestantism in need of the unsweetened truths of Calvinism. McGiffert's Edwards was thus a figure who could provide answers to the religious crisis of the 1930s.[29]

Perhaps the Prelude to Joseph Haroutunian's influential *Piety versus Moralism* (1932), the classic study of the Edwardsean theology and its eventual demise, suggests most clearly the neo-orthodox sensibility that helped ignite interest in Edwards: "It is probable that a revival of the 'tragic sense of life,' together with the wisdom and sobriety which grew out of it, should be forthcoming. It is necessary that men discover the truths once signified by the doctrines of divine sovereignty and divine grace, of predestination and election, of depravity and regeneration." [30] Divine sovereignty, the means of grace, original sin—these are the themes of Christian orthodoxy and, of course, the subjects of Jonathan Edwards' major treatises. It is not surprising that a generation inspired by the teachings of the Niebuhrs would find another spiritual master in Edwards. As Clyde Holbrook correctly predicted in an essay surveying the history of Edwards and his "detractors": "another age may return to find in this man an interpretation of humanity and god which the liberalism of the post-Edwardsean era falsified by its extravagant optimism about man and its sentimentality about God." [31] Locating in Edwards the claims of orthodoxy against the "falsifying" liberalism of his own time, Holbrook articulated the assumptions of those who during the neo-orthodox revival of the 1930s (and later, of the 1950s) would embrace the colonial "realist" as "our" Edwards.

Ola Winslow's prize-winning biography of 1940 did not attempt to remake Edwards into a contemporary; her effort to rehabilitate the figure of Edwards was directed instead at the historiographic method of Parkes's harsh caricature. Answering Thomas H. Johnson's call for a biographer who would examine the vast piles of letters, sermons, and diaries by and about Edwards and his society which were available in various manuscript collections,[32] Winslow embedded Edwards in the social history of early eighteenth-century New England; she detailed Edwards' family life, his frontier childhood and Yale education; she revealed an Edwards embroiled in family feuds and occupied with bitter religious controversies that characterized fractious Northampton throughout the century.

Perry Miller recognized the importance of Winslow's subject—"Edwards 'the man' "—and congratulated her for setting Edwards "in his period." [33] But Miller was left bemused by her conclusions. For Winslow's Edwards was "a thinker denied the gathering of his own harvest," "a leader forgotten," though a figure whose "personal story bears inspection." Yet after the story had been told, from triumph to eventual tragedy, Winslow could only evaluate Edwards in words ironically reminiscent of Parrington and Brooks: Edwards' mistake, she concluded, was "in choosing to speak through an outworn, dogmatic system" rather than formulating his "new truth" in a form commensurate with its message. Thus her Edwards "lacked the mellowness and flexibility" to judge with detachment the theology he inherited; in effect, Edwards was chained to an anachronistic Calvinism, a "bondage" which "seems almost a tragic pity." [34] Miller must have bristled at this estimate. If Edwards the *man* was rendered in Winslow's biography, Edwards the American *artist* was yet to be unveiled.

III

There is undoubtedly a personal dimension to Perry Miller's portrait of Jonathan Edwards—an embattled intellectual hounded by the crass businessmen of the Connecticut Valley, fighting their money, power, and Arminianism with the weapons of his "modern" mind—the "lone wolf" of Northampton one might style him.[35] Edwards' response to the mind of the Valley was heroic, in Miller's view, for he was able to synthesize the revolutionary advances of Newton and Locke and adapt them to the needs of an America in crisis. Against the Arminianist challenge of Charles Chauncy (from whose theology grew the seeds of nineteenth-century Unitarianism and the Social Gospel of the early twentieth) Edwards answered with a new intellectual formulation of Protestantism which for Miller signaled "America's sudden leap into modernity." By modernity, Miller meant that Edwards abandoned a metaphysics based on feudal dogma and, true to his Lockean inheritance, set forth a theology of "ideas" grounded in "experience," validated by the testament of history and nature. He was America's first great artist, as well as prophet pronouncing judgment upon the emerging "free and catholic" sensibility of Boston. Thus Edwards became a modern Jeremiah awakening his people to "the terror of modern man, the terror of insecurity." It was Edwards' burden, in Miller's account, to remind America that "its practice ha[d] become hopelessly sundered from its ethos." Repudiating the ideological stance of the antirevivalists, Edwards symbolized "the most formidable defiance yet leveled against the liberal spirit, against the cult of progress" in the history of the culture.[36]

Of course, Edwards' modernity was not to be found in his rebuke to the American business ethic; rather, it was his response to and participation in the Great Awakening—the cultural crisis Miller believed fundamental for an understanding of America—which made him the most modern man of his age. The idea of revival was central to Miller's vision of America; it was, he asserted in *The Life of the Mind in America*, "the central mode of this culture's search for national identity." [37] Edwards joined that search in *A Faithful Narrative* and *Some Thoughts on the Revival*, both written during the frenzy of revival effusions, and later, after the flames had been extinguished, in *Religious Affections* and the very popular *Memoir of David Brainerd*. The experience of revival, however, finally proved enigmatic, as Edwards confessed at one point in *A Faithful Narrative*, his subjective chronicle of Northampton's "famed awakening":

> There have indeed been some few instances of impressions on persons' imaginations, that have been something mysterious to me, and I have been at a loss about them; for though it has been exceeding evident to me by many things that appeared in them, both then (when they related to them) and afterwards, that

they indeed had a great sense of the spiritual excellency of divine things accompanying them; yet I have not been able well to satisfy myself, whether their imaginary ideas have been more than could naturally arise from their spiritual sense of things. However, I have used the utmost caution in such cases; great care has been taken both in public and in private to teach persons the difference between what is spiritual and what is merely imaginary.[38]

The Awakening posed Edwards with the dilemmas of interpreting the perplexing ambiguities of history. Its excesses (his Uncle Hawley's suicide, the book-burning antics of James Davenport) thrust upon Edwards "a concept of the career of things in time"—or, as Miller defines it throughout *Edwards*, the problem of history, of "America's role in the sequence of things throughout time, which is what men call history." [39]

As if to startle his readers into a recognition of Edwards' modernity, Miller opened each chapter of the intellectual biography with epigraphs from a gallery of moderns: Bergson, Eliot, Kafka, William James, Veblen. Only in the last chapter, significantly entitled "History," does Miller dramatically depart from his modernist texts, citing Augustine. The choice is indeed fitting. It recalls, first, Edwards the Christian historian, providentially plotting the signs of the times for revelations of God's will. At the same time the example of Augustine highlights Edwards' distance from medieval historiography; his thoroughly modern (again, in Miller's view) consciousness of the "historicity" of history, the problem of time, and so on. Most important, however, by linking together these two giants of the Reformed tradition, Miller wished to remind us of their relevance to *his* own time. Both Edwards and Augustine sought to fathom the meaning of historical process; both sought an answer to the problem of history through art. More than any chapter in the biography, the coda to the *Edwards* leads us to the heart of Miller's vision of Jonathan Edwards as artist; it also reveals (in its invocation of Paul Tillich) the importance of the neo-orthodox mode—especially, the example of Reinhold Niebuhr—for Miller's understanding of the Edwardsean legacy to America.[40]

IV

Both Perry Miller and Reinhold Niebuhr shared a passion for the intellectual and religious history of America; from their very different affiliations they both recorded the tragic story of the failure of American experience to correspond to the ideal—or, as Miller phrased it in *From Colony to Province*, "a failure of reality to conform to theory." [41] Niebuhr reviewed the second volume of *The New England Mind* and *Jonathan Edwards* and later joined in the testament to Miller's achievement. "Perry Miller and Our Embarrassment," Niebuhr's *Harvard Review* appreciation, records an indebtedness to Miller's revaluation of the Puritans. Miller's act of demystification, Niebuhr wrote, "allowed these heroes and villains to speak . . . to our generation." After Miller, the Puritans "ceased to embarrass our democratic hearts," for their drama "simply revealed that there were many settings in which the human capacity for self-deception and lust for power could be expressed." Thus Miller's errand issued in an "ironic" exposé, in Niebuhr's words, of "our vaunted democratic civilization." Niebuhr clearly perceived Miller as a "realist," though not within the fold of neo-orthodoxy, nevertheless "a believing unbeliever" in the ironies of American history.[42]

Miller's own debt to Niebuhr has been noted before, usually in terms of a shared "ironic" historiographic perspective, but the question of Niebuhr's intellectual influence remains unanswered. Miller did review Niebuhr's *Faith and History* and *Pious and Secular America*, and there are references to Niebuhr scattered through the essays. Miller opened his review of *Faith and History* (published the same year as *Edwards*) by recalling the "shock" that Niebuhr's critiques sent through an American Protestantism that "had lost touch with its own

creed." Against the "cosmic optimism," "ethical compla-
cency," and assumptions of "universal progress," Niebuhr
"spoke for a fundamental tradition" which, although "driven
underground," had appeared earlier in Jonathan Edwards.
Significantly, Niebuhr's strategy of critique was to use the
"new" science of Freud and Marx (as Edwards had appropriated Newton and Locke) "to show that the scientists and
psychologists do not comprehend their own data." [43] The evidence from this review and from various passages in *Edwards*
suggests that Miller understood Niebuhr as a Jonathan Edwards redivivus; in turn, Miller fashioned his Edwards as a
Jeremiah in the neo-orthodox grain, a critical realist exposing
the naive doctrines of American exceptionalism in his own
time, after the millennial fires of the Awakening had died
away, and to Miller's, in the wake of God's judgment on
postwar America.

In their effort to show America that "its practice" was
"hopelessly sundered from its ethos," both Edwards and Niebuhr discovered the problem of history—the ambiguity of
Hawley's suicide; the ironies of Cold War arrogance. Sadly,
however, Edwards' heroic labors were "lost to the American
tradition," as Miller summarized 200 years of negative response to the figure of Edwards:

> the belief that he was an anachronism, a retrograde leader of a
> rear-guard action against science, became a premise of Amer-
> ica's opinion about its past. Even in the twentieth century, when
> the smiling aspects largely ceased to smile, and Hawthorne, Mel-
> ville, and Mark Twain were re-evaluated, Edwards remained
> identified with what Dr. Holmes called "the nebulous realm of
> asiatic legend," and therefore could not be supposed of value
> for critical realism. Edwards was thus relegated, through failure
> of comprehension, even further into an unusable past.

The telling phrase is "critical realism," the epithet linked re-
flexively with the neo-orthodox stance. And the following
passage, appearing right after Miller's counter-progressive lit-

any, could be taken for the preface to *The Irony of American History*:

> a distinctive mark of the contemporary crisis has been a rediscovery of history—not only of the reality of the crimes and terrors of the past, made convincing by those of the present, but still more of the applicability of the world's experience to America. Conflicts, anxieties, and cruelties, which in the air of freedom were supposed the lot of other men and nations but never of the United States, now appear as much the heritage of Americans as of Europeans. Faith in democracy can no longer be maintained by ignorance of the recurrent lessons of history.

Thus Miller's Edwards, the colonial Niebuhr invoking the lessons of history, "called upon America not to submit to time-worn dogma, but to surrender its pretensions to exceptionalism, to acknowledge its share in the propensity of the race"—to become, in effect, a humble America.[44]

Reinhold Niebuhr called for humility too. The Edwardsean (or better, perhaps "Millerean") dimension of his vision can be discerned in this passage from "The Dilemma of Modern Man" (1947), later incorporated into the opening chapter of *Faith and History*: "The one unifying element in all strands of modern culture was the idea of progress. We had faith in a redemptive history. This faith, which suppposedly made all other interpretations of life completely incredible, is now progressively disclosing itself as the most incredible of all interpretations of life. This refutation of the culture of modern man by contemporary history may be regarded as the real spiritual crisis of our day."[45] Niebuhr, like Edwards before him, summoned a Gospel faith and preached the somber realities of human nature in response to crisis. For Edwards, the crisis issued from the Arminians, who, "like modern sociologists," clung "to the fallacy of a causal sequence with no inner coherence"; for Niebuhr, the betrayal of the dream was linked to the latter-day Arminianist ideology of the American Way.[46]

Midway in the "History" chapter Miller quotes Paul Tillich on the distinction between "nonhistorical" and "historical" interpretations of history. In contrast to the nonhistorical mode (read naturalistic, cyclic, salvation *from* time and history) Edwards penned "the first truly historical interpretation in American literature"—that is, a progressive history of salvation, a history interpreted "through history itself." [47] Edwards' historicism, in Miller's reading, was a prophetic answer to the "naturalistic histories" of both the eighteenth and twentieth centuries; moreover, his method offered a solution to "the contemporary crisis, wherein the nonhistorical has at last been challenged." [48] Both the American Augustine and the American Tillich, as well as the link between the nascent Reformed tradition and its modern analogue, Edwards had already solved what in the 1930s Tillich had labelled as *the* problem of the modern period—that of creating historical order out of apparent historical chaos. [49]

Of course Perry Miller did not share either Niebuhr's or Edwards' faith in redemptive history or belief in the Gospels. Still, as an "atheist for Niebuhr" (in Morton White's description) Miller felt an intellectual kinship with the contemporary Jeremiah and clearly recognized in Niebuhr a type of America's first native artist. [50] If Parrington's Edwards led the country back into an unusable past, Miller's anticipated the future; appropriately, Niebuhr rejected (as did the young Miller) the progressivist ideology of Parrington and, like Edwards, imposed history and nature upon the popular doctrine of American destiny. Miller recovered and proclaimed Edwards a major American artist because, like Hawthorne, Twain, and Niebuhr after him, Edwards refused to smile at the darker aspects of American life.

V

In retrospect, Perry Miller's intellectual biography of Jonathan Edwards was his own attempt to make Edwards usable; to recover a figure who for more than a generation had been labeled a reactionary. The *Edwards* should thus be read as yet another of Miller's errands into a wilderness of misinformed, misguided opinion about the American past. With the same dramatic intensity that had characterized his rehabilitation of the Puritans, Miller overcame the limitations of the traditions in Edwards studies he inherited and virtually ignited a revival of scholarship. Significantly, too, the *Edwards* holds a crucial transitional place in the chronology of Miller's writings. As Alan Heimert has noted, "It was not till after World War II" that Miller "explored the relationship of ideas . . . to the assumptions of a whole society." [51] Miller explored the dialectic of mind and history in *From Colony to Province* (1953), generally regarded as his historiographic masterpiece. Yet the *Edwards* was the necessary prolegomen to that work. As Miller stood behind Edwards, watching the historian (or, at times, theologian, anthropologist, psychologist) confront the meaning of the revival, Miller fashioned a laboratory to observe how ideas impinge upon the mind in historical process—or, to recall his later description of the burden and dilemma of modern intellectuals: "the responsibility of mind in a civilization of machines." Above all else, Edwards preserved the integrity of mind "amid the terrifying operations of the machine" [52]—a terror which Miller embryonically located in the Arminian metaphysic.

In retrospect, too, Miller's *Edwards* effected a kind of "paradigm shift" in the appreciation of Edwards; its critical stance objectified the growing recognition (through the 1930s and 1940s) of Edwards' importance and, at the same time, became the locus classicus of Edwards scholarship for a new generation. Though in 1949 the response to the *Edwards* was divided, Miller looked back to it with "considerable pleasure"; in contrast to the first volume of *The New England Mind* (1939), whose reception Miller later deemed "a sorry mess," he recalled that the *Edwards* "excited full and genuinely critical discussion" of its subject and enabled its author "to assume a kind of leadership" in Edwards studies.[53] As the first General Editor of the Yale *Works of Jonathan Edwards*, Miller explained the current Edwards revival by citing the impact of recent history:

> The very existence of the project is itself testimony to the deepening appreciation in the mid-twentieth century of the importance of Edwards to the intellectual as well as the religious history of America. A generation or so ago, outside a restricted circle of professional theologians, he was popularly known only as one who had preached a distasteful and happily outmoded brand of hell-fire and brimstone. There was, in fact, a general disposition to pass him over as an anachronism, as retrograde. Recent events in world history have no doubt stimulated drastic re-examination of such complacent assumptions. Whether because of that prodding or because of the logic of intellectual development, we find today a new urgency to confront and reinterpret the historic, philosophical and theological cruxes with which Edwards grappled so courageously.[54]

That new urgency, prompted at least on one level by the hell-fire of war, was echoed by H. Richard Niebuhr (who also inspired fresh readings of Edwards) in an address commemorating the two-hundredth anniversary of Edwards' death: "We have changed our minds about the truth of the many things he said. No rather, our minds have been changed by what has happened to us in our history. We have seen evil somewhat as he saw it, not because we desired to see it, but because it thrust itself upon us." [55] Far from being unusable, the figure of Edwards offered a heroic example to a generation facing an anxious future.

In the thirty years since *Jonathan Edwards*, Edwards has become enshrined in the American pantheon; Miller's biography, however, has been the target of revisionist challenge: Conrad Cherry has re-emphasized the traditionality of Edwards' Calvinism; Roland Delattre has modified in important ways Miller's distinction between the objective and inherent good in terms of Edwards' concept of "beauty"; John F. Wilson has resolved the debate over the "modernity" of Edwards' historical method, clarifying the tradition of Reformed historiography that shaped Edwards' vision; and Norman Fiering and Wallace Anderson have argued against Miller's formulation of Edwards' Lockean inheritance.[56] Still, the critiques of a later generation should not blur the achievement of the *Edwards*. To be sure, the Edwards who emerges in Miller is a figure unnaturally forced into a variety of modernist poses that simply cannot be defended. Miller claimed too much for Edwards' "modernity"—perhaps an ironic example of the constraints of progressive/counter-progressive categories of his time. But the fact remains that Miller revolutionized the study of Edwards. In the process of unraveling the meaning of Jonathan Edwards, he found yet another touchstone that could register the meaning of America.

NOTES

1. Stuart Pratt Sherman to Carl Van Doren, 30 October 1915, in *Life and Letters of Stuart Pratt Sherman,* ed. Jacob Zeitlin and Homer Woodbridge, 2 vols. (New York: Farrar and Rinehart, 1929), 1: 263. The "Beecher" whom Van Doren was thinking of is Henry Ward, whose judgment upon "Sinners in the Hands of an Angry God" is quoted in the second volume of the *Cambridge History*: "I think a person of moral sensibilities, alone at midnight, reading that awful discourse, would well nigh go crazy" (*The Cambridge History of American Literature,* ed. W. P. Trent et al. [New York: Macmillan, 1943], 2: 215–16).
2. Sherman to Van Doren, 18 September 1913, *Life and Letters,* 1: 257.
3. Perry Miller, *Jonathan Edwards* (New York: Sloane, 1949), pp. 270, xiii, xiv.
4. David A. Hollinger, "Perry Miller and Philosophical History," *History and Theory,* 7 (1968), 189. The best evaluation of Miller is by Robert Middlekauff. See his "Perry Miller," in *Pastmasters: Some Essays on American Historians,* ed. Marcus Cunliffe and Robin W. Winks (New York: Harper & Row, 1969), 167–90; the literature on Miller continues to grow. See Gene Wise, *American Historical Explanations,* 2d ed. rev. (Minneapolis: University of Minnesota Press, 1980), especially pp. 315–43, and John C. Crowell, "Perry Miller as Historian: A Bibliography of Evaluations," *Bulletin of Bibliography,* 34 (1977), 77–85.
5. Alan Heimert, "Perry Miller: An Appreciation," *Harvard Review,* 2 (Winter–Spring 1964), 35.
6. R. W. B. Lewis, "The Drama of Jonathan Edwards," *Hudson*

Review, 3 (1950), 135; Reinhold Niebuhr, review of *Jonathan Edwards* by Perry Miller, *The Nation*, 169 (31 December 1949), 648.

7. Although he was dismayed about an Edwards stripped of his Calvinist heritage, Joseph Haroutunian still admitted that Miller had "recovered Edwards." Haroutunian, review of *Jonathan Edwards* by Perry Miller, *Theology Today*, 7 (1950–51), 554.

8. Perry Miller, *Errand into the Wilderness* (New York: Harper & Row, 1956), pp. 98, 49, 50.

9. Van Wyck Brooks, " 'Highbrow' and 'Lowbrow,' " in *America's Coming-of-Age* (Garden City, N.Y.: Doubleday, 1958), pp. 6, 5. For a discussion of early twentieth-century American literary history see Howard M. Jones, *The Theory of American Literature* (Ithaca: Cornell University Press, 1965), pp. 118–59 and Robert E. Spiller, "The Battle of the Books," in *Literary History of the United States*, ed. Robert E. Spiller et al. (London: Macmillan, 1963), pp. 1135–56.

10. James Hoopes, *Van Wyck Brooks: In Search of American Culture* (Amherst: University of Massachusetts Press, 1977), pp. 60–61.

11. Barrett Wendell, *A Literary History of America* (New York: Scribners, 1900), pp. 102–3. On Wendell, see Alan Heimert's introduction to Wendell's biography, *Cotton Mather: The Puritan Priest* (New York: Harcourt, 1963), pp. vii–xxxix.

12. Carl Van Doren, ed., *Benjamin Franklin and Jonathan Edwards: Selections from their Writings* (New York: Scribners, 1920), pp. ix, xii, xvi–xvii, xix.

13. Ibid., p. xxxiii. By 1930, however, in a review of H. B. Parkes's *Jonathan Edwards: The Fiery Puritan*, Van Doren had become more sympathetic. Edwards' life still remained tragic, but it was a tragedy "profound and moving." This "metaphysical Messiah," in Van Doren's new account, by virtue of his "eloquence," "singleness of . . . aims," and "blamelessness of conduct" had attained an eminence throughout New England. Van Doren had come to view Edwards as a misunderstood yet important figure whose "superb" treatises still went "unread," and whose life remained "incomprehensible, even repulsive" to those few who could be brought to consider it (Carl Van Doren, "A Metaphysical Messiah," New York *Herald Tribune Books*, 21 September 1930, p. 7).

14. See, for example, Parrington's conclusion to the chapter on Franklin: "What was best in that century Franklin made his own. In his modesty, his willingness to compromise, his open-mindedness, his clear and luminous understanding, his charity—above all, in his desire to subdue the ugly facts of society to some rational scheme of things—he proved himself a great and useful man, one of the greatest and most useful whom America has produced" (V. L.

Parrington, *Main Currents in American Thought*, vol. 1, *The Colonial Mind* [New York: Harcourt, 1927, 1954], p. 181). Of course Edwards' meaning for the 1920s was the exact opposite of that of Franklin.

15. Jones, *Theory of American Literature*, p. 141; Perry Miller, "Nineteenth-Century New England and Its Descendents," in *The Responsibilities of Mind in a Civilization of Machines: Essays by Perry Miller*, ed. John Crowell and Stanford J. Searl, Jr. (Amherst: University of Massachusetts Press, 1979), p. 165.

16. Parrington, *The Colonial Mind*, pp. 153, 159.

17. Ibid., p. 162.

18. Henry B. Parkes, *Jonathan Edwards: The Fiery Puritan* (New York: Minton, Blanch, 1930), pp. 253, 254.

19. Between Parkes's study of 1930 and Ola Winslow's *Jonathan Edwards* (New York: Macmillan, 1940), A. C. McGiffert, Jr., published *Jonathan Edwards* (New York: Harper, 1932).

20. This observation about Parrington's categories has been noted often, most recently by Gene Wise, *American Historical Explanations*, p. 266.

21. Henry F. May, "The Recovery of American Religious History," *American Historical Review*, 70 (1964), 81.

22. The discussion of neo-orthodoxy that follows is indebted to these studies: Donald B. Meyer, *The Protestant Search for Political Realism, 1919–1941* (Berkeley and Los Angeles: University of California Press, 1960); Sydney E. Ahlstrom, "Neo-Orthodoxy and Social Crisis," in *A Religious History of the American People* (New Haven: Yale University Press, 1972), pp. 932–48; W. L. Miller, "The Rise of Neo-Orthodoxy," in *Paths of American Thought*, ed. A. M. Schlesinger, Jr., and M. White (Boston: Houghton, 1963), pp. 326–44; Cushing Strout, "Crisis Theology from the Crash to the Bomb," in *The New Heavens and New Earth: Political Religion in America* (New York: Harper & Row, 1974), pp. 265–84. On Reinhold Niebuhr see Nathan A. Scott, Jr., ed., *The Legacy of Reinhold Niebuhr* (Chicago: University of Chicago Press, 1975), especially the essay by Martin E. Marty, "Reinhold Niebuhr: Public Theology and the American Experience," pp. 8–35.

23. Sydney E. Ahlstrom, "The Romantic Religious Revolution and the Dilemmas of Religious History," *Church History*, 46 (1977), 151.

24. Ahlstrom, "New-Orthodoxy and Social Crisis," p. 945.

25. Ibid., p. 946.

26. H. Richard Niebuhr, *The Kingdom of God in America* (New York: Harper, 1959), pp. xvi, 126, 197. The Edwardsean dimension of Niebuhr's thought is outlined in Sydney E. Ahlstrom, "H. Richard Niebuhr's Place in American Thought," *Christianity and*

Crisis, 25 (23 November 1963), 213–17 and Leo Sandon, Jr., "Jonathan Edwards and H. Richard Niebuhr," *Religious Studies*, 12 (1976), 101–15.

27. Austin Warren, review of *Jonathan Edwards* by H. B. Parkes and *Jonathan Edwards* by A. C. McGiffert, Jr., *American Literature*, 4 (1932–33), 315, 317.

28. Letter received from A. C. McGiffert, Jr., 1 September 1977.

29. A. C. McGiffert, Jr., *Jonathan Edwards* (New York: Harper, 1932), p. 173.

30. Joseph Haroutunian, *Piety versus Moralism: The Passing of the New England Theology* (New York: Holt, 1932), p. xxv. See Haroutunian's essays on Jonathan Edwards: "Jonathan Edwards: A Study in Godliness," *Journal of Religion*, 11 (1931), 400–19, and "Jonathan Edwards: Theologian of the Great Commandment," *Theology Today*, 1 (1944), 361–77.

31. Clyde A. Holbrook, "Jonathan Edwards and His Detractors," *Theology Today*, 10 (1953), 395. See also, in this context, the introduction to Conrad Cherry, *The Theology of Jonathan Edwards: A Reappraisal* (Garden City, N.Y.: Doubleday, 1966): "The leading doctrines of the Calvinist tradition have been reinterpreted as symbols laden with meaning and relevant to the contemporary situation. Whatever quarrel one may have with specific features of the theologies of such thinkers as Karl Barth and Reinhold Niebuhr, they have, in diverse ways, reclaimed Augustinian and Calvinist categories in order to prick the contemporary conscience, wean man away from religious sentimentality, and throw him up against the hard reality of a God who judges as well as forgives" (p. 6).

32. Thomas H. Johnson, review of *Jonathan Edwards: The Fiery Puritan* by H. B. Parkes, *New England Quarterly*, 4 (1931), 354–56. An index to the shift in Edwards' image may be seen in the bold headline introducing H. M. Jones's review of Winslow's *Edwards* in the Boston *Transcript*, 16 March 1940: "Preached Heart Religion, Not Hard, Inhuman Creed" (p. 1).

33. Perry Miller, review of *Jonathan Edwards* by Ola E. Winslow, *Saturday Review of Literature*, 30 March 1940, p. 7.

34. Ola E. Winslow, *Jonathan Edwards* (New York: Macmillan, 1940), pp. 1–2, 326–27.

35. The reference, of course, is to Miller's autobiographical "The Plight of the Lone Wolf" (1956) in *The Responsibilities of Mind*, pp. 8–14.

36. Miller, *Jonathan Edwards*, pp. 147, 113, 257.

37. Perry Miller, *The Life of the Mind in America* (New York: Harcourt, 1965), p. 6, as well as the further elaboration in Book One, "The Evangelical Basis." See also Miller, *Edwards*, pp. 135, 148, along with "Jonathan Edwards and the Great Awakening," in

Errand, pp. 153–66, and his famous "From the Covenant to the Revival," in *The Shaping of American Religion*, ed. J. W. Smith and A. L. Jamison (Princeton: Princeton University Press, 1961), pp. 322–68.

38. Jonathan Edwards, *A Faithful Narrative*, in *The Great Awakening*, ed. C. C. Goen (New Haven: Yale University Press, 1972), p. 189 (vol. 4 of *The Works of Jonathan Edwards*).

39. Miller, *Jonathan Edwards*, pp. 140, 263. The phrase, "the problem of history," is a refrain throughout *Edwards*; indeed, the idea of history becomes Miller's subject.

40. Miller's juxtaposition of Edwards and Augustine highlights the remark of Sydney Ahlstrom (and others) that H. Richard Niebuhr's *Kingdom of God* was perhaps the most important book of the neo-orthodox movement. See Ahlstrom, "Neo-Orthodoxy and Social Crisis," pp. 942–43.

41. Perry Miller, *The New England Mind: From Colony to Province* (Boston: Beacon, 1961), p. 49.

42. Reinhold Niebuhr, "Perry Miller and Our Embarrassment," *Harvard Review*, 2 (Winter–Spring 1964), 49–50. Niebuhr reviewed *The New England Mind: From Colony to Province* in *The New Republic*, 31 August 1953, p. 18, remarking that Miller was able "to bring out the full flavor of the ironic history of a settlement which was based upon presuppositions which proved in almost every case to be totally different from those which govern our American culture this day."

43. Perry Miller, review of *Faith and History* by Reinhold Niebuhr, *The Nation*, 169 (6 August 1949), 138. For a later response, see Miller, "The Influence of Reinhold Niebuhr," a review of *Pious and Secular America*, in *The Reporter*, 18 (1 May 1958), 39–40. Other spokesmen whom Miller included in that "fundamental tradition" were Emerson and Horace Bushnell.

44. Miller, *Jonathan Edwards*, 270–71.

45. Reinhold Niebuhr, "The Dilemma of Modern Man," *The Nation*, 167 (22 February 1947), 208. See also Niebuhr's "The Sickness of American Culture," ibid., 168 (6 March 1948), 267–70.

46. Miller, *Jonathan Edwards*, 314.

47. Ibid. The material in the "History" chapter is based on Paul Tillich, *The Protestant Era* (Chicago: University of Chicago Press, 1948), especially chapter 2, "Historical and Nonhistorical Interpretations of History: A Comparison," pp. 16–31. On Tillich's view of history see James L. Adams, "Tillich's Interpretation of History," in *The Theology of Paul Tillich*, ed. C. W. Kegley and R. W. Bretall (New York: Macmillan, 1959), pp. 294–309. See also Adams' excellent essay, "Tillich's Concept of the Protestant Era," in Tillich, *The Protestant Era*, pp. 273–316.

48. Miller, *Jonathan Edwards*, 314.

Introduction

49. See Paul Tillich, "History as *The* Problem of Our Period," *Review of Religion*, 3 (1938–39), 255–64.
50. That "telling phrase," Miller wrote in the review of Niebuhr's *Pious and Secular America*, "justifiably pokes fun at those who, like myself, have copiously availed themselves of Niebuhr's conclusions without pretending to share his basic and, to him, indispensible premise" ("The Influence of Reinhold Niebuhr," p. 40).
51. Heimert, "Perry Miller: An Appreciation," p. 34.
52. Miller, "The Responsibilities of Mind," p. 213.
53. Perry Miller, Preface to *Jonathan Edwards* (Cleveland: Meridian, 1959), n.p.; Miller, *The New England Mind: The Seventeenth Century*, p. xii; Miller, Preface to *Jonathan Edwards*, n.p.
54. Perry Miller, General Editor's Note, in Jonathan Edwards, *Freedom of the Will*, ed. Paul Ramsey (New Haven: Yale University Press, 1957), p. viii (vol. 1 of *The Works of Jonathan Edwards*).
55. H. Richard Niebuhr, "The Anachronism of Jonathan Edwards," quoted in Sandon, "Jonathan Edwards and H. Richard Niebuhr," p. 112. Niebuhr delivered the address at the First Church of Christ, Northampton, Massachusetts, March 1958.
56. Cherry, *The Theology of Jonathan Edwards,* pp. 110ff. (on covenant theology); Roland A. Delattre, *Beauty and Sensibility in the Thought of Jonathan Edwards* (New Haven: Yale University Press, 1968), especially pp. 4ff. (Delattre cites his indebtedness to H. Richard Niebuhr in the Postscript, pp. 217–26); and John F. Wilson, "Jonathan Edwards as Historian," *Church History*, 46 (1977), 5–18. Wilson effectively answers Peter Gay's misguided interpretation of Edwards in *A Loss of Mastery: Puritan Historians in Colonial America* (Berkeley: University of California Press, 1966), pp. 88–117. Gay subtitles the Edwards chapter "An American Tragedy" and severely criticizes Miller's *Edwards* on p. 113 and in the bibliographic essay, p. 154. Important reassessments of Edwards' historiography include C. C. Goen, "Jonathan Edwards: A New Departure in Eschatology," *Church History*, 28 (1959), 25–40; Stephen J. Stein, Introduction to Jonathan Edwards, *Apocalyptic Writings* (New Haven: Yale University Press, 1977) (vol. 5 of *The Works of Jonathan Edwards*); and Sacvan Bercovitch, *The American Jeremiad* (Madison: University of Wisconsin Press, 1978), especially pp. 97–109. Norman S. Fiering, "Will and Intellect in the New England Mind," *William and Mary Quarterly*, 3d ser., 29 (1972), 515–58; Wallace E. Anderson, Editor's Introduction to Jonathan Edwards, *Scientific and Philosophical Writings*, ed. W. E. Anderson (New Haven: Yale University Press, 1980), pp. 101, 113, 119 (vol. 6 of *The Works of Jonathan Edwards*). On the question of Edwards and Locke see David Laurence, "Jonathan Edwards, John Locke, and the Canon of Experience," *Early American Literature*, 15 (1980), 107–23.

Foreword

THE REAL life of Jonathan Edwards was the life of his mind. Hence, in order that the emphasis may fall in the proper measure, this book is focussed upon the drama of his ideas, and the external biography is restricted to the basic essentials.

Yet, paradoxically enough, no one more than Edwards ever insisted that the individual is immersed in a context of time and place. No writer ever emerged more directly out of the passions, the feuds, and the anxieties of his society. His peculiar kind of objectivity must, in fact, be interpreted, not as insensitivity to his surroundings, but as an effort to protect himself against their clutch. Edwards does not—in contrast to his contemporary Franklin—deal with the surface appearances of his epoch; he is not given to descriptions of scenes, persons, and events, yet he comes out of the heart of his culture. He is one of those pure artists through whom the deepest urgencies of their age and their country become articulate. Consequently, my analysis endeavors to reconstruct as much of the historical conditions and biographical factors as is needed to make his achievement intelligible—enough, but not, I trust, more. My excursions into the history of New England or into the century take account only of what centers upon Edwards or illuminates his thought.

A Scottish admirer, introducing Edwards' posthumous *History of Redemption*, described it as the only one of his works on the level of the average comprehension; he explained that elsewhere Edwards was an acute philosopher and a deep controversialist, who composed highly abstract and metaphysical reasonings. If even in addressing the congregation of the Kirk, which presumably had a bowing acquaintance with the theological terminology, an eighteenth-century parson had to confess that Edwards was not for the vulgar, there is all the more reason to fear that he may appear difficult to an American audience in the twentieth century. Except in fairly sheltered groves, systematic theology, once the proud possession of all Protestant Americans, seems to be nearly a lost art. But theology was Edwards' medium, as blank verse was Milton's. Consequently, in the effort to make him understandable, I have hewn rough passages through the uncongenial thicket which was Edwards' tradition. These have been held to a minimum, but if to the professional theologian they seem rough indeed, may he remember that the book seeks wherever possible to simplify.

Yet, on the other hand, Edwards is a writer who, like Dante or Milton, cannot be simplified. The student quickly reaches a point where he realizes that further reduction to popularity becomes downright falsification, and on most topics I have striven without apology to keep pace with his thought, conscious of a responsibility resting upon me to secure for his ideas as full a hearing as the space permits or as the contemporary reader has time for.

The truth is, Edwards was infinitely more than a theologian. He was one of America's five or six major artists, who happened to work with ideas instead of with poems or novels. He was much more a psychologist and a poet than a logician, and though he devoted his genius to topics derived from the body of divinity—the will, virtue, sin—he treated them in the manner of the very finest speculators, in the manner of Augustine, Aquinas, and Pascal, as problems not of dogma but of life. Furthermore, the conditions under which he labored, in pioneer America, make his achievement the more remarkable, and his failures the more poignant, not as an episode in the history of creeds and systems, but as a prefiguration of the artist in America. He is the child of genius in this civilization; though he met the forces of our society in their infancy, when they had not yet enlarged into the complexity we now endure, he called them by their names, and pronounced as one foreseeing their tendencies. If the student penetrates behind the technical language, he discovers an intelligence which, as much as Emerson's, Melville's, or Mark Twain's, is both an index of American society and a comment upon it.

If I read him correctly—though Edwards remains, as he was even to himself, an enigma—he repays study because, while he speaks from a primitive religious conception which often seems hopelessly out of touch with even his own day, yet at the same time he speaks from an insight into science and psychology so much ahead of his time that our own can hardly be said to have caught up with him. Though he had followers, he was not the sort of artist who really can found a "school." He is unique, an aboriginal and monolithic power, with nothing of that humanity which opens every heart to Franklin; but he is a reminder that, although our civilization has chosen to wander in the more genial meadows to which Franklin beckoned it, there come periods, either through disaster or through self-knowledge, when applied science and Benjamin Franklin's *The Way to Wealth* seem not a sufficient philosophy of national life.

The student of Edwards must seek to ascertain not so much the peculiar doctrines in which he expressed his meaning as the meaning itself. In terms of what he strove toward rather than of his creed, Edwards is a spokesman, almost the first, for the deep, the most rooted, the really native tradition. His opponents, who are customarily called the liberals, often prove upon analysis to speak for limited and particular interests which, because of their circumscribed conception of the goal, were bound, upon gaining their private ends, to become vested interests. Edwards was a Puritan who would not permit mankind to evade the unending ordeal and the continuing agony of liberty. As a Protestant, he protested against the tyranny of all formalism, especially of that which masquerades as sweet reasonableness. He preached a universe in which the nature of things will permit no interest to become vested. My contention is that no American succeeded better, even though his experience was set within narrow limits, in generalizing his experience into the meaning of America. It is this Edwards, the artist and the writer, that my volume seeks to expound.

May I add that, if to show him for what he was, the presentation seems too eagerly to take his part in order to overcome the prejudice against him which certainly exists, it is not out of partisanship for his creed. It is rather out of a sincere conviction that a major American must be appreciated for his greatness, and upon the assumption that an ability so to estimate a man, regardless of our personal beliefs, along with an adequate documentation of his temporal and personal circumstances, is one test of a truly great America.

My thanks are due to the Yale University Library for granting access to, and permission to quote from, the yet unpublished mass of Edwards' journals and papers. I am indebted to the Library of Andover Newton Theological Seminary for permission to use the manuscripts in their possession, especially the transcripts which assist in deciphering Edwards' difficult handwriting. I am obliged to the Forbes Library in Northampton for my quotations from the Judd manuscripts. I have the gracious permission of Professor Harold Laski and Professor Mark Howe to use a sentence from an unpublished letter of Mr. Justice Oliver Wendell Holmes. It is a pleasure to acknowledge how much I profited from the reading given my manuscript by the editors of this series, and by Professor I. Bernard Cohen, Mr. Leo Marx, and Mr. Sherman Paul. To Mrs. Sarah Cabot Sedgwick I am indebted not only for assistance out of her own researches into Stockbridge history but for the opportunity of composing several of these paragraphs on the very ground where Edwards walked and meditated. Throughout, I have had the invaluable editorial assistance of Mrs. Elizabeth C. Moore, who also compiled the index.

The published sources are acknowledged at the end of the volume.

P. M.

Harvard University
February 25, 1949

For
E. B. W. M.

As soon as the prayer was closed, Mr. Moody turned round, and saw Mr. Edwards behind him; and, without leaving his place, gave him his right hand, and addressed him as follows, "Brother Edwards, we are all of us much rejoiced to see you here to-day. . . . I didn't intend to flatter you to your face; but there's one thing I'll tell you: They say that your wife is a going to heaven, by a shorter road than yourself." Mr. Edwards bowed, and after reading the Psalm, went on with the Sermon.

The changes that alter the face of national life have small beginnings; the traceable initial process having commonly set in with some overt act on the part of a small and distinctive group of persons, who will then presently be credited with insight and initiative in case the move proves itself by success. Should the movement fail of acceptance and consequent effect, these spokesmen of its propaganda would then prove to have been fanciful projectmakers, perhaps of unsound mind. To describe the course of such a matter by analogy, the symptoms of the new frame of mind will first come in evidence in the attitude of some one individual, who, by congenital proclivity and through an exceptional degree of exposure, is peculiarly liable to its infection. In so far as the like susceptibility is prevalent among the rest of the population, and so far as circumstances of habituation favor the new conceit, it will then presently find lodgment in the habits of thought of an increasing number of persons,—particularly among those whom the excursive play of a hybrid heredity has thrown up as temperamental variants peculiarly apt for its reception, or whom the discipline of life bends with exceptional rigor in the direction of its bias. Should the new idea also come to have the countenance of those in authority or in a position to claim popular deference, its vogue will be greatly helped out by imitation, and perhaps by compulsory observance, and so it may in a relatively short time become a matter of course and of common sense. But the reservation always stands over, that in such a hybrid population the same prevalent variability of temperament that so favors the infiltration and establishment of new ideas will at the same time render their tenure correspondingly precarious.

THORSTEIN VEBLEN

When the mind is affected with a thing much, it is led into such schemes of thought about it, as, if they were written down, would seem very impertinent to one that was not affected. It is so in all matters. The scripture falls in with the natural stream of one's thought when the mind is affected with the things of which they speak; but are very wide of their series of thought, who are not affected. For instance, the text that says "one generation passeth away and another cometh, but the earth abideth forever," seems to me in a common frame of mind insipid; the latter part of the verse seems impertinently to be brought in, as what may better tend to illustrate the former: the thought of the earth being the same, does not seem very naturally and affectingly to fall in after the thought of one generation passing, and another coming. What is it to the purpose whether the earth remains the same or no? This makes not the changes of the inhabitants either more or less affecting.

But yet when, upon an occasion, I was more than ordinarily affected with the passing of one generation after another; how all those, who made such a noise and bluster now, and were so much concerned about their life, would be clean gone off from the face of the earth in sixty or seventy years time, and that the world would be left desolate with respect to them, and that another generation would come on, that would be very little concerned about them, and so one after another: it was particularly affecting to me to think that the earth still remained the same through all these changes upon the surface: the same spots of ground, the same mountains and valleys where those things were done, remaining just as they were, though the actors ceased, and the actors just gone. And then this text came into my mind.

JONATHAN EDWARDS

Trial of a Successor

JONATHAN EDWARDS rode from Northampton to
Boston to give the Public Lecture on Thursday, July 8,
1731. The Thursday lecture, held in the First Church,
had originated with the settlers of Massachusetts. They were
so insatiate of hearing the word of God preached, from which
they had been prevented in old England, that two sermons on
the Sabbath were not enough; they gathered on Thursday
morning at the First Church, there to listen to all ministers
in rotation and savor all eloquences. Conducted as a lecture
rather than as a service, the discourse was always more theological than hortatory; it institutionalized the Puritan thirst
for abstract, logical formulations, and from the beginning
assumed that while a minister might dispense his ordinary
rhetoric on Sundays, when it came his turn to deliver the lecture, he pulled himself together and gave his best.

By the fourth decade of the eighteenth century, Boston was
a busy town of about 13,000 persons, most of whom no longer
had time to leave their affairs on a weekday. The lecture continued, but with a primarily clerical audience. It was the only
time the ministers had a chance to hear—and appraise—each
other. Thus the lecture became increasingly a professional
exhibition, and if a man had anything to say, here he said it. If
in the judgment of the capital he passed the test exceptionally

well, a committee signalized his success by arranging for publication. Only the best of Puritan utterance became the printed word out of this highly critical screening process.

By 1731 New England had expanded far beyond the collection of seaboard clearings of 1631. As far as York in Maine and Hampton in New Hampshire there were settlements, each with its educated minister; Connecticut was a separate and remote province, relations between Boston and Connecticut clerics being friendly but formal, since communication was difficult. But there were also settlements to the west, thriving towns that legally pertained to Massachusetts Bay, but which, in vigor and self-sufficiency, were as remote as Connecticut if not more so. Passage by sea from York or New London to Boston was relatively easy, but the trip overland, across hills that still are waste, between Worcester and Springfield, was tedious. It cost the town of Northampton £3 for horses and escort "waiting on Mr. Edwards to Boston." Western Massachusetts in 1731 was, in anthropological terms, a distinct cultural entity, with more ties down the river to Hartford and New Haven than to Boston or Salem. Yet because this virtually independent satrapy was economically essential to the Bay Colony, because it was the source of new lands, furs, timber, and Indian fighters, because it was wealthy and becoming wealthier, it had to be wooed and cajoled by gentlemen of the metropolis, by the Governor's mansion and by "the United Ministers of Boston."

Distances were great; only on rare occasions could a man come from farther than Plymouth, Concord, or Ipswich, and the Thursday lecture was usually delivered by a minister resident in Boston or within a day's riding. When "Father" Moody of York or Eliphalet Adams of New London could make it, all the clergy of eastern Massachusetts attended, out of both courtesy and curiosity. The first week in July was Commencement at Harvard College, when degree-holders held reunion, and to give the lecture at that time was a special honor, a chance to address the largest available concentration of New England scholarship and influence. But when Jonathan Edwards came out of the Connecticut Valley, we may indeed be certain that all ministers not bedridden or in their dotage, together with the President, professors, and tutors of Harvard College, as well as many substantial citizens, were on hand. This was no routine performance. The twenty-eight-year-old youth standing before the distinguished gathering on this 8th of July was about to reveal whether the future of New England would be peace or strife, and everybody in the company knew it.

Edwards was of special interest, first of all, because he was not a Harvard man. Unlike his grandfather, Solomon Stoddard of the class of 1662, who had gone out to Northampton, or William Williams of 1683, who went to Hatfield, he had not learned his doctrine and rhetoric in Cambridge before heeding a call to a frontier post; he was not now returning to renew old friendships. Valley-born and Valley-bred, a product of that wild frontier where massacre was a constant threat and where traffic of all sorts, from Indian scalps to land grants, was booming, he had received his training at the little college in New Haven, founded only thirty years before, and only thirteen years since known as Yale. He was a product of its turbulent second decade, when it was a scandal and a stumbling block to the righteous. As Edwards stood up in Boston, it was the first time so large a collection of Harvard men, on the alert to be critical as well as hospitable, had had an opportunity to take the measure of a Yale education. (Three months earlier a Yale man had spoken and published in Boston, but that, as we shall see, did not make Edwards' task easier.) He had entered the "Collegiate School" in 1716, when it was still unable to get itself organized in one place; his senior year and his degree in 1720 were taken under Rector Timothy Cutler, and he then had two years of graduate study, up to the very eve of that terrible Commencement of September 12, 1722, when Cutler stunned the Corporation and threw Connecticut into panic by announcing that he, two tutors, and four ministers were going over to the Church of England. The shock of this "Great

Apostasy" was still reverberating through orthodox New England in 1731. Cutler, of course, was thrown out, and several attempts were made to get a rector, the newly appointed Hollis Professor at Harvard being one of the solicited, but Edward Wigglesworth was a shrewd man and pleaded his deafness to excuse him from the thankless job of salvaging Yale. For four years the distracted school got along without any head, during two of which Edwards, who had gone to a New York church in 1722 and so was free of any charge of complicity in Cutler's heresy, was one of its brace of tutors. In 1726 the powers of Connecticut finally settled Elisha Williams in the Rectorship. Nobody doubted that he was an able man. For one thing, he was the son of William Williams of Hatfield, whom many considered an even greater man than Stoddard of Northampton, being a son by the first wife and so stepson to one of Edwards' innumerable aunts. Everyone agreed when speaking of Williamses, whether mothered by Stoddards or by others, that "they were all men of more than common understanding." In the days before unity was forced upon Yale, Elisha maintained one segment of the school at Wethersfield, where among his fourteen devoted students was Jonathan Edwards; he had been at one point so disgusted that he meditated moving with his charges to Cambridge and joining Harvard College—in which case the religious history of America would have been radically altered; but a Boston minister, Benjamin Colman, genuinely eager that Yale be put on its feet, dissuaded him. Elisha Williams was bidding fair to achieve the primacy of his prolific, aggressive clan, which already exercised a "peculiar leadership" in the Connecticut Valley; and after he became Rector, the great oligarchs of western Massachusetts—the "river gods" as they were being called—even those who were Harvard men, began to divert their sons toward New Haven.

None of this would have troubled easterners had it not been that, despite the positive assurances of Williams that Yale taught nothing but the strictest Calvinism, they had reason to fear that the place was still unsound. Perhaps only gossip, but it all went in one direction. A Boston businessman, who was in fact one of the two Yale graduates then living in Boston (both of them businessmen!), traveling through Guilford in 1731 was told "that Y. Coll. was corrupted & ruined with Arminianism & Heresy." He repeated this to Rector Williams, who descended on the rumormonger with a process for libel, but the story got around. It did not help that at intervals since 1722 a succession of Yale graduates had gone "back to Egypt," and that concerning two others then occupying Connecticut pulpits there were more than suspicions.

Meanwhile Samuel Johnson, one of the tutors joined with Cutler in the Apostasy, having been ordained in England, was spreading episcopal poison over all Connecticut from his church in Stratford; while Timothy Cutler himself, also ordained in England, turned up in Boston, and at Christ Church was preaching the arch-Jacobite doctrine of passive resistance, than which nothing was more repugnant to Puritan ears. Harvard, of course, might share the blame for Cutler, since he was class of 1701, but alumni figured that it was the friends he had made in New Haven who had corrupted him; we may be sure that on July 8 of 1731 he was not invited to hear his former pupil.

The sorrow of Boston over the miseries of Yale was the greater because many of the first movers had been Boston men convinced that "the College at Cambridge was under the Tutorage of Latitudinarians." But now the rumors were spreading that Yale had erred not only in spawning Latitudinarians who went all the way to episcopacy, but that it was running into the opposite and even more shocking extreme of "enthusiasm." There was said to be a clique of students, with good old names like Davenport, Pomeroy, and Wheelock, gathered around an insidious character (some said he was a Quaker) from New Milford named David Ferris, who "with his plausible Craft, and insinuating Behaviour, and His Books" was corrupting the lot. Friends of the Mathers used to say bitter things about Harvard while Leverett was president, but no one could say that its Latitudinarians were out-and-out traitors to the New England polity, and nobody, ever, accused Harvard of enthusiasm.

The condition of Boston's nerves on the subject of Yale at the time of Edwards' lecture may be exhibited by an episode of the following year, when the news came that the College had received a noble present of 880 books from an English bishop. The tidings awakened memories of the unhappy fruits of Yale's last receipt of books: in 1714 the agent for New England in London had been Jeremiah Dummer, who was considered so ambiguous a character that despite his European postgraduate work and a good Dutch degree in theology he was not able to secure a New England church or a post at Harvard; he got together an imposing library, by working upon English philanthropists or by appealing to the vanity of authors pleased at the thought of being read in the wilderness, and sent it to Yale. The collection was better than anything Harvard could boast, yet out of it Cutler and Johnson garnered their arguments for episcopal ordination. So in 1732 when the news arrived of a second great donation, and Boston realized that it came from a certain Bishop Berkeley (vaguely known to be a dangerous philosopher and indubitably a friend of Johnson of Stratford), the dean of the Boston clergy, Benjamin Colman—who in 1718 persuaded tutor Williams to keep his fourteen boys at Wethersfield for the sake of Yale's future —wrote in haste to Rector Williams to ask if this donation meant new apostasies. Williams replied that had the gift been "clogged in the manner you hint," Yale would have rejected it, but since it was made in "a true Catholick Spirit, as much (if I mistake not) as Mr. Hollis's to Harvard College," Yale was adding it to the already fine library.

This was a palpable hit. Colman's favorite and insistent shibboleth was "catholick," and he had been chiefly instrumental in persuading Thomas Hollis to endow Harvard with two professorships which, at the moment, were occupied, one by a man whom the phalanx of the orthodox regarded with suspicion, and the other by a well-known toper. Edward Wigglesworth was a discreet man, but he smelled as much of Latitudinarianism as anybody in New Haven, and he talked even more about the catholic spirit than Colman. Graduated in 1710 and frequently a candidate for vacant pulpits, he could persuade no church to call him, and upon his appointment as Hollis Professor in 1722, there were murmurings throughout New England which his friends tried to silence with a campaign of reassuring propaganda. The only reason, said one of these, that Wigglesworth had not got a pulpit was "the ignorance and unskilfulness of the rabble, who make the majority," and who "disgust every thing but noise and nonsense, and cannot be content to sit quiet, unless their auditory nerves are drummed upon with a voice like thunder." As for Isaac Greenwood, appointed in 1728 to be the first "Professor of Mathematicks & Natural & Experimental Philosophy," by 1731 it was becoming evident, even to the long-suffering Corporation, that despite his managing to deliver during April a public "philosophical discourse" in which he expounded Sir Isaac Newton, he was, through "various Acts of gros Intemperance, by excessive drinking," reaching the condition which made necessary in 1738 the severance of his connection with the College.

Thus, when the tall, soft-spoken member of the Yale class of 1720 came before his Boston audience, he confronted an initial distrust born of Harvard's apprehensions. But there was a still more pressing reason why the Boston leaders were anxious about his performance: Edwards was not only a son of the Valley and of Yale, he was the grandson and heir of Solomon Stoddard, of the "Pope" who for over half a century had ruled Northampton and from it built an empire, like some Biblical Pharaoh, along both banks of a river, from Deerfield to the Sound. He had detached Hadley, Hatfield, Springfield, Westfield, Longmeadow, Suffield, Deerfield, from the dominion of Boston, and made them into a new principality with Northampton their capital. His quarrel with Boston, it is important to note, was not theological but ecclesiastical. True, his great dissertation, *The Safety of Appearing at the Day of Judgment*, published in 1687 and reissued the year of his death, 1729, one of the monuments of seventeenth-century Puritan literature, did contain certain radical emphases, though no real departures from the body of orthodox doctrine. It conspicuously asserted the naked sovereignty of God at a time when most leaders were endeavoring to present the God of Calvinism as inherently a rational being. To compare his statements with contemporaneous utterances of the Mathers is to get the first faint hints of a philosophical division that roughly coincided with an emerging difference of temper between the west and the east. Without any of the mitigation by which preachers of the Matherian stripe softened their discourse, Stoddard put the case for an absolute divinity who chooses one man rather than another solely because He pleases, and who still would be a God of mercy "if it had pleased him never to exercise any." This was the tradition in which Edwards had been brought up, and Boston would be curious to see if, in a year in which Greenwood was expounding Newton to the citizenry, he saw any reason to modify his grandfather's absolutist theology.

Still, no one anticipated that differences upon theological views would make for real trouble; it had never been Stoddard's doctrine of the divine will that separated the regions. Stoddard's great book bore all the hallmarks of the peculiarly New England version of Calvinism, the language of the "Covenant Theology," and all New England professed to believe, even if with varying degrees of conviction, that God chose and rejected men at His pleasure. What had made the strife was that Stoddard, an immensely practical man, decided that the old Congregational principle of limiting the membership to those who could give a profession of their faith, and of restricting the Lord's Supper to those who offered evidence of conversion, would not work on the frontier. So, while the rest of New England, notably the Mathers, waited for lightning to strike him, he announced that we have no reason to take the practices of our fathers on trust, and opened the church doors to everybody in town (except the "openly scandalous"). He offered them the communion, calling it a "converting ordinance," on the highly pragmatic ground that "All Ordinances are for the Saving good of those that they are to be administered unto." When Increase Mather wrung his hands and cried to the heavens that Stoddard was depriving New England churches of their glory, Stoddard dryly remarked, "Mr. Mather all along intermingles Passionate Lamentations with his Arguments," and went serenely ahead to reorganize the churches of the west into his program.

Historians have incautiously saluted this innovation as "democratic." It was exactly the contrary. Bringing all the people officially as well as nominally under his ecclesiastical rule, Stoddard was New England's greatest autocrat. "The Elders," he said, "are to Rule over the Church, and therefore not to be over-ruled by the Brethren." He maintained on the frontier Governor John Winthrop's theory that the people should be seen and not heard: "The Community are not men of understanding." And further, Stoddard joined his innovation in the membership with a campaign to combine particular churches into regional associations, similar to Presbyterian classes, which were to assume (the Mathers called it usurp) dictatorial power over discipline and the choice of ministers. The royal government of Massachusetts refused to countenance such organizations; nevertheless, Stoddard proceeded on his own and set up the Hampshire Association, which, without any legal warrant, ruled the churches of the Valley. In 1705 Connecticut, by officially adopting his plan in the form of the *Saybrook Platform*, gave legal status to the associations, so that Congregationalism in Connecticut was transformed into a "semi-Presbyterianism." The Mathers shouted that New England churches were autonomous bodies founded on the church covenant, but Stoddard calmly answered that there was no such thing as a covenant in the Bible, and in western New England "neither is there any need of it."

The pamphlet warfare raged between 1700 and 1710 without impeding Stoddard's succession of conquests, while the Mathers suffered from dissension in their own ranks. In 1699 the Brattles organized the Brattle Street Church and published a "Manifesto" declaring that they would imitate Stoddard to the extent of dispensing with public relations of conversion. Benjamin Colman, then in London, accepted the pastorate, but thought it wise to get himself ordained by English Presbyterians so that the Mathers could not interfere at his installation; this was another affront to the old system, which always maintained that a minister could be ordained only by the election of his own congregation. In the midst of their fight with Stoddard, the Mathers weakened their own position by their *Proposals* of 1705, in which they sought to organize in eastern Massachusetts regional associations similar to Stoddard's but not so authoritarian. The government would not help, the churches objected, the Mathers could not bully their colleagues as Stoddard did his, and in 1710 and 1717 the *Proposals* were riddled by the pamphlets of John Wise, after which there was no future for such schemes in the Boston area. The cup of defeat was filled to overflowing for the Mathers in 1707 when Leverett, the Brattles, and Colman captured Harvard. By 1710 the Mathers cried quits and let Stoddard have his way, since they were powerless to stop him. Increase Mather died in 1723, Cotton in 1728, both of them unhappy men, persevering by sheer stubbornness, but knowing they were beaten. In 1729 Solomon Stoddard died in all his glory, the undisputed master of the Connecticut Valley, having hand-picked and personally trained his crown prince, selected with an eye to the preservation of the empire.

Stoddard's ecclesiastical revolt was an affirmation of the autonomy of the Valley. Meetings of the Great and General Court in these decades were diplomatic congresses, in which it is not fanciful to see prefigurations of the east-west struggle that runs through American history down to Jackson, Lincoln, and Bryan. In 1731 the west had become so self-contained that it had not only its peculiar ecclesiastical system—Stoddard's—but also its own political boss, the greatest of the river gods, who held the Valley in the palm of his hand and who came to Boston nominally as the representative of Northampton, but actually more like a feudal duke attending the parliament of a king whose power he was ready to defy. This archon was none other than the son of old Solomon, Colonel John Stoddard, who lived in the manse on Prospect Street and was not only the uncle but the avowed champion of his pale nephew. The Colonel graduated from Harvard in 1701 (being a classmate of Cutler), but had proved his mettle in Indian fighting and land speculation rather than in scholarship. Once he stopped by the Governor's gate and sent in word that he was waiting: the Governor left his shocked guests at table, saying, "Excuse me, gentlemen; if it is Colonel Stoddard, I must go to him." The considerate attention which Boston was prepared to pay to Edwards was not solely a tribute to his reputation for intellect, it was homage to the majesty of the name of Stoddard; behind it there was, more or less concealed, a hope that the old war might now be ended and an era of coöperation be ushered in. Solomon and the Mathers were dead, with all their noise and bluster, and the world was left desolate with respect to them. If this youth, now occupying the one pulpit in New England that could challenge Boston's eight, would prove amenable, a reign of amity might follow the generation of virtual civil war. The figure who stood before the congregation on this Thursday morning was the newly crowned successor of a rival principality, and the Boston clergy turned out to greet him as some privy council might greet the fledgling heir of a competing power.

In the 1720's even Pope Stoddard had known he was getting old. In 1725 the town paid out £13 for a young minister to assist him, and in 1726 Deacon Clark collected 4s. for going twice to Hadley, and then 38s. for hunting as far as Hartford, a trip that took him eight days. Solomon Stoddard sired six daughters, five of whom were married to ministers—Esther to Timothy Edwards of East Windsor, and Christian to William Williams of Hatfield. Stoddard genes made tall children, and there was no lack of grandsons—Mixes, Whitmans, Hawleys, Williamses. For two decades, Yale B.A.'s came to Northampton to learn theology from Stoddard; his library was the first school of graduate studies for Yale College. Stoddard could have had his choice of successors. In 1726 he chose, and after the proper formalities the town dutifully voted 48s. for sending horses and the constable—a man named Miller—down to New Haven, in February 1727, to fetch grandson Edwards.

As late as 1719 Stoddard used to go every year to Boston, generally at Commencement time, to stop with his rich merchant brother, Anthony, and to dine with his lifelong friend, Judge Sewall. Whenever he came, they gave him the Thursday lecture, or the election sermon, or whatever would show their respect and awe. In 1721 he had to write to Sewall, "I am never like to see my Friends in Boston any more." Upon his death, Benjamin Colman—who always maintained friends on both sides of all conflicts—delivered a sermon that declared Stoddard much honored in Northampton, but no less in Boston, "where both Ministers and People receiv'd his annual Visits with a peculiar Reverence and Pleasure." We know that Edwards traced his grandfather's route in 1729, but on that invasion he remained as silent as he had upon his first visit to the city in 1723. The whole colony could read in the funeral sermon which William Williams had delivered over the Pope's body how the town was called upon to pray that the spirit of Elijah might rest upon the grandson and successor, "under the weight of so much Work as is now rowl'd upon him." By 1731 Edwards had been at work two years. Was he the man for Stoddard's post? Boston thought it time to find out, and so invited him to give the lecture in Commencement week.

This would be the trial. If Edwards failed, Boston could relax, unless it had to refigure its strategy against the possibility that some Williams might prove the real heir. After all, Timothy Edwards was no great shakes compared with Williams of Hatfield, and besides he had begot ten girls—"my sixty feet of daughters," he is supposed to have lamented—with only this delicate man-child to sit in Stoddard's seat. Also, there was supposed to be bad blood between Christian and Esther, and everybody knew to what lengths a feud between New England cousins could go. Would Esther's son ever amount to anything in the Valley if he had the Williamses against him? If Edwards did not impress his critics, Col. John Stoddard would be that much lessened. But if he made clear that he had to be reckoned with, Boston would have no choice: it would perceive that the present lull was only a truce, and that as soon as it found a qualified spokesman among the younger Harvard men, the struggle would be resumed. There was one obvious way in which the recognition would be marked: if the Harvard community saw that they had a real adversary, they would publish his sermon.

He preached on July 8, and within a month his discourse was printed, under the title, *God Glorified in the Work of Redemption, by the Greatness of Man's Dependence upon him, in the Whole of it.* Two Boston ministers, William Cooper and Thomas Prince, wrote the preface. With some difficulty, they said, Edwards' youth and modesty had been prevailed upon by many of the ministers and "others" (was Col. Stoddard there?) to yield the manuscript to the printer. They praised the discourse, but concluded in phrases which, to all New England readers in 1731, were highly charged:

> And, as we cannot but wish and pray, that the College in the neighboring colony, as well as our own, may be a fruitful mother of many such sons as the author; so we heartily rejoice, in the special favour of Providence in bestowing such a rich gift on the happy church of Northampton, which has, for so many lustres of years, flourished under the influence of such pious doctrines, taught them in the excellent ministry of their late venerable pastor, whose gift and spirit we hope will long live and shine in his grandson, to the end that they may abound in

all the lovely fruits of evangelical humility and thankfulness, to the glory of God.

Neither Prince nor Cooper claimed the gift of prophecy, but Prince had a sense for history; three years earlier he had issued the prospectus for his *Annals of New England*, the first volume of which, appearing in 1736, was to begin with the Creation. At this moment he was seeing through the press a *Vade Mecum for America; or a Companion for Traders and Travellers*, which surveyed towns, counties, and roads, and gave tables of commodities and rates of interest. He was one, in other words, who appreciated actualities. Hence he wrote of Edwards, "We quickly found him to be a workman that need not be ashamed before his brethren." No Williams could miss the point of that language! For two decades Edwards was to work in the shadow of the late venerable pastor, a shadow which grew greater with the years. The life of Edwards is a tragedy; but it was not Boston alone that defeated him. Alone, the eighteenth-century metropolis could not have overthrown him had it not enlisted against him the image of his own grandfather, who for two generations had been Boston's dedicated opponent, or had it not found willing allies, filled with a vindictiveness the city seldom bred, among collateral descendants of Stoddard's loins.

A detached observer, unversed in the secret currents of American life, studying the audience that listened to Edwards, would at first view have been struck by its show of unanimity. The violent debates of thirty years before seemed buried with the Mathers. Here and there churches were occasionally splintered by disputes between pastor and people over salaries or personalities, but no fundamental controversies were being raised. Issues of organizational theory had ceased to be disturbing since the churches had learned, or Stoddard had obliged them to learn, to tolerate variation. Few leaders were any longer worried about Harvard; most of the clergy by now were products of the Leverett regime, and under the presidency of the mild Benjamin Wadsworth, who contrived to succeed Leverett in 1725 with the approbation of both parties, Harvard no longer offended anybody. Also, the clergy had the unprecedented experience of standing solidly together in defense of inoculation during the epidemic of 1721. Furthermore, the ministers were convinced that piety and not polity was the real problem; week after week they regularly bewailed New England's declension from the founders, castigated tavern haunters and backbiters, and went home to solid dinners and a glass of Madeira. In 1727 the seaboard was shaken by an earthquake; on the next Sabbath the ministers expatiated upon the long overdue vengeance of God toward a degenerate people, and about thirty of their sermons were published, with no noticeable effect on New England manners. The social order had become dignified and polite—at least in the eastern townships—and, while everybody agreed that it was depraved, it was on the whole comfortable.

As the ministers and "others" gathered for the lecture on this July noon, the dominating figure easily was Benjamin Colman, nearly the eldest, and in reputation certainly the most famous, of the divines. He was mainly responsible for changing the social tone from the pedantry and querulousness of the Mathers to a genial piety, solid but relaxed, serious but decorous. He was urbane, neat and clean in dress (eulogies stress this point); he prided himself on the twin virtues of "learning and moderation." His prose style, which owed everything to Addison, had become the fashion, and was echoed in the meanest villages by adoring Harvard men. He had lived four years in London, after a romantic capture by a French privateer, and had cultivated, by sentimental standards successfully, an infatuation with a minor poetess. Leverett was his tutor at Harvard, the Brattles were his backers in the "Manifesto Church"; he was Leverett's staunch supporter during the presidency, and having secured the Hollis bequests, he endorsed Wigglesworth for the professorship. He corresponded with a host of English divines, imported the newest books, and in 1731 had just received the highest Puritan accolade, a D.D. from Glasgow. The

Matherian spirit, three years after Cotton Mather's lingering death, seemed not only extinct but forgotten.

Colman is worth dwelling upon because, while he was a friend to everybody, he proved a good friend to Jonathan Edwards. His sermons breathed the spirit which he and Leverett made synonymous with that of Harvard, "free and catholick." It was his practice, after delivering a series on some topic, to publish it as a sort of provincial *Spectator*. His *Government and Improvement of Mirth*, in 1707, defended indulgence in mirth to the extent that it can be indulged without a sacrifice of sobriety. His masterpiece, still readable, was *A Humble Discourse of the Incomprehensibility of God*, which, while laboriously attesting the fact that God is not comprehensible, exhaustively demonstrated that the fact itself is eminently understandable; it was a principal vehicle, anticipating Cotton Mather's *The Christian Philosopher* of 1721, for the popularization of the new science. From the frame of the universe, he argued, it is evident that there must be some "Mighty Mind" that comprehends "Universal Nature"; he celebrated "Tellescopes" as aids to piety, and made Newton known, if not exactly understood, by exclaiming of the earth, "How Unsearchable is the Law of its Center or Gravitation, wherein it is fixt?" He shared the joy of the new century in the happy concord between man and nature, though he showed himself a New Englander by taking his pleasure a trifle sadly:

> What Wonders of Wisdom for our musing Minds? What Beauties for our gazing Eyes? What Pleasing Sounds for our Ears? What Delicacy of Food for our Palates? What a Paradise the Earth—if by our Sins we had not blasted it?

After the excitement of founding the Brattle Street Church, Colman exhibited no further radical tendencies, although he continued to voice New England's firm adherence to the Whig conception of the British Constitution, hailing the accession of George II in 1727 with a profession of New England's "sincere and fervent zeal for the Religion of Christ and the Protestant Succession in the Royal Family."

It would be both inaccurate and unfair to represent Colman as a full-fledged rationalist. No one more deplored the decadence of piety or more called for an awakening. But it is essential for our story, in order to make Edwards' relation to his age comprehensible, to understand that Colman, who mainly formed the style and sensibility of New England between 1720 and 1730, was a rationalist who luxuriated in emotion, a kind of Calvinist sentimentalist. He partook, although from afar, in that maneuver at the very center of English culture which, immediately upon the triumph of the scientific reason, instinctively sought a counterbalance in the exploitation of the passions, especially, out of an overwhelming urgency, the "benevolent" passions. Colman may not have known exactly what he was encouraging, but he was capable of deriving from his hazy grasp of Newton such a statement as this: "All Creatures are Emanations of Overflowing Goodness, and all do continuously subsist by it." (Puritan congregations had always understood that the universe was created by God, and Colman's remark might not seem especially novel; but, on second thought, a few might reflect that were it advanced by one more thoroughly grounded in the new physics and more strenuously concerned about comprehending its God, in a mind less neat and clean in intellectual dress, this concept of emanation might have rather staggering and unorthodox implications.) In order to suggest the quality of his influence upon the rising generation, it is not amiss to quote a characteristic passage:

> Now out of the South comes the Whirlwind, and Cold out of the North, and Frost is the Breath of God; Presently again He quieteth the Earth by the same South-wind, and we know not how our Garments grow warm upon us. Now He Persecutes a guilty World by His Tempests, and makes them afraid by His Storm; again He Mercifully Fanns and Purges the Air for us, by bringing the Winds out of His Treasures, and the pleas'd Mariners improve the Welcome Gale, the Ships Stagger under their Courses, and are driven with their rich Fraight to their Port. Thus the Greatness and Goodness of GOD is seen in the blowing of the Wind.

Colman set the model for the habit of ornamenting sermons with quotations from polite literature. He not only cited familiarly Milton and Plutarch, or the standard Puritan authorities revered by the previous century, but also the new poetry and the elevated prose of the age of Queen Anne; above all, he brought into New England pulpits the names of rationalistic, moderate Anglican writers like Tillotson and Addison. Broadened by his experience of the great world, Colman deprecated the parochialism of New England, and although hostile to Popery, he yearned for formulae of accommodation, not only among the several camps of Congregationalism, but more especially between New England and the mother country. He entreated all alike to stress, not their peculiarities, but their common Protestantism. The open revolt of Cutler and Johnson was to him distressing because it widened the breach; it set up a reaction which so "alarmed and narrowed us" that New Englanders were now in danger of becoming more sectarian than ever, just as they had begun to acquire a taste for cosmopolitanism. Even persons who, under his and Leverett's tutoring, "before received the Writings and Gentlemen of the Church of England with most open Reverence and Affection" were so enraged by the "high-flying" Jacobitism of Cutler that they began to frown upon the reading of the gentle Tillotson.

By 1731 Colman was an elder statesman, as was Wadsworth, the ultra-conciliatory president of Harvard, or Simon Bradstreet of Charlestown, who also quoted Archbishop Tillotson and exalted "practical" above "doctrinal" sermons. Their generation had grown up in the shadow of the Mathers and their rebellion had taken the form, in sheer self-defense, of the genial and irenical. Now they were grave and reverend seniors, who vaguely sensed that among the newer generation lines were again being sharply drawn, that the clash of fundamental differences could no longer be muted by the free and catholic approach. Colman must have had some intimation that the era of pacific modernism was over, because he became interested in William Cooper, of the Harvard class of 1712, and in 1716 engineered his election as his own colleague at the Brattle Street Church. Cooper at once became a popular preacher, and aroused more enthusiasm among the people by portraying the agonies of the damned than Colman could excite by improving mirth or expatiating on the earthly paradise. At his ordination Cooper insisted upon publicly drawing up a confession of his faith in the articles of Calvinism, a far from "catholick" act, which ran directly counter to Colman's dislike of specific formulations.

Two centuries later, with the advantage of hindsight, it is not difficult to guess in what direction these men were tending; yet as early as 1731 there were signs that the generation following Colman's was drifting into a more profound division than New England, with all its history of internal dissension, had yet known. The lines of cleavage were forming. Cooper, as we have seen, signed the laudatory preface to Edwards' sermon. The other signer, Thomas Prince, graduated from Harvard in 1707, spent eight years abroad attending Gresham College, enjoyed "the company of Wonderfull Rope Dancers," and returned with "a Wigg and Russet coat"; yet he, unlike Colman in 1700, brought back no liberal ideas. Instead, he was even more convinced that the plea for revival, advanced in vain by three generations of the clergy, ought now to be heeded. Although his ordination at the Old South in 1718 was followed by an entertainment at Judge Sewall's which included wine and cost the congregation 5*l.* 17*s.*, although he was almost as learned as Cotton Mather and certainly knew more about science than Colman, he believed passionately that man is really sinful and that grace is strictly predestined.

Prince and Cooper had a kindred spirit in Joseph Sewall, son of Judge Sewall and beloved of Cotton Mather, who became minister of the Old South in 1713 and soon achieved fame for a species of sermonizing that won him the name of "the weeping prophet." He welcomed his classmate Prince to the partnership, and they worked in perfect harmony. They and Cooper admired Thomas Foxcroft of the class of 1714, who in 1717 was joined with Wadsworth at the First Church, thus to become its senior pastor after Wadsworth disappeared into Harvard College; he could be as eloquent about hell-torments as Cooper and Sewall, but could also be as "polite and elegant" as Colman, and he knew as much New England history as Prince. The group found support in Joshua Gee, whom Cotton had called to the Second Church when Increase died in 1723; however, Gee, although temperamentally "fiery hot, his principles rigid to the highest degree, and his charity as cold as death in regard of all but those who tho't as he did," was the most indolent man in Boston; still, when he could be roused he would work with Cooper and Prince. The kind of man these clerics admired was another classmate of Prince and Sewall, William Shurtleff, who went up to Portsmouth in 1732 and, finding the place rife with Pelagianism and Socinianism, the richly dressed congregation fallen into the supposition that mankind "had nothing further in View than to smoke and eat together, to tell a pleasant Story, and to talk of the common and ordinary Affairs of Life," commenced his pastorate by telling them he would not give "a nice and Philosophical Account of the Nature, Influences and Motions of the Stars."

The lull that had come around 1720 with the fading out of the Mathers, by which Colman, Leverett, and Wadsworth had prospered, was now being repented. Old-style Calvinism, in a new and harsher, a self-consciously reactionary mood, was taking a new lease on life, for reasons which to the Colman generation were obscure. An endorsement by Prince and Cooper therefore meant that one of the two rapidly cohering factions among the clergy of eastern Massachusetts put the stamp of their approval upon Edwards. Strangely enough, the spiritual parentage of this group went back, often through direct contacts, to the Mathers, whom Stoddard had fought. But simultaneously the members claimed to be followers of Colman, because he had taught them the value of emotion and he, rather than the Mathers, had provided their style. The majority of the clergy in and around Boston, most of whom were probably in the audience on July 8, still looked askance upon such extravagances as Sewall's weeping; they were solid enough Calvinists, and they too deplored the decline of New England, but they could not yet get so excited about it. Each of these, the rank and file of the clergy, was a power in his own community, and if a movement was to be organized for the awakening of piety and the reform of manners, these solid citizens would need to be enlisted. As he preached the lecture, Edwards was aware of them.

But he was most aware of another element, numerically the smallest, but already the greatest in prestige and intellect. In order to challenge these men, he came to Boston, just as his grandfather used to come to beard the Mathers. It is of the essence of the situation that this group considered themselves inheritors of the Colman tradition no less—such are the ambiguities of liberalism—than did the Cooper-Prince faction. "Free and catholick" was their motto, but to Jonathan Edwards, conditioned by the tumult of primitive Yale and trained by Stoddard to the standards of frontier autocracy, they incarnated everything most corrupt and complacent in the metropolis. If he was to hold together the provinces his grandfather had conquered, it was against these minions of the Enlightenment he must fight. If he found allies in men like Cooper, Prince, or Sewall, that only showed how Jehovah could raise up partisans even in Babylon. But if the faith of the Valley and of primitive New England was to be vindicated, then the Harvard of Leverett and of Wigglesworth and of the platitudinous Wadsworth—which was the American outpost of "the prodigious prevalency of infidelity and heresy in this nation at this day"—had to be told that God can be glorified by, and only by, man's absolute dependence upon Him.

Edwards had little difficulty in picking out his antagonists. Nathaniel Appleton of Cambridge, who exerted a constant influence on Harvard, pleaded for caution in judging those who differ "in some points," opposed cheap money, could be "very merry at whist," and was known to be the source of certain stories about "indecent freedoms with women." Wigglesworth himself, who unwittingly twice escaped becoming Edwards' preceptor, and whose students were annually infiltrating the churches of the seaboard, was a candid man, "no ways rigid in his attachment to any scheme, . . . charitable to others, though they widely differed from him." Thirty years later he was to confess, what he had suspected all along, that "notwithstanding any thing in the decrees of God, there may be a certain connection between striving to enter in at the strait gate, and admission to it." In 1730, Governor Belcher, who shared Wigglesworth's admiration for Tillotson, secured him a D.D. from Edinburgh, which was a citadel of Calvinism no less than Glasgow.

There was also Peter Clark of Danvers, who argued that nothing should be admitted for truth but what a rational judgment can accept upon convincing evidence; then there was Barnard of Marblehead, all his life called "Johnny," who once suffered ecclesiastical censure for playing cards, and whose favorite phrase was: "zeal guided by knowledge, tempered with prudence, and accompanied with charity." There was Edward Holyoke, weighing 235 pounds, who had been a tutor under Leverett and was now minister at Marblehead, of whom Johnny Barnard said, "I think Mr. Holyoke as orthodox a Calvinist as any man; though I look upon him as too much of a gentleman, and of too catholic a temper, to cram his principles down another man's throat." Then there was Ebenezer Gay of Hingham, endowed with a sense of humor and famous as a conciliator of disputes. And finally, there was the short, sturdy, thin-lipped colleague of Foxcroft at the First Church, Charles Chauncy of the class of 1721, who had been ordained in 1727, the same year in which constable Miller escorted Edwards to his consecration at Northampton.

Did Edwards recognize in Chauncy the man designated by providence to be his arch-opponent? Unless he was even more unworldly than his wife and friends supposed him, he should have sensed it. Chauncy was known in the west; he had gone out there after his graduation because he had relatives in Hatfield, where the predecessor of Williams had been a Nathaniel Chauncy. Charles stopped long enough to collect first-hand impressions of the Williamses: "They were all too apt to be governed in conduct by an undue regard to self." He read the works of Stoddard, and "was never able to see in them that strength of genius some have attributed to him." But also on this expedition he went down to Wallingford in Connecticut to spend six weeks with Samuel Whittelsey, who, having married Sarah Chauncy of Hatfield, was his cousin-in-law, and in this member of the Yale class of 1705 he found a man after his own heart, with "the clearest way of expressing his thoughts upon any difficult subject of any one I have been acquainted with." In all modesty, Whittelsey confessed that "when he had in his mind clear ideas of a subject, he could communicate them with the same clearness they lay in his mind, and do it with ease," which to Chauncy was a definition of genius.

To appreciate what this group meant by clarity, we must consider the history of the Whittelseys. Samuel's "clear and strong head" brought him in 1722 to testify with Cutler against Congregational ordination, but it also had proved strong enough to bring him rapidly back into conformity with what in Connecticut was called the "standing" order. His son, Samuel, Jr., Yale 1729, studied for a year at Harvard, received an M.A. in 1732, and then settled at Milford, where he soon made so clear his free and catholic sentiments that in 1739 half his congregation seceded from him. The second son, Chauncy Whittelsey, graduating in 1738, was a tutor at Yale during the Awakening, when enthusiasm of the Ferris variety became rampant among the students; one of the most intense was a feverish young man named David Brainerd, and one day in hall, after Tutor Whittelsey had been "unusually pathetic in his prayer," a friend asked Brainerd what he thought of him, and Brainerd replied that Whittelsey "had no more grace than this chair." A freshman told "a certain woman in the town," who told Rector Clap, who unceremoniously expelled Brainerd from Yale. Years later, Edwards told the story in his tender biography of Brainerd, and still later, ten years after Edwards' death, Chauncy Whittelsey was to assert that if Edwards' scheme were received for orthodoxy, many would become Deists and more atheists by substituting in their minds "necessity in the Room of an Intelligent Moral Governor." The Whittelseys, in short, were to prove the leading opponents in Connecticut of the Awakening, and were from the beginning cut from the same cloth as Charles Chauncy.

To return to 1731, was it, then, a coincidence that on April 4, three months before Edwards spoke at Commencement, Chauncy invited Samuel Whittelsey to preach in the pulpit of the First Church? Did it just happen that Whittelsey, "being occasionally in Town," perhaps to arrange for his son's graduate work at Harvard, was available? Was it a spontaneous move, or did Chauncy contrive that a motion should arise "from one and another" to have Whittelsey's sermon published? Did he know, as he must have, that the Boston ministers had already invited Stoddard's successor, and did he hasten to place this other voice of Yale on the record? In the light of the actors' characters and subsequent conduct, the presumption is that they all knew what they were doing.

At any rate, Whittelsey's *The Woful Condition of Impenitent Souls in their Separate State* was in the bookstalls by the time Edwards came to town. Although admirably clear, it is not a memorable document; its thesis, laid out in the conventionally logical heads, is that the souls of wicked men go immediately at death without delay to hell, and that "the Doctrine of the Soul's sleep, is exploded as an unreasonable and groundless phansie." The choice of subject was a demonstration to Cooper and Sewall that the Chauncy-Whittelsey *entente* was sound on the doctrine of future torments. The first "application" was addressed to rich men, "who spend your days in Mirth, and your years in Vanity," warning them that they will weep and howl. But for us the interest of the sermon is not so much the sermon as the preface, which was signed by Foxcroft (out of courtesy to his colleague's guest, but also out of endorsement of the doctrine) and by Chauncy. As ultimately proved to be the fact, this was the opening maneuver of the free and catholic faction to establish alliances in the Valley, to offset possible coalitions of Cooper and Prince with Edwards; Chauncy was already capturing outposts inside the Stoddard territory, among those who, as he put it, "in retired places of service, out of the way of Fame or any worldly Reward, . . . are diligent in their Studies." Eulogy of Whittelsey was a bid for further support among Yale men and back-country devotees of clarity:

> And we take this occasion to express our Joy in the Increase & Flourishing of Yale-College, which may well boast of being the happy Mother of our Author, who stands in the first Rank of her learned Sons, and who is (we think) the only Instance as yet, of a Father and his Son named in her Catalogue of Graduates. May that Society be ever a fruitful Seminary of pure Religion, and the most useful Learning from whence shall spring up many Plants of Renown, to enrich and adorn the Garden of Christ.

The meaning behind this preface, taking it along with the preface to Edwards' sermon, is simply that Yale, although obviously a doubtful constituency, was being wooed by two separate factions in the rapidly shaping alignment of Boston. She might well cast the deciding vote. Chauncy was not an eloquent man; he had so little relish for poetry that he "wished that some one would translate *Paradise Lost* into prose, that he might understand it," and when he once prayed God not to make him an orator, a friend replied that his prayer was long since granted. Still, he presumed to praise Whittelsey as one whose lips were touched with fire, whose discourse was "full of Tho't and sacred Flame." What seemed flaming to Chauncy and his friends appears in Whittelsey's highest reach of rhetoric, where devils are pictured waiting round the bed of a dying man: "When they have him in their power, they torture him with their bitter invectives, their biting sarcasms and cutting exprobations." The ultimate in anguish, as conceived by the apostles of clarity, was exactly this: "What a torment to endure the lashes of their unceasing Insults." Chauncy was junior to the powerful Foxcroft, but in the First Church he had a rostrum from which, it was expected, he and his scholarship would be heard. He had the most distinguished post in New England—except for the eminence to which Stoddard had elevated the Northampton desk. Undoubtedly Chauncy was present on July 8. There is no record that he spoke. (Indeed, there is no record that he and Edwards ever exchanged words directly.) But assuredly he would have listened with care to the inexorable assertion that the only way God can be glorified is through the abasement of man. Just three months before, his friend Whittelsey, who knew the back-country well, had said that a man can be subjected to no greater abasement than bitter invectives, biting sarcasms, and unceasing insults.

Thus Edwards spoke on July 8 not merely as a casual visitor from out of town. He represented Yale, and he was Stoddard's heir; half his audience was prepared to embrace him, a certain element was watching him with suspicion. It is in the light of these ominous circumstances that the sermon must be read; yet it concealed, with a deliberateness more eloquent than any open reference would have been, his complete awareness of the situation. At first hearing the discourse would seem no more than a conventional assertion of a thesis held in New England from the beginning. Perhaps the manner was a trifle haughty, and there were certainly no flourishes of eloquence, no similes, no metaphors of ships staggering into Boston harbor with rich freight. If Chauncy had not so recently exhibited a contrasting specimen, Harvard might have concluded that oratory at Yale had not yet been blessed by Colman's "learning and moderation." There was indeed learning, but the old-fashioned, narrowly Biblical sort instead of the more flowing and allusive kind that took cognizance of Tillotson and *The Spectator*. There was also a kind of fierce moderation in the baldness of the assertion, but it was the restraint of an inward discipline, not of catholicity.

The thesis was that conversion is "in every thing, directly, immediately, and entirely dependent on God," that man is holy, if ever, "from mere and arbitrary grace." The sermon affirmed, without mitigation, "that the creature is nothing, and that God is all," that God is under no obligation to redeem anybody, and that if any are saved, it is by "God's arbitrary and sovereign good pleasure." This doctrine Cooper and Prince were pressing upon the people, while it was being noticeably scanted by such gentlemen as Appleton, Gay, and Johnny Barnard. However, the latter group could not disavow it, and Professor Wigglesworth paid lip-service to it in lectures from his Hollis chair. So they must have recognized the strategy: Edwards did not deign to acknowledge that anyone in New England did or could protest his doctrine; instead, he contented himself with a carefully sustained paragraph declaring that "schemes of divinity" which in any respect hedge upon such absolute dependence are "repugnant to the design and tenor of the gospel." In his concise catalogue of all gradations and shades of opinion that tend toward a "partial dependence," Edwards served notice that he was skilled in detecting nascent defections. Amid the decorum of the lecture, the paragraph was a gage of battle, a challenge to a combat that would be waged, not as in the time of Stoddard over ecclesiastical forms, but over fundamental theological and philosophical issues. Such a conflict, once joined, could not conclude with a stalemate of the kind Stoddard and the Mathers accepted by 1710. In the war to which Edwards invited the Harvard liberals, there would be no quarter. So Cooper and Prince were delighted, and underscored their joy: "Our satisfaction was the greater, to see him pitching upon so noble a subject, and treating it with so much strength and clearness, as the judicious will perceive in the following composure."

But were even they judicious enough to understand what they admired? It is true that New England from the beginning had held that the redeemed depend directly on God. Still, even before the migration of 1630, theologians of the Congregational way had qualified this assertion by declaring that the relationship between God and man was cast, by God's own appointment, into the form of a "covenant." At the moment of conversion, their doctrine ran, the saint is received into a compact with the divine, and thereafter depends for his security upon the fact that the transaction is on record. The sacraments are then given him as "seals of the covenant," testifying to what had been nominated in the bond. The advantage of this "Federal Theology," as it was called, was that by conceiving of regeneration as the drawing up of a covenant, requiring assent on both sides, the clergy could, even while professing absolute predestination, offer to rational men certain inducements for their attempting to open negotiations. Hence they could preach with vigor, on the assumption that energetic sermons become "means of grace" by working upon the reason and will of an auditor. Though grace was indeed a free gift of God, and was not a reward to human merit, still no man signs a deed or a lease without his own consent, and surely not without the assurance that the terms are binding upon both the signatories. By this adroit and highly legalistic formulation, seventeenth-century New England found a way for human enterprise in the midst of a system of determinism.

But Edwards put the pure doctrine without the slightest mitigation. The Federal Theology is conspicuous in his sermon by its utter absence. "The nature and contrivance of our redemption is such, that the redeemed are in every thing directly, immediately, and entirely dependent on God: They are dependent on him for all, and are dependent on him every way." No one in Puritan New England could quarrel with this statement as it stood; but some might note the omission, the insistence upon "contrivance" instead of "covenant," and the emphasis upon the "direct" and the "immediate." If they began to wonder, their suspicions could be further aroused as he went on to play down the rôle of the "means," declaring that while they are made use of, still God gives them, and God alone makes them effectual, not any efficient or causal power of their own. "It is of God that we have ordinances, and their efficacy depends on the immediate influence of his Spirit." New England had learned in dealing with Antinomians and Quakers that people who insist inordinately upon the "immediate" influence of God could easily come to conclude that no means or ordinances were any longer necessary. For a century the usual method was to point out that while grace is indeed from God, nevertheless means must be used. The whole ecclesiastical order of New England, which is to say the whole society, was built upon that "nevertheless." But Edwards' emphasis was clearly different: the Holy Ghost is from God, and grace is the gift of God. "And God is under no obligation to any man: He is sovereign, and hath mercy on whom he will have mercy." This is very different from saying that God will have mercy on those who take up a covenant.

Furthermore, the New England theology had always assured the elect that once the covenant was signed, sealed, and delivered, they were safe. Solomon Stoddard had hammered at this theme in his *Safety of Appearing:* once inside the covenant, the saints were guaranteed their salvation. They could work thenceforth in the conviction of memory, though their sense of the event might grow dim. But Edwards said before all Boston, "As grace is at first from God, so it is continually from him, and is maintained by him, as much as light in the atmosphere is all day long from the sun, as well as at first dawning, or at sun-rising." Again there was nothing here to which any could take exception—unless perhaps the equating of a continuous influence of God on the saints with such a natural phenomenon as light in the atmosphere. For a major contention of the Federal Theology was always that man, while in nature, is not of nature; in the Covenant of Grace he is treated, at least formally, as a power in his own right. If man is as an atmosphere in which the light of the sun shines, and if without that light he is mere void and darkness, what then is man?

All this might have given even Cooper and Prince pause, were it not that in their enthusiasm for the doctrine they did not stop to consider the implications of so stark a version. Yet even they might have wondered about certain peculiarities of diction. Did they forgive these as the crudities of strength, as signs of a lack of Harvard training? Certainly there was something a little strange in the vocabulary, at least as compared with the use of words in other sermons of that year. There was, for example, an odd concentration upon the term "excellency." Early in the sermon Edwards described the fallen state of man as wanting "excellency to merit," which might be easily comprehended; then he made a logical distinction between two kinds of good which the redeemed find in God—an objective good and an inherent. He defined the objective, barely allowing his audience time to take it in, as "that extrinsic object, in the possession and enjoyment of which they are happy." Then he introduced the second point, not stopping to elucidate, with a brusque dictum: "Inherent good is twofold; it is either excellency or pleasure." Two sentences later, the sense seemed to be merely that the saints are both excellent and happy, which was safe ground. But was this all he meant? What queer metaphysic, or what hidden assumptions, lay behind this abrupt definition? What, as Edwards was using the terms, is the difference between excellency and pleasure, and what do they signify when subsumed under an "inherent" good?

Still more puzzling to the judicious was a repeated, though unexplained, emphasis upon conversion as "sensible." Because the holy have previously been polluted, "the production of the effect is sensible." Of course, Puritanism had always understood that conversion is an experience, and the Congregational system, limiting church membership to "visible" saints, had always assumed that it was distinguishable enough to be tested. Unfortunately, difficulties had arisen in applying the test to specific individuals, and the Half-Way Covenant had been devised to take care of persons who were not positively sure they had had the experience. Solomon Stoddard had then drawn his own deduction—the center of his quarrel with the Mathers—that because the problem of particular diagnosis was impossibly complicated, everybody should be taken into the church and given the Lord's Supper. But all parties to this dispute were agreed that theoretically the experience was, or might be, actual. But why "sensible"? Why the assumption, made as though all understood it, when everybody knew the problem to be complex, that it pertains exclusively to the senses? The senses, as Colman had shown, were the eyes (which gaze upon beauties), the ears (which receive pleasant sounds), and the palate (which tastes delicate food); our sins have blasted this earthly paradise—although Colman still made it attractive. But this notion that conversion is sensible seemed to imply, if it meant anything, that the converted would revel uninhibited among beauties, harmonies, and delicate foods. By the same token, if damnation is the opposite of salvation, was it, too, sensible? Did this mean that the damned would be subjected by devils, not only to unceasing insults, but to actual physical pain?

All this was enigmatic enough, but there appeared to be at the back of the lecturer's mind still another concept somehow associated with that of the sensible: if a man fails to apprehend the difference between God and himself, he is not sensible of it, and so "will not be disposed to give God the glory due to his name." Now, apprehension of the difference between God and man is a function of reason, which is a faculty superior to the senses; at least, this was the way New England had always thought of it: why, then, should an intellectual faculty be described as sensible? And then, what was the connection between the sensible and the disposed?

To dispose means simply to arrange in order; does a man become disposed one way or another only through the sensible? If Edwards was insinuating anything of this sort, he was suggesting something that to Harvard men of 1731, to either of the varieties of Harvard men, was utterly strange.

The suspicion that he meant something that he was not yet willing, or perhaps not yet able, to speak of outright might have become a certainty to any clear-headed enough to sense the logical inferences when, upon completing his proof that views of a partial dependence are unscriptural, he abruptly introduced a paragraph with another disturbing sentence: "Faith is a sensibleness of what is real in the work of redemption." Surely this was a deliberate conjunction of terms. It seemed to say that on the one side is something rooted in the senses, a physical matter, and on the other a reality which is difficult for the physical to reach, which must be stripped of appearances in order for sense to come into relation with it. This was even more of a foreign language to the students of Leverett and Wigglesworth. Did this distinction, if it was a distinction, have anything to do with the previous distinction of the objective from the inherent? What was its relation to the talismanic definition of the inherent as consisting either of excellency or of pleasure? And then faith: it appeared to be a linking of the sensible and the real, a new solution to an epistemological question nobody had asked. Where was the problem, anyway? Why could not the sensible, by eating a peach or tasting honey, by kicking a stone, or by killing an Indian, get at what is real, and so distinguish it from appearances? And how could faith—which everybody knew is that by which some of us go to heaven—have anything to do with joining the human senses to objective reality? By weaving into his discourse, otherwise so conventional, such gnomic words, was Edwards not only challenging his opponents to a duel, but himself making the choice of weapons?

THE EXTERNAL BIOGRAPHY I

Edwards' great-great-grandfather was an English clergy-man who taught in the school of the Coopers' Company in London; he died of the plague in 1625, leaving a widow and a son named William. She married a cooper, one James Cole, and with him migrated to New England. They settled in Hartford about 1640.

William Edwards inherited his stepfather's trade and tools, but his son Richard, born at Hartford in 1647, was not only a cooper but a merchant, and so became a man of wealth. Richard and his wife, Elizabeth Tuttle, had six children, of whom the eldest was Timothy, born in 1669. Elizabeth proved, by the most charitable account, to be of unsound mind; at any rate, she bore a seventh child by another man, and her husband invoked a council of ministers to justify his petition for divorce. There were other scandals in the Tuttle family: Elizabeth's brother killed a sister with an ax and was hanged for it; another sister murdered her own child. However, her son Timothy was eminently sane.

Timothy, with his father's wealth behind him, could afford to go to Harvard, where he was graduated in the class of 1691. He was ordained minister in the east parish of Windsor, Connecticut, in May 1694.

In colonial New England most men of twenty-five were already married and had become fathers. Intellectuals were obliged to postpone that bliss until they acquired their college degrees and found themselves a pulpit. If they did not have a bride-elect by that time, they quickly found one. Wives and husbands made, on the whole, devoted couples, but they were not sentimental, and courtships were realistic. By November 6, 1694, Timothy was married—to Esther Stoddard, the second child of the Rev. Solomon Stoddard of Northampton. Timothy's merchant father bought him a farm and built him a house that was considered elegant at the time. Esther was twenty-two at her marriage; she lived to be ninety-eight, dying on January 19, 1771. Stoddards were usually a long-lived clan.

Physically and mentally, if the language be permissible, Jonathan Edwards was more a Stoddard than a son of Timothy. From the beginning in New England the Stoddards were aristocrats. Anthony Stoddard, a merchant among the founding fathers, married Mary Downing, a niece of Governor Winthrop. Solomon, his son, was graduated from Harvard in 1662, when he maintained as his commencement thesis the then conventional Puritan affirmative to the question, "Whether God punishes sin by a necessity of nature"— a prophetic commitment in view of the altered connotations his grandson was ultimately to find in the terms "nature" and "necessity." In 1669 Solomon accepted the call to the frontier town of Northampton, where the first minister, Eleazar Mather, brother of Increase, had recently died. Solomon promptly married the widow, Esther Warham Mather, and took unto himself her three children; to these Solomon and Esther added twelve more. Esther continued to the last, though "lame of the Sciatica," to work "at the Linen-wheel"; she died in 1736, aged ninety-two.

Solomon Stoddard dominated the Connecticut Valley and contested the ecclesiastical leadership of New England with Increase and Cotton Mather. Through the marriages of his children and stepchildren, he became the center of an intricate web of family relationships that virtually covered Western Massachusetts and Northern Connecticut. For the understanding of Edwards' story it is essential to remember that while one daughter, Esther, married Timothy Edwards, another daughter, Christian, became the second wife of the Rev. William Williams of Hatfield. The Williamses were a numerous, hard-driving crowd. William Williams was much older than Christian; by his first wife he already had one son, Elisha. Christian bore him two sons, Solomon (later minister in Lebanon, Connecticut) and Israel. These two were thus full cousins to Jonathan. Elisha we might call a stepcousin. Another daughter of Stoddard married the leading merchant of pioneer Northampton, Joseph Hawley, and bore him a son named Joseph.

Timothy and Esther Edwards had eleven children, ten of them girls. Jonathan, the fifth child, was born on October 5, 1703. He received his elementary schooling, along with his sisters, from his father, who, like most New England ministers of the period, conducted a school on the side. Two surviving letters of Timothy's, written while he was absent as chaplain on an abortive invasion of Canada in 1711, exhort Esther to prosecute Jonathan's studies in Latin grammar.

It seems likely that Jonathan wrote his thousand-word essay, "Of insects," as early as 1715, or at the latest in 1716. His father was then corresponding with an English friend who had asked for information about American spiders. Presumably about 1716 he also wrote a short demonstration that the soul is not material, and analyses of the rainbow and of colors. These pieces all exhibit a precociousness that has, of course, made Edwards into a legend. From the essay on colors it appears that he had already studied Newton's *Opticks* or else had learned its contents in some manner. His earliest datable writing is a letter to a sister, May 10, 1716, describing a "pouring out of the Spirrit of God" in East Windsor—one of those premonitory local awakenings that presaged the great upheaval of 1740. It indicates that from the beginning his life was attuned to the rising crescendo of back-country revivalism.

Edwards was entered in Yale College in September 1716, aged thirteen. A few weeks after the matriculation at New Haven, the class moved to Wethersfield, only ten miles from East Windsor, where they were tutored by Elisha Williams, nine years older than Edwards and five years out of Harvard. Contention over the location of the College endured for three years, and only after June 1719 was Edwards resident in New Haven.

In the Wethersfield period, then, Edwards read Locke and commenced writing the "Notes on the Mind." Out of his reading in science, and especially in Newton, came "Notes on Natural Science." Whether all of these entries date from his undergraduate years, or whether some belong to his postgraduate studies, is impossible to determine. In his senior year he was college butler, and during it had a disagreement with his freshman roommate, who was also his cousin; Elisha Mix evidently rebelled against paying the customary duties to his student superior. Timothy was informed, and wrote an insulting letter to Elisha's father, the Rev. Stephen Mix. Since Mix had married still another daughter of Stoddard, the episode may be interpreted, considering the nature of New England families, as a further indication of latent stresses within the Stoddard connection.

Edwards finished his collegiate course in September 1720, and remained in the college preparing for the ministry until August 1722, when he accepted the call to a Scotch Presbyterian church in New York, which met in a building on William Street between Liberty and Wall. That a Yale man should go to a Presbyterian church speaks much concerning the ecclesiastical complexion of Connecticut; after that colony, following the teachings of Stoddard, adopted the Saybrook Platform in 1708, its polity, with its regional associations of ministers, so closely approximated the Presbyterian system that cordial relations with the Presbyterian centers of New York and New Jersey became increasingly easy. That Edwards, the child of New England Congregationalism, should take his first pulpit in a Presbyterian body indicates how indifferent to him had become the forms of church polity, at least in the sense in which they had been of fundamental importance to the founders of New England.

In New York he lived in the family of one John Smith, a currier, who became and remained his "dear friend." In this attachment may first be detected, as later friendships and letters sometimes reveal, what Stanley Williams has called "that elusive sweetness of nature, which somehow brings the student back, even when his gorge rises at the dreary doctrines of Calvin, to Edwards himself."

By the spring of 1723 it was evident that the church was not prospering, and Edwards left in April in response to a call from Bolton, Connecticut. He spent the summer at East Windsor, and by November had completed his arrangements with Bolton, when he received an offer from Yale College. He took his Master of Arts degree in September, and assumed the office of tutor on May 21, 1724.

The period of his youth and his collegiate and graduate career was later recollected, in 1739, in his *Personal Narrative.* However, since this was written after the ebbing of the "Surprising Conversions" at Northampton, and while he was laboring and praying for a new awakening, it cannot be taken as an altogether factual record of his earliest years. Yet even in this highly self-absorbed narrative there are glimpses of Connecticut pastures and of a solitary place on the banks of the Hudson which testify to the vividness of his experiences. In his last year of study at New Haven and through the summer at East Windsor he put down the series of his "Resolutions," and on December 18, 1722, commenced his "Diary," which he kept up with regularity only through the first year. It is believed that in 1723, probably at East Windsor, he wrote the apostrophe to Sarah Pierrepont. In June he made his first recorded visit to Boston, but found nothing worth noting in his diary but that he was to blame during the journey in respect to strict temperance in eating, drinking, and sleeping; while in the city he concluded with himself that it would be to his "advantage" never to do anything but his duty, whatever the unpleasant circumstances, and not to please any man.

As senior tutor at Yale, Edwards was effectually in charge. There was still no president, and with but one colleague he instructed sixty students. In June 1724, he conceded in his diary, "I have now, abundant reason to be convinced, of the troublesomeness and vexation of the world and that it never will be another kind of world." During September 1725, he was seriously ill at the house of a friend in North Haven, and his mother came down from East Windsor to nurse him. In that month the trustees added £5 to his salary in reward for his extraordinary services and for his pains in sorting books and making a catalogue.

The church at Northampton voted in April 1725 that the time had come to find a colleague pastor for the aging Stoddard. Edwards was first invited to preach in August 1726, and having proved satisfactory—and being wanted by Stoddard—he was invited "to Settle" on November 21, 1726. He was ordained on February 15, 1727, and married at New Haven to Sarah Pierrepont on July 28, she being then seventeen years of age. Their first child, Sarah, was born on August 25, 1728. On February 22, 1729, Solomon Stoddard died, and William Williams preached the funeral sermon.

Edwards' second child, Jerusha, was born in April of 1731, and in July he went to Boston to deliver the Public Lecture.

I call him an amateur in philosophy who accepts just as they come the terms of a given problem, believes it definitely posed, and limits himself to choosing between the patent solutions which necessarily exist previous to his choice. But to philosophize in earnest would here consist in creating the formulation of the problem as well as creating its solution. How could it be otherwise? Is it not evident that if the problem has long since been posed, and is not yet resolved, that is because it embraces, in the form in which it is framed, two or more solutions equally possible, which are mutually exclusive? The true philosopher cannot, must not, rest there. Hence I call him an amateur who chooses between solutions already reached, as one chooses the political party in which he wishes to enroll. And I call him philosopher who creates the solution, in this event necessarily unique, of the problem which he has posed anew by the very fact that he has attempted to resolve it. There is thus between the two a radical difference, but one which will escape readers of both if they do not penetrate, by an exertion which necessarily demands an effort analogous to the philosopher's, to the new sense which the words take on in the new conception of the problem.

HENRI BERGSON

The Inherent Good

MAKE YOUR PORK on a few legs," said Ebenezer Phelps of Northampton, "and get your milk from a few bags." For two years after the lecture, Edwards published nothing. We know he was busy. After Stoddard's death the Hampshire Association continued to meet, with Williams of Hatfield in the chair, and Edwards attended; it organized lectures, copied after Boston's Thursdays, among the six towns in rotation, and Edwards took his turn; it set up rules for admitting candidates to the ministry, continuing to defy the laws of the colony which gave each congregation the right, at least in theory, to call whom it wished. The Association ruled that a woman who had a bastard and would not name the father could be admitted to a church if her repentance was sincere, and it passed resolutions against "growing vice and immorality, and particularly tavern-haunting and disorderly night-walking."

Edwards took part in these decisions, governed his church, preached every Sabbath, and received £200 a year. Three deacons kept the parish in order. In politics the town was full of turmoil, having for twenty years been divided into what was called the "Court" party—"some of the chief men in the town, of chief authority and wealth, that have been great proprietors of their lands"; and the "Country" party—"which

has commonly been the greatest, have been of those, who
have been jealous of them, apt to envy them, and afraid of
their having too much power and influence in town and
church."

From the beginning, Northampton was exceptionally ex-
plosive: during Stoddard's time the heat of strife between the
two parties once rose to such a degree "that it came to blows,"
and often "Mr. Stoddard, great as his authority was, knew not
what to do with them." Still, when Deacon Ebenezer Hunt's
felt-making shop burned in January of 1734, everybody in
town contributed to buy him a new stock, turned to and re-
built the house, and had him back in business within nine
days. Only five men wore white shirts, on Sunday or any
other day; the rest, including some of the chief men of the
Court party, wore checkered shirts. In the summer of 1733
there were locusts, and in October an influenza. In August
Edwards delivered a sermon which, according to legend, so
delighted his people that they persuaded him to publish it.
I suspect he did considerable rewriting; he could hardly have
devised a more carefully constructed sequel to the Boston lecture than the treatise that came off the press early in 1734
bearing the title, *A Divine and Supernatural Light, Immediately imparted to the Soul by the Spirit of God, Shown to be
both a Scriptural, and Rational Doctrine.*

It is no exaggeration to say that the whole of Edwards'
system is contained in miniature within some ten or twelve
of the pages in this work. Yet it, no less than its predecessor,
is a puzzle. Edwards was not the sort who undergoes a long
development or whose work can be divided into "periods."
His whole insight was given him at once, preternaturally
early, and he did not change: he only deepened. Whatever he
suffered and whatever mistakes he committed, though he
would criticize himself unmercifully—"If I had had more
experience, and ripeness of judgment and courage, I should
have guided my people in a better manner"—he altered little
from his adolescence at Yale to his death in Princeton. His

works are statement and restatement of an essentially static conception, worked over and over, as upon a photographic plate, to bring out more detail or force from it clearer prints. Perhaps this is because, being the apotheosis of Puritanism, he was committed to rigidity and would not put his thought at the mercy of changing circumstances, biographical or social. If this explanation be allowed—and there is much in Edwards' thought and behavior that is simply irrefrangible— it coincides with a now widely current theory of Puritanism, or at least of American Puritanism, which holds (in Harold Laski's words) that it refused to see the individual in his context as a member of a particular society, and instead— putting the individual outside society—left him to assure his own regeneration "by an act of will, sometimes called faith." However, seventeenth-century Puritanism had a highly developed social philosophy and Edwards' tradition certainly was not one of "inaction."

Application of this thesis to Edwards encounters the initial difficulty that while he was indeed intractable, he always exalted experience over reason. He could remember being so young that he thought two objects, one twice as far off as the other, were the same distance away, one above the other; his senses, he reflected, made the same representation of them then as now, and in themselves the senses do not deceive: "The only difference is in *experience*." In his latest thinking he condemned as nonsensical all views that regard reason as a rule superior to experience, that build upon "what our reason would lead us to suppose without, or before experience, . . . even in those matters that afterwards are tried by experience, and wherein experience shews things in a different light from what our reason suggested without experience." The riddle of Edwards is that this (as his townsmen came to believe) monstrously intransigent man scorned the doctrinaire: "History, observation, and experience, are the things which must determine the question."

In these respects Edwards must be called, as this study will call him, an empiricist. This is not to say, however, that Edwards held tentative hypotheses subject to constant alteration by further experiment. Critics filled with the spirit of modern positivism rashly declare that because at the age of twelve Edwards wrote a masterpiece of microscopic observation upon a species of flying spider, and as an undergraduate put down a series of "Notes on Science" which exhibit a phenomenal mastery of Newton, he was a potential scientist thwarted by his environment and forced into the uncongenial wastes of theology. The precocious piece on the spider does indeed indicate, as his nineteenth-century biographer put it, "a fondness, minutely and critically to investigate the works of nature"; but Edwards went to nature and experience, not in search of the possible, but of the given, of that which cannot be controverted, of that to which reason has access only through perception and pain, that of which logic is the servant and from which dialectic receives its premises. "And thus it is we actually determine, that experience is so good and sure a medium of proof."

That the mold of Edwards' mind set so early and so indestructibly is to be explained, not on the easy generalization that the Puritan "neo-Platonist" rigorously guarded his sensitive conscience from contamination by the particular, but rather by his proud conviction that into his primary vision he had incorporated the terms of his age in such basic simplicity that he could give a meaningful account of all particulars. Undoubtedly, after he left the Yale library, he suffered a poverty of books, but the evidence of his journals is that this was no handicap, for he read other thinkers, not for new ideas, but to check their arguments against his own, and to appropriate occasional pages for his own devices. Thus he was passionately interested in experience, his own, his wife's, his people's—or the universe's—because in experience was to be detected the subtle working of the pattern; but he was supremely uninterested in personality, his own or anybody else's. Especially, we may add, in his own. Being nominated to the presidency of the College of New Jersey in 1757, he brought forward the list of his disqualifications:

"I have a constitution, in many respects peculiarly unhappy, attended with flaccid solids, vapid, sizy and scarce fluids, and a low tide of spirits; often occasioning a kind of childish weakness and contemptibleness of speech, presence, and demeanor, with a disagreeable dulness and stiffness, much unfitting me for conversation, but more especially for the government of a college."

This is to be taken, I believe, not so much for description as for estimate. Had he been permitted to finish out a term as president of Princeton, he would have presented to the rest of America the challenge of a character capable simultaneously both of complete self-distrust and of absolute confidence—a mixture he possessed to so sublime a degree that even among Yankees, for whom inner conflict was assumed to be the lot of man, he was frightening. His point was that a person's peculiar eccentricities are not of interest except in so far as they are part of the judgment that life passes upon him. Nothing innate, nothing claiming royal rights previous to experience, ever had value for him, and he simply assumed that no person could be an end in himself because he was unique. A man achieved significance by becoming a focus of experience, not by indulging in eccentricity. The contrast between his mind and Chauncy's, whose letters to Stiles in the 1760's hit off the foibles and quirks of his contemporaries with brilliant malice, is complete.

Consequently two reflections must be borne in mind if one is to read Edwards perceptively. In the first place, he was entirely satisfied to express himself, so far as content goes, in the received tenets of Calvinism. The body of dogma was an adequate formal account of reality. This can hardly be said of any other New Englander of his time. He expended no ingenuity on extracting novel or arresting theses out of Biblical texts or in trying to phrase old doctrines in idiosyncratic ways, as did those progeny of Cotton Mather, Joseph

Sewall and Thomas Prince. Nor did he follow the cavalier method of his grandfather: according to a Yale graduate who studied with him, Stoddard chose his subject as though writing an essay, worked it out, "and last of all looked a Text & wrote it with an Introduction to his Doctrine"—a method increasingly cultivated by the free and catholic wing of the clergy, whose sermons were rapidly becoming literary orations to which a text was mechanically prefixed.

Edwards took each verse of the Bible for an object in experience, drew from it the baldest, most obvious doctrine, reasoned it out, and applied it in the standard Puritan form. In contrast to the straining for effect and the experimentalism of a Foxcroft or a Cooper, or to the studied Addisonianism of Chauncy, or to the colloquial ease that Mayhew was shortly to bring into the pulpit, Edwards' sermons are overwhelmingly commonplace in their propositions and as conventional in form as Elizabethan sonnets. He was an artist working in a tradition, and for him the tradition was sufficient. Therefore to read him in the hope of discriminating between what is his and what is traditional, one must seize upon occasional passages, definitions by the way, the peculiar use of key words, and above all the use of words as incantation. His originality was not substantive but primarily verbal—which justifies calling him an artist—although his innovation in language portended an ultimate revolution in substance. His technique remained that of the Boston lecture, a rigorously unornamented prose and a stark, logical dissection of some Calvinist platitude, where the deceptive simplicity concealed the fact that certain immense metaphysical assumptions had been smuggled in through the vocabulary. He never sought out or recognized the terms used by his opponents, or tried to equate theirs with his, or helped them to comprehend him; he simply assumed that his own were the only terms available and infuriated his enemies by taking their words in his sense. By steadfastly refusing, not so much to compromise as to admit that there was anything to compromise, he forced his antagonists or his listeners to come up to his level, or to fight against words they could not understand. Certainly many of them—Charles Chauncy and, after twenty years of it, the majority of citizens in Northampton—did not understand. To follow Edwards sympathetically requires of the reader an effort analogous to his own, a seizing on the new sense of his words in the framework of his conception. Edwards would be the first to agree that this is not easy: he had resolved, when still a boy, "To live with all my might, while I do live."

Secondly, Edwards never did set forth the framework, once and for all, in black and white. He was trying to do so in the great project on which he worked all his life, "A Rational Account of the Main Doctrines of the Christian Religion Attempted," which was to show "how all arts and sciences, the more they are perfected, the more they issue in divinity." This was to be the *summa* of Calvinism, for which his youthful notes on the mind and on science were the first drafts, which lay behind every sermon, for which he stored up meditations in his notebooks, of which the published works are fragments. "I am fitted," he remarked after his people expelled him from Northampton and he knew not what would become of him or his numerous and chargeable family, "for no other business but study. I should make a poor hand at getting a living by any secular employment." He composed out of such deep recesses of study that in his mind every sentence pertained to a place in the "Rational Account," but readers and listeners, ignorant of the piles of notebooks on his desk, could not always see the connections.

Yet, even had the "Rational Account" been completed, it still would have presented the system obliquely. Not because Edwards' system was unmanageably complicated, like Kant's or Hegel's: there are numerous paragraphs in which the essence is compacted; but rather because at the center of it was a conception so simple that to attempt complete enunciation was (as he realized while still at Yale) to go "so far beyond those things for which language was chiefly contrived, that, unless we use extreme caution, we cannot speak, except we speak exceeding unintelligibly, without literally contradicting ourselves."

One hardly knows, therefore, whether the cryptic element in Edwards' writing is deliberate artistry—he early determined not to let it "look as if I was much read, or was conversant with books, or with the learned world"—or a psychic inhibition (to use his own phrase, a moral inability) that kept him from what Samuel Whittelsey found so easy and Chauncy so admirable, the communication of ideas with the same clearness in which they lay in the mind. We are not sure whether we have to deal with a pathological secretiveness or an inherent inexpressibility in the thought itself. Both interpretations can be put upon a passage in the private notebooks which declares that we may go farther into abstraction than any have yet gone, far enough at last to see reality and truth in part, "and yet we may not be able more than just to touch it, and to have a few obscure glances"; strength of mind may fail us, he predicted even in his youth, and then, "We had better stop a degree or two short of this, and abstract no farther than we can conceive of the thing distinctly, and explain it clearly: otherwise we shall be apt to run into error, and confound our minds." In every utterance of Edwards, even his most personal letters, there is an implication that can become unbearably painful, a suggestion that powerful though any argument is, strength of mind falls short, and that he is stopping a degree or two this side of ultimate truth, where things can still, though just barely, be distinctly conceived. What is not clear is whether the stopping short is out of mercy to the audience or simply because he has reached the limits of language. If the latter, then the temptation was always present to push the limits a bit farther, and then possibly still farther.

So his second publication, like his first—and his last—contains an exasperating intimation of something hidden. There is a gift held back, some esoteric divination that the listener must make for himself. Edwards' writing is an immense cryptogram, the passionate oratory of the revival no less than the hard reasoning of the treatise on the will. The way he delivered his sermons is enough to confirm the suspicion that there was an occult secret in them: no display, no inflection, no consideration of the audience. "Mr. Edwards in preaching," remembered one of the townspeople, "used no gestures, but looked straight forward; Gideon Clark said 'he looked on the bell rope until he looked it off.' " His writings are almost a hoax, not to be read but to be seen through. In the manuscripts of his ordinary sermons, most of which are mere jottings of topic heads, he patiently recounts the obvious as though to a child; that he was keeping much back is clear, but in the published works his strategy of assertion without full revelation is constant. He makes a dogmatic thrust that startles by its very dispassionateness, delivers a blow upon the ear or eye so violent and yet so calculated that the stunned victim has no time to ask why he should have been struck in the first place, or just what he was hit by.

In his controversial tracts—and all except *The Nature of True Virtue* are polemics—the method is a sustained attack, never a defense; he demolishes at tedious length all possible positions of his opponents, including some that they do not hold but might hold, and all the time hardly declares his own. He seems to work upon the grim assumption that if all other philosophies are totally demolished, survivors of the bombardment will crawl out of the ruins, prepared to decipher, from the few clues he gives them, the unuttered secret of his smashing power. To the end he remained the child who studied with concentration the pretensions of flying spiders, which are not the sort "that keep in houses" or the sort "that keep in the ground, and those that keep in swamps, in hollow trees, and rotten logs," but the sort who construct "curious network polygonal webs"; the chief end, he found even that early, of their wondrous faculty "is not their recreation, but their destruction."

In *A Divine and Supernatural Light,* the way for the cryptic utterance is carefully prepared by pushing aside the false lights: the occasional conviction of sin men have because they are miserable, some reach of their imagination, some new philosophical notion, or the emotion experienced upon reading a romance, seeing "a stage play," or being affected "by any other tragical story." What is it then? It is, as he had said in Boston, a sense. And then comes the carefully planned elaboration of the Boston discourse: it is "that which consists in the sense of the heart: as when there is a sense of the beauty, amiableness, or sweetness of a thing; so that the heart is sensible of pleasure and delight in the presence of the idea of it." With the insertion of the word "idea" into the foldings of the logic, Edwards held out another clue; his people might take it simply for a word, but to those conversant with books it was a signal from which they might at last get some glimmering of what he was driving at—provided, that is, their conversation with books included converse with John Locke's *An Essay Concerning Human Understanding.*

Not only had Jonathan Edwards' converse, unlike that of even more erudite contemporaries, included Locke's *Essay,* but the reading of it had been the central and decisive event in his intellectual life. He discovered it in 1717 when still at Wethersfield, two years after the essay on spiders, and read it with far more pleasure "than the most greedy miser finds, when gathering up handfuls of silver and gold, from some newly discovered treasure." History cannot scrape together out of all America as early as 1717 more than a handful of men who had read the *Essay,* and none with any such realization that the "new way of thinking by ideas" would determine the intellectual career of the eighteenth century. The boy of fourteen grasped in a flash what was to take the free and catholic students of Professor Wigglesworth thirty or forty years to comprehend, that Locke was the master-spirit of the age, and that the *Essay* made everything then being offered at Harvard or Yale as philosophy, psychology, and rhetoric so obsolete that it could no longer be taken seriously.

What prepared Edwards for the insight? At first view nothing in the history of thought is more incongruous than the instinctive seizure by this backwoods adolescent upon the doctrine that emerged from the sophisticated entourage of the first Earl of Shaftesbury, and yet one can, I believe, make out the logic of it. The boy had walked in his father's pasture, looking upon the sky and clouds until "the appearance of every thing was altered" and "there seemed to be, as it were, a calm, sweet, cast, or appearance of divine glory, in almost every thing"; he used to sit and view the moon, "singing forth, with a low voice, my contemplations of the Creator." His mind became "greatly fixed on divine things; almost perpetually in the contemplation of them," until his inability to express what he felt became a torturing clog and a burden: "The inward ardour of my soul, seemed to be hindered and pent up, and could not freely flame out as it would." Then he read Locke, and the divine strategy was revealed to him. God's way, Locke made clear, is indirection, which is the only way, because speaking the unspeakable is impossible; God works through the concrete and the specific, and the mind (Edwards would add, the regenerate mind) must know enough "to stop when it is at the utmost extent of its tether." The way to cope with the problem was not to raise questions and multiply disputes, as did M.A. candidates in the public "commonplacings" by which they qualified themselves to be ministers in New England, but "to take a survey of our own understandings, examine our own powers, and see to what things they were adapted." Otherwise, we shall either come to a "perfect scepticism" or else "let loose our thoughts in the vast ocean of Being; as if all that boundless extent were the natural and undoubted possession of our understandings, wherein there was nothing exempt from its decisions, or that escaped its comprehension."

For a young man on the verge of drowning in the vast ocean of Being, the disclosure of "this historical, plain method," which gave at last a full account of the ways whereby our understandings attain their notions and which prescribed tests of the certainty of knowledge, was not only a rescue, it was a directive for living. It saved him from the fire of his own intensity, or from the scepticism which in moments of depression seemed the only alternative, by teaching him that the one legitimate field of both speculation and worship is the content of the human mind. Out of his study of Locke, remote as such a result was from Locke's aim of bringing philosophy "into well-bred company and polite conversation," Edwards was able to solve his problem, and (as he believed) the problem of American culture, by achieving a permanent and abiding sense "how meet and suitable it was that God should govern the world, and order all things according to his own pleasure."

From the beginning Puritan education was organized into a hierarchy of the liberal arts culminating in a blueprint of creation, taught as the crowning subject in the curriculum and called "technologia," which was supposed to be an organon of all the arts and was therefore an exhaustive chart of the order by which God did govern the world. Therein were laid out all things, concepts, relations, propositions, principles, as in a graph which, with endless branches and subdivisions and "dichotomies," looked like a genealogist's diagram of some gigantic family tree. At the moment he read Locke, Edwards was learning technologia from Elisha Williams. Locke showed him that technologia was "some of the rubbish that lies in the way of knowledge," a "learned but frivolous use of uncouth, affected, or unintelligible terms" that had to be cleared away before the "master-builders"—Locke mentioned specifically Boyle, Sydenham, Huygens, "and the incomparable Mr. Newton," names that echoed ominously in the air of Wethersfield—might get on with the proper business of philosophy, "which is nothing but the true knowledge of things."

The elaborate structure of technologia, which was taught

not as a knowledge of things but of "arguments," collapsed in Edwards' mind like a house of cards as he learned from Locke that men can acquire the materials of reason and knowledge solely from (Locke printed it in capitals) "EXPERIENCE." Men have to deal with things, but not with things as they lie in the divine mind or float in the ocean of being, but simply as they are registered on the human brain. When perceived by the mind, a thing is, to speak accurately, no longer just a dead thing by itself, but the mind's "idea" of it. An idea, said Locke, is "the *object* of the understanding when a man thinks." This is, in fact, only common sense, but the point is that one does not need an elaborate scholastic ritual to grasp the definition of ideas: "every one is conscious of them in himself." Yet just that simplicity of the first principle was what delivered Edwards from the maze of technologia a generation in advance of his fellows. Thenceforth Edwards' fundamental premise was Locke's, the assurance that what the mind knows is no more than its ideas, and consequently (Locke again resorted to capitals) that "this great source of most of the ideas we have, depending wholly upon our senses, and derived by them to the understanding, I call SENSATION."

Edwards read this work with ecstasy, the burden of an insupportable weight lifted with every page. No longer, he saw, need mankind struggle through life on the supposition that certain innate concepts were implanted in them which did not originate out of the world about them, which were supposed to be part of the image of God and therefore to exert absolute authority in advance of any experience or any actual problem. Locke made it evident that to believe in such an imperative was to submit to something so out of kilter that it was bound to become an excuse for self-indulgence. Hence Edwards' thought cohered firmly about the basic certainty that God does not impart ideas or obligations outside sense experience, He does not rend the fabric of nature or break the connection between experience and behavior. The universe is all of a piece, and in it God works upon man through the daily shock of sensation, which (here Locke resorted to italics) *"is such an impression or motion made in some part of the body, as produces some perception in the understanding."*

The best of it was, for Edwards, that Locke accounted for, even while destroying, such monstrosities as technologia: those sublime constructions, "which tower above the clouds, and reach as high as heaven itself," all take their rise from (and so can be resolved back into) the lowly senses; "in all that great extent wherein the mind wanders, in those remote speculations it may seem to be elevated with, it stirs not one jot beyond those ideas which *sense* or *reflection* have offered for its contemplation." Therefore Edwards was enabled to understand the predicament of New England civilization: if religion remained bound to an antiquated metaphysic, false philosophy would drag theology deeper into the morass. The free and catholic spirit, confessing by its scorn of cramming principles down another man's throat that it had no principles to cram, was setting up an ideal of candor attached to no particular scheme, a position which was as great an evasion of sensation as the rubbish of technologia. Here was the secret of that decline of piety which all the clergy lamented, but which none was able to arrest.

Furthermore, did not Locke, by supplying the diagnosis, also point the way to rectification: "As the bodies that surround us do diversely affect our organs, the mind is forced to receive the impressions; and cannot avoid the perception of those ideas that are annexed to them." If the way to make living impressions on the minds of men is through the senses, did it not follow that a Christian oratory which would put aside all those vague and insignificant forms of speech, all those abuses of language that have passed for science, which with the help of Locke would "break in upon the sanctuary of vanity and ignorance," which would use words as God uses objects, to force sensations and the ideas annexed to them into men's minds through the only channel ideas can be carried to them, through the senses—would such an oratory not force upon New England the awakening that three generations of prophets had called for in vain? It was central to Locke's analysis that the mind, having no innate faculties of its own, is so dependent upon the outer world that it is wholly passive in receiving impressions, "and whether or no it will have these beginnings, and as it were materials of knowledge, is not in its own power."

Critics of Locke, even in his own day and more ardently in the nineteenth century, have called his doctrine of "passivity" the fatal weakness of empirical psychology; the mind of Edwards, however, was trained by the doctrine of New England, in which it had always been held that man is passive in the reception of grace and that he is bound to sin if he tries to earn salvation by his own efforts or on his own terms. Was it not precisely here that the new metaphysics and the old theology, the modern psychology and the ancient regeneration, came together in an exhilarating union? The whole reach of the vision unfolded before Edwards as he read Locke's innocent observation that simple ideas, "when offered to the mind, the understanding can no more refuse to have, nor alter when they are imprinted, nor blot them out and make new ones itself, than a mirror can refuse, alter, or obliterate the images or ideas which the objects set before it do therein produce." The empirical passivity became for Edwards, in the context of eighteenth-century New England, not an invitation to lethargy, but a program of action.

The question that teases historians is where Edwards got his copy of the *Essay*. In Boston, although Locke's treatises on government were being cited, the *Essay* appears not to have been digested until the middle of the century; a copy was in the Dummer gift, but in 1717 that collection was still in crates at Saybrook. Obviously a stray volume came somehow, from some hand, to his, possibly from Tutor Samuel Johnson's, because he, as we now know, had an experience similar to Edwards' only two years before. At his graduation in 1714, Johnson prepared, as every student was required to do, a manuscript summary of technologia, the surviving copy of which bears a marginal notation, "And by next Thanksgiving, November 16, 1715, I was wholly changed to the New Learning." In other words, he, too, almost as youthful as Edwards, rejected Puritan scholasticism the moment he read Locke; in 1716 he was a tutor with whom Edwards could have had a brief contact at New Haven before he followed Williams to Wethersfield. However, the Williams connection disliked Johnson and gloated when he proved a traitor. Perhaps the awful example of Johnson had something, possibly too much, to do with Edwards' morbid secrecy, after he had given his heart to the new philosophy, about disclosing overt signs of his conviction.

It may be, of course, that Edwards and Johnson, both reacting against the sterility of technologia, read separate copies of Locke and independently found their liberation; certainly, from this time forward Locke meant something altogether different to the Anglican who became the first president of King's College from what he meant to the Calvinist who became the revivalist of Northampton. No doubt the condition of learning in the colleges in this decade, and especially in Yale during the contest about its location, was low, possibly as low as Johnson remembered. At the time of his graduation, he says, there were rumors "of a new philosophy that of late was all in vogue and of such names as Descartes, Boyle, Locke, and Newton, but they were cautioned against thinking of them because the new philosophy, it was said, would soon bring in a new divinity and corrupt the pure religion of the country."

All the evidence suggests why Edwards had to be extremely cautious about avowing what Locke meant to him, and why his resolution "to be very moderate in the use of terms of art" has to be taken as meaning specifically the art of John Locke. At any rate, one element in the peculiarly cryptic character of all of Edwards' creations is simply that he con-

tinued to use words in the Lockean sense without confessing
or defining it, and that much, though not all, of the mystery
is solved if he is read with the *Essay* in mind. His people, of
course, could not gather from his statements the inward meaning unless they too had studied Locke, as few Ebenezer
Phelpses and Hunts had. But that did not hinder Edwards,
who could use Lockean principles to work effects upon
people ignorant of Locke; so when he came to argue with
Chauncy about the Awakening, he used the same tactics, and
put the case for the revival in a language that Chauncy assumed they understood in common, but for which Chauncy
did not have the key.

Edwards presumably prepared a manuscript technologia
for his graduation in 1720, as Johnson had in 1714; it does
not survive, probably because he did not think it worth keeping. But in the seclusion of his chamber, fired with his new
enthusiasm, he started a private one. Whatever the defects of
technologia, it did at least require the student to organize
the little he knew; Edwards confessed that he had been
pleased "with study of the Old Logick" because it taught
him to range his thoughts in order and to distribute them into
categories, "so that I could tell where they all belonged, and
run them up to their general heads." Now that he was gone
over to the "other Logick," he set himself to compose a new
technologia, characteristically undertaking nothing less than
a *summa* of all knowledge at the first essay. As an undergraduate and possibly as a tutor he progressed as far as the
manuscripts called "Notes on the Mind" and "Notes on Science," which, being published in 1830, made his reputation
as a philosopher and won him a place in the textbooks. Actually they are mere drafts, crude but full of the spontaneous
excitement of discovery, for the design he was to prosecute
during the rest of his life. I shall come back to them frequently, but for the moment the "Notes on the Mind" may
be said to show primarily how immense was the impact Locke
made upon him, and how, from the sensationalist premises,

he reached his startling disjunction of the good and his conception of the inherent good which, distinguished from the objective, consists either in pleasure or in excellency.

Modern criticism has been fascinated with the "Notes" mainly because Edwards made the brilliant stroke of extending to primary qualities the critique which Locke applied to the secondary. As the history of philosophy is written, at least in this country, Edwards' lonely performance appears so astounding that the remainder, the major portion of his undertaking, goes unnoticed. Undoubtedly this feat is testimony to Edwards' genius for abstract speculation, or at least to his knack for improving upon his sources. According to the mechanics of sensation as Locke conceived them, the color, sound, or taste habitually attributed to objects actually exists only in the senses of spectators, and therefore such qualities, which he called secondary, had to be "mental." But the qualities which, by his reasoning, were inseparable from the nature of body itself—solidity, bulk, extension, number, figure, mobility—by any honest consideration must be granted the status of objective reality; these characteristics impress upon the senses a motion which "must be thence continued by our nerves, or animal spirits, by some parts of our bodies, to the brains or the seat of sensation, there to produce in our minds the particular ideas we have of them." The blue color and the sweet scent of the violet, although effects upon our senses, are ideas that God has "annexed" to the violet, not the flower itself; but the bulk and figure are really there, "whether any one's senses perceive them or no." Edwards began by dutifully repeating this logic: "there never can be any idea, thought, or act of the mind, unless the mind first received some ideas from Sensation, or some other way equivalent, wherein the mind is wholly passive"; still following his master, he argued that it was now agreed "by every knowing philosopher" that colors are no more in things than pain is in the needle, "but strictly no where else but in the mind." At this point, having stripped off all subjective attributes, Edwards asked the question that has proved the fatal question of modern metaphysics: how can we have an idea which will correspond faithfully to uncolored space since our ideas of color do not correspond to the external causes of color? To simplify the problem, he reduced Locke's solidity, number, figure to the single term "resistance," and then was able to show how it, being no less a concept than color, was no less mental. "And how is there any Resistance, except it be in some mind, in idea?"

After Locke, the intellect of western Europe became obsessed with epistemology. After Kant, obsession became mania despite the protests of Mill and of William James that the separation of the synthetic judgment from the thing in itself is false, unnecessary, unprofitable, and paralyzing. When Edwards' "Notes" appeared in 1830, amid a generation to whom the subject-object relationship was all-engrossing, they were hailed as a phenomenal achievement (which they are) because they gave America, to its vast surprise, a pioneer "idealist." "The world is therefore an ideal one; and the Law of creating, and the succession, of these ideas is constant and regular." Such a sentence, rent from its context, has so excited the awe of students that where Edwards is known as anything more than the preacher of hell-fire, he is considered the one American who saw through Locke's halfway and half-hearted arguments, who roundly concluded that if color is subjective, then so is mass. "Hence it is manifest, there can be nothing like those things we call by the name of Bodies, out of the mind, unless it be in some other mind or minds."

Unable to believe that anyone in primitive America could make such a leap unaided, critics have advanced the hypothesis, still current, that Edwards got at least the essential hint from Berkeley, whose *Treatise Concerning the Principles of Understanding*, published in 1710, likewise transmuted primary qualities into subjective perceptions. Actually there is no evidence whatsoever that Edwards read Berkeley, then or later; his journals meticulously acknowledge his debts to every philosopher he managed to read, and nowhere is there any sign of a first-hand acquaintance with Berkeley. Belief in the Berkeleyan influence springs from a reluctance to credit a mere boy with achieving such maturity—a strange inference for the century of Mozart—or else upon a superficial reading of the parallel. In Edwards, "idealism" is an incidental argument, and except for the fact that his mind moved for a few paragraphs along the same path as Berkeley's, a path that was unmistakably laid out by Locke, Edwards and Berkeley have little in common. Berkeley wanted to destroy Locke's thesis that out of repeated sensational experiences with particulars the mind constructs "abstract general ideas"; Berkeley contended that the mind has ideas only of particulars and that abstract ideas simply do not exist. Not only was Edwards innocent of such a concern, but on this score he remained incurably Lockean, and took abstract or complex ideas to be as much true mental entities as the simple.

Also, it is obvious that Edwards would have protested with every fiber of his being against the tendency of Berkeley's logic, which eventuated in freedom of the will and a thoroughgoing doubt of the "external world." To anticipate what will, I trust, become still more evident, it was a constant in Edwards' philosophy that the only "sense" to be trusted is one which is "in an agreement with the nature of things," which gives accurate representations of concrete objects and "a right understanding of things in general." The simplest, and most precise, definition of Edwards' thought is that it was Puritanism recast in the idiom of empirical psychology, and since it was Puritan before it was Lockean, all the logic converges upon a condemnation of those who hold, in any fashion, that the external world is not external and factual. Dogmatic though he is, Edwards is the least solipsistic of modern thinkers.

Hence for Edwards, from the beginning, the world was real. "Things are where they seem to be." His so-called idealism was a stratagem, not to deny objective existence, but to affirm it, and he recognized at once (so deeply did he comprehend what Locke had wrought) that this "way of expressing, will lead us into a thousand difficulties and perplexities." He tried to assure himself (not always successfully) that when he spoke of the material universe as existing only in the mind he spoke merely of the world as it is known, and only of that world did he claim "that it is absolutely dependent on the conception of the mind for its existence." Metaphysically, this led to the immense conclusion that the entire universe exists in the divine idea; but for practical purposes Edwards was persuaded that "it is just all one, as to any benefit or advantage, any end that we can suppose was proposed by the Creator, as if the Material Universe were existent in the same manner as is vulgarly thought." We may continue, even after we have agreed that matter is dependent upon idea, to speak—that is, to preach—"in the old way, and as properly, and truly as ever." We may still talk as though bodies are where they appear to be whether or not anybody perceives them, because our problem as sentient beings is to find our way among them, truthfully and without sin.

Warning himself to be careful lest he confound himself by mere imagination, Edwards kept his speculations hidden, but he did not, he could not, altogether succeed in speaking in the old way, not even in Boston. He was so thoroughly saturated with the *Essay*, and reworked its concepts with such concentration, that as soon as he opened his mouth, he used words with the denotations acquired in his interior meditations. The words and phrases he could not keep out of his discourse, which make his attempt to speak in the old way persistently become a new way, are those that pertain not to his explorations of epistemology but of perception. When Edwards stood up among the New England clergy, it was as though a master of relativity spoke to a convention of Newtonians who had not yet heard of Einstein, or as though among nineteenth-century professors of philosophy, all assuming that man is rational and responsible, a strange youth began to refer, without more ado, to the id, ego, and super-ego.

In *A Divine and Supernatural Light* Edwards threw out to the townsmen, and by publishing it to all New England, for what they could make of it, this crucial passage:

> It is out of reason's province to perceive the beauty or loveliness of any thing: such a perception does not belong to that faculty. Reason's work is to perceive truth and not excellency. It is not ratiocination that gives men the perception of the beauty and amiableness of a countenance, though it may be many ways indirectly an advantage to it; yet it is no more reason that immediately perceives it, than it is reason that perceives the sweetness of honey: it depends on the sense of the heart. Reason may determine that a countenance is beautiful to others, it may determine that honey is sweet to others; but it will never give me a perception of its sweetness.

His auditors, to judge from the semilegendary accounts, were aware of some wondrous mystery behind the passage, but they must also have felt bewilderment, unless by chance they could turn to the second book of Locke and find the explanation: "Our Senses, conversant about particular sensible objects, do convey into the mind several distinct perceptions of things, according to those various ways wherein those objects do affect them." From this principle came the real discovery, for which Edwards' dialectical idealism was merely preliminary: because an object is never just an object, it is never the same for all men, or for the same man at all times, and must vary in their apprehension as the senses variously take it in; hence men perceive variously, and according to how they perceive, they are "affected," and thus they act. Nothing Edwards got from Locke was more important or more fundamental to his thought than this: lacking innate or transcendental standards within themselves, men must encounter objective reality—call it as you will, either mental or material—in the form of ideas given through the senses. For human discourse, things or people or doctrines exist solely within the configuration of a perception. To ask what the thing may be in itself is to ask what the sleeping rocks do dream of, since always, as soon as men take cognizance of anything, they deal with what they themselves have perceived. And perception being the form in which men apprehend, in which they actually see, it is that through which and by which they perform. Perception, for this American empiricist, and on the basis of a strict empiricism, was the way a man conducts himself in the face of reality. It was the irreversible sentence of judgment.

Puritanism had always recognized a distinction between what it called "speculative" religion and living religion. Any man could understand intellectually what a verse in the Bible or a doctrine of theology said, but not all could feel what it meant. Furthermore, the individual who felt it one day found himself incapable of feeling it the next. Puritan diarists, acutely aware of the fluctuation, abound with lamentations over the periods when they are "in a cold, dull, lifeless frame." Puritanism of the seventeenth century had no explanation for the phenomenon except the caprice of God: sometimes He gave the emotion and sometimes He did not. But Edwards entered upon his mission of reawakening New England armed with a scientific psychology wherewith to account, in the finest detail, for this riddle of experience. From Locke's demonstration that a thing cannot be the same to all perceptions, that it must exist for each perceiver as it is perceived, and from Locke's assertion that perception is an immediate, irresistible response of sensation to the impact of an object, Edwards concluded that as a man perceives, so is he—and that as he will perceive, so he is predestined to be! If he perceives in a cold, dull, lifeless frame, the coldness is not in the inert object, but is his own. "He that is spiritually enlightened truly apprehends and sees it, or has a sense of it." To see is to have a sense; to have a sense is to have an inclination; and as a man inclines, he wills.

The process from the form of the perception to the act of the will thus became, for the Edwardsean psychology, not what it had been in the scholastic physics of his predecessors, the complicated transmission of a phantasm through the senses to the common sense, to the judgment of reason, to the command of the will, to the response of the passions; it became an instantaneous and single moment. To perceive became to do. A man's act is not the result of a meshing of gears, but the expression—the "image" he was later to say—of the whole man. "This evidence that they that are spiritually enlightened have of the truth of the things of religion, is a kind of intuitive and immediate evidence." Locke constructed mankind out of sensations in order to rebuke the passions of zealots and to convey the admonition that a natural religion based on experience might be less subject to doubt and uncertainty than a dogma based on fiat; his frontier disciple remodeled the Lockean man into a being radically passionate in religion, and then made him available to the democracy: "persons with but an ordinary degree of knowledge, are capable, without a long and subtle train of reasoning, to see the divine excellency of the things of religion." All a man needs is his senses, which no one in Northampton was lacking; then perforce he perceives, and perception depends not on social status or a Harvard degree, it "depends on the sense of the heart."

As the "Notes" make clear, vistas of empiricism opened indefinitely before Edwards' hard-driving logic. The most enticing, to his first vision as to his last, was the realization that because an object participates in the human mind not as itself but through the idea, it plays an active and double rôle: as a stimulus to action it invites the organism to choose what appears to be the most pleasurable; as an image it has the charm of a purely aesthetic spectacle in the mind. To the extent that the heart is affected by it, both the enjoyment and the beauty are the greater. In the first sense, as a stimulus, the good inherent in an idea—not necessarily in the object which is the source, but in the idea—is a degree of pleasure; in the second, as a timeless essence, it is a degree of excellency. "Excellency," he wrote, "to put it in other words, is that which is beautiful and lovely." The highest degree of pleasure and the nearest approach to excellency are given to man through those ideas which he can positively love. Because objects, persons, doctrines have no ascertainable existence apart from being perceived, they can become through perception the inherent sources of pleasure and excellency to those capable of "a real sense and apprehension of them."

If the mind could conceivably hold converse directly with things instead of going through the medium of ideas, then pleasure would amount to what profits the organism, and excellency to what is useful: a pleasant meal, an excellent spade to dig with, a pleasant banker who reduces the rate of interest, an excellent preacher who is eloquent, and a pleasant and excellent heaven where the saints will get what they want. To this connotation New England had, bit by bit, become accustomed, and by now could comprehend no other. Precisely this, said Edwards—employing what was henceforth to be his peculiar method, a paraphrase in the language of sensationalism of an historic concept—was what in Lockean terms could be defined as the merely "speculative" understanding of that good of which God has made man capable, "as when a person only speculatively judges that any thing is, which, by the agreement of mankind, is called good or excellent, viz., that which is most to general advantage, and between which and a reward there is a suitableness." The fallacy behind the conventional attitude, Edwards was saying, is a misconception of the way God causes the human spirit to operate, which is not by the calculation of rewards, but by ideas. The miracle of an idea is that by its very nature, even while it acts as a stimulus to advantage, it is also an invitation to pleasure and a testament of beauty. This coördination of utility and glory in the very act of perception was the great, the original and creative, result of Edwards' deep immersion in Locke.

In *A Divine and Spiritual Light* Edwards expounded the difficult and yet simple doctrine with care, but he could not put into one short sermon everything he had packed into the

"Notes on the Mind." Today the sermon is often cited as the finest expression of his "mysticism," and its point accordingly lost, the point he was striving to make, that spiritual light is imparted not as a mystical infusion but as a rational conveyance through the senses. Supernatural conviction, he was trying to say, arises out of perception, it "is an effect and natural consequence of this sight." A regenerate man is one who perceives in such a fashion that in his heart he cannot help knowing the delight and the beauty. As against all merely speculative notions, "the will, or inclination, or heart, is mainly concerned."

This was Edwards' defiance, as explicit as he could make it in 1733, of Boston, of Harvard, of the century. If we take reason to mean only ratiocination, "a power of inferring by argument," then the perception of excellency is no business of the reason. By this contention he offered to lift from the shoulders of troubled spirits the weight of the rationalism, or of the scepticism, of the age. But still the sermon is baffling. Was Edwards not in effect debasing the religious insight by equating it with something merely sensational? And was he not, despite the "rational" in his title, verging upon stark irrationality when he declared that reasonable persuasions could "have no proper causal in the affair"? He held out new and enticing definitions of grace in terms of pleasure and excellency, but after all, this was the eighteenth century, which was dedicated from the beginning not alone to empiricism but more particularly to an absolute certainty that events have causes. Nobody, not even in New England, could any longer pretend in enlightened society that any occurrence, even regeneration, might flout the law of cause and effect. Had Edwards, remote as was Yale College from enlightened society, not heard of Sir Isaac Newton and the three laws of motion?

In vulgar modern terms Newton was profoundly neurotic of a not unfamiliar type, but—I should say from the records—a most extreme example. His deepest instincts were occult, esoteric, semantic—with profound shrinking from the world, a paralyzing fear of exposing his thoughts, his beliefs, his discoveries in all nakedness to the inspection and criticism of the world. . . . His peculiar gift was the power of holding continuously in his mind a purely mental problem until he had seen straight through it. . . . Anyone who has ever attempted pure scientific or philosophical thought knows how one can hold a problem momentarily in one's mind and apply all one's powers of concentration to piercing through it, and how it will dissolve and escape and you find that what you are surveying is a blank. I believe Newton could hold a problem in his mind for hours and days and weeks until it surrendered to him its secret. . . . He looked on the whole universe and all that is in it *as a riddle*, as a secret which could be read by applying pure thought to certain evidence, certain mystic clues which God had laid about the world to allow a sort of philosopher's treasure hunt to the esoteric brotherhood. He believed that these clues were to be found partly in the evidence of the heavens and in the constitution of elements (and that is what gives the false suggestion of his being an experimental natural philosopher), but also partly in certain papers and traditions handed down by the brethren in an unbroken chain back to the original cryptic revelation in Babylonia. He regarded the universe as a cryptogram set by the Almighty—just as he himself wrapt the discovery of the calculus in a cryptogram when he communicated with Leibnitz. By pure thought, by concentration of mind, the riddle, he believed, would be revealed to the initiate.

JOHN MAYNARD KEYNES

The Objective Good

ASTRAY COPY of Locke might have found its way to Wethersfield in 1717, but that Williams' little band owned a copy of *Principia* is unlikely. Many entries in the "Notes" probably attained their present form only after Edwards had moved back to New Haven in 1719, and some passages may date from his tutorship in 1724-26. After the College forcibly reclaimed the Dummer collection from Saybrook, Edwards could hold in his hands the actual *Principia* and *Opticks* Newton himself took down from his shelves and gave to Dummer for a gift to the new college in the wilderness. (In 1723 Harvard owned the *Opticks* but no *Principia*.) We know that Samuel Johnson read this *Principia* and vainly tried to teach himself enough mathematics to understand it. Edwards never understood fluxions or other higher mathematics, but to the extent that a man can read Newton without such proficiency, he read him, and though like most admirers he accepted the "sublime geometry" on Newton's say-so, he appreciated the more literary "Scholia" with a profundity not to be rivaled in America until the great John Winthrop took over the Hollis professorship as successor to Greenwood in 1738, or until a printer in Philadelphia succeeded in keeping his shop until it kept him in sufficient leisure to allow time for reading. Consequently, when we go behind Edwards' early publications to find the hidden meanings, we discover in the "Notes" not one key but two, a dual series of reflections, often intermingled but not yet synthesized. The one proceeds out of Locke and becomes what posterity has called his "idealism"; the other begins with Newton and becomes what has been less widely appreciated, his naturalism. In his mind there was an equilibrium, more or less stable, of the two, which is the background of his cabalistic dichotomy, set up in the Boston lecture as though it were too apparent to need explaining; if his proposition about the "inherent good" requires for full comprehension a knowledge of Locke, his assertion of the "objective good" demands an equally rigorous study of Newton.

Edwards would not compartmentalize his thinking. He is the last great American, perhaps the last European, for whom there could be no warfare between religion and science, or between ethics and nature. He was incapable of accepting Christianity and physics on separate premises. His mind was so constituted—call it courage or call it naïveté—that he went directly to the issues of his age, defined them, and asserted the historic Protestant doctrine in full cognizance of the latest disclosures in both psychology and natural science. That the psychology he accepted was an oversimplified sensationalism, and that his science was unaware of evolution and relativity, should not obscure the fact that in both quarters he dealt with the primary intellectual achievements of modernism, with the assumptions upon which our psychology and physics still prosper: that man is conditioned and that the universe is uniform law. The importance of Edwards—I cannot insist too strongly—lies not in his answers, which often are pathetic testimonies to his lack of sophistication or to the meagerness of his resources, but in his inspired definitions. Locke is, after all, the father of modern psychology, and Newton is the fountainhead of our physics; their American student, aided by remoteness, by technological innocence, and undoubtedly by his arrogance, asked in all cogency why, if the human organism is a protoplasm molded by environment, and if its environment is a system of unalterable operations, need mankind any longer agonize, as they had for seventeen hundred years, over the burden of sin? By defining the meaning of terms derived from Locke and Newton in the light of this question, Edwards established certain readings so profound that only from the perspective of today can they be fully appreciated.

"The whole burden of philosophy," said Newton, "seems to consist in this—from the phenomena of motions to investigate the forces of nature, and then from these forces to demonstrate the other phenomena." Conceiving the universe as motion—which, unlike the concepts hitherto taught in New England, such as substance, form, and accident, could be expressed in mathematical formulae—Newton arrived at such an earth-shaking discovery as this: "If you press a stone with your finger, the finger is also pressed by the stone." Of course, no farmer in Connecticut needed to be told, "If a horse draws a stone tied to a rope, the horse (if I may say so) will be equally drawn back towards the stone." But every farmer was told, and professed to believe, what Luther had put succinctly over a century before the *Principia:* "For though you were nothing but good works from the sole of your foot to the crown of your head, yet you would not be righteous, nor worship God, nor fulfill the First Commandment, since God cannot be worshipped unless you ascribe to Him the glory of truthfulness and of all goodness, which is due Him." By the logic of that other science, called divinity or theology, upon which New England was founded, the best of deeds were "insensate things," which in themselves reflect no slightest glory upon the Creator. "Faith alone is the righteousness of a Christian man." If a man has faith, according to Luther—and after him Calvin and the Puritans—he "is free from all things and over all things."

For a century Yankees had believed this, but they had not been free from and over such things as the stones in their pastures, which broke both their own and their horses' backs.

In the old-fashioned physics a stone was a concatenation of form and substance, with a final cause, and so its weight could be "improved" in theology as a trial laid upon man in punishment of his sin; but if now the obstinacy of the resisting body was an inherent mathematical product of its density and its bulk, if it lawfully possessed an inertia of its own which man must comprehend by the analogy of muscular effort, how could a man struggling with a rock in his field become persuaded that by faith he might be "free" of it? A more logical conclusion was that since weight is a natural force, the profitable method of freeing himself from it was by the law of levers, by a better breed of horses, but not by moralizing that the presumption of good works means the instant loss of faith and its benefits. There was—as Edwards perceived the situation—an organic connection between Newton's laws of motion and that law of salvation by faith which Calvin had made, once and for all, "the principal hinge by which religion is supported."

Luther, Calvin, and the founders of New England frequently utilized the physics of their day, which was still scholastic, for illustration or confirmation of their doctrines, but they never dreamed of resting the case for Protestantism upon the laws of nature. Edwards saw in a glance that no theology would any longer survive unless it could be integrated with the *Principia*. Newton claimed that in so far as we can learn the first cause from natural philosophy, "so far our Duty towards Him, as well as towards one another, will appear to us by the Light of Nature." This was not a boast, it was a threat. The *Principia* meant that henceforth there was to be no intelligible order apart from the actual. Although Newton discreetly left unanswered certain basic queries, he did show beyond question that the method of inquiry, in theology no less than in science, must be conformed to physical reality: "For Nature is pleased with simplicity, and affects not the pomp of superfluous causes."

In 1734 Edwards preached a series of sermons on justification by faith, the "principal hinge" of Protestantism; he reworked them into a sustained tract which he published in 1738. It was the most elaborate intellectual production he had yet attempted, and it figures in his development—or rather in the public exhibition of the development he had already undergone—as the first effort in American history to coördinate with the doctrine of Puritan revelation the new concept of science, in which such a superfluity of causes as had been the stock-in-trade of Edwards' predecessors became an affectation of pomp. He was resolved to prove that justification must in all simplicity be merged with the order of causality, and that if salvation was to be called an effect, of which faith was in some sense the cause, then the sequence must be formulated anew in language compatible with Newton's.

The still regnant doctrine, which no respectable Puritan had openly questioned, went back to Calvin himself, who as usual reduced Lutheran eloquence to legalism. Justification by faith, he said, is entirely a "forensic" transaction: a sovereign God is pleased, for no other reason than that He is pleased, to accept the righteousness of Christ in place of the obedience which no man can achieve, and He "imputes" Christ's perfections to a chosen few who in fact fall far short of perfection. These are saved "as if" they were Christ Himself: "He is justified who is considered not as a sinner, but as a righteous person, and on that account stands in safety before the tribunal of God, where all sinners are confounded and ruined." In the realm of objective fact, salvation was conceived by the Puritans as the transfer of a balance on the divine ledger, wherein God arbitrarily accepted another's payment for the debt which all men owed Him by the sin of Adam, and condemned those for whom the debt was not paid, though in life there might be little to distinguish one from another. In its published form, Edwards' treatise on justification reaffirmed the stereotyped doctrine: "A person is said to be justified, when he is approved of God as free from the guilt of sin and its deserved punishment; and as having that righteousness belonging to him that entitles to the reward of life." Had he been concerned, like Prince and Sewall, with no more than restating old doctrines, his tract would have said only this, as indeed no other American publication of the 1730's did.

The necessity of saying something more was, to Edwards' sense of the times, thrust upon him. For over a century Puritans in both Englands had drifted into the habit of calling faith the "condition" of justification. They started speaking in this fashion because they adhered to the "Federal Theology." At first it was merely a manner of speaking. They meant simply that if you believe you may be saved. Their rhetoric, in its early stages, was a natural result of Calvin's version of the whole procedure as a forensic transaction in which the recipient got credit for deeds he had not done. But the legalistic bent of primitive Calvinism, once carried to England, was there accelerated by the alliance of the English Puritans with the Parliamentary lawyers. Concepts taken from the common law pervaded theology, and even before the founding of New England the Puritans had theorized Calvinism anew into an idiom of what the lawyers called a contract or a covenant. Every New Englander before Edwards was a "Federalist," and because he put aside all this sort of thinking, he became a new point of departure in the history of the American mind. All his predecessors would have denied that Federalism was anything different from Calvinism—or Protestantism. They believed that it was simply a more precise way of phrasing the doctrine, on the premise that an absolute God, like an absolute monarch, could be held to nothing but what He had covenanted. Federal theologians, of whom Stoddard was a great example, liked to say that Jehovah, out of sheer indulgence, signed a set of contracts with both Christ and Abraham, in which He covenanted to accept the performance of Christ as though it had been rendered by individuals among the seed of Abraham, on the "condition" that they believe in Christ. As long as the theorists also pointed out that belief was an act of God, and that no man could muster it by himself, they were technically good Calvinists; they merely obtained in the language of the contract a greater precision, or at least a more precise metaphor, with which to argue that God does all, while man is impotent, but that nevertheless there exists a recorded transaction in which the recipient of grace can be accorded, and is assured, the bounty.

Actually, with a century of repetition, and after the political triumphs of 1649 and 1689, the Covenant of Grace came to mean in Puritan circles, in both the Englands, not what God was pleased to grant, but what He was obliged to concede. Faith gradually became so identified, at least in general parlance, with the condition of the covenant that it ceased to mean a decree enacted outside and above the human sphere. It became, bit by bit, something which a man might obtain, and which, once he had it, gave him a claim that God was bound to honor. Even in a theology of predestination, it was declared that a man could do his part and then relax, waiting upon God to do His. The theory of faith as a condition, said Edwards in 1734, is "ambiguous, both in common use, and also as used in divinity." New England had so perverted the language of the founders—the language lent itself rather too easily to perversion—that faith had come to mean "any thing that may have the place of a condition in a conditional proposition, and as such as is truly connected with the consequent."

In these sentences Edwards spoke with restraint, but he was none the less declaring a break with the New England past, a break which his Boston sermon only subtly insinuated. He was putting his finger upon the point at which, as he saw it, the real declension of New England had set in. He maneuvered a revolt by substituting for seventeenth-century legalisms the brute language of eighteenth-century physics. He cast off habits of mind formed in feudalism, and entered abruptly into modernity, where facts rather than prescriptive rights and charters were henceforth to be the arbiters of human affairs. If the experience of regeneration is real, then "what is real in the union between Christ and his people, is the foundation of what is legal." The language of revolution in this undramatic sentence is difficult to catch across the centuries, but taken in the context of the 1730's it is as decisive, and as fundamental, as that of the more historic declarations. In 1734 Edwards was applying to theology a critique which assumed that theology should derive from experience and not from logic or from convention. His society, having slipped into a way of calling faith the condition of a covenant, had made the gratuitous assumption that faith was therefore the actual producer of the effect. It was heedlessly supposing that faith is the cause of salvation, and had insensibly come to assume that a man's belief worked his spiritual character exactly as by his physical exertion he shoved a stone out of a meadow. The people had succumbed to a metaphor, and had taken a shallow analogy for a scientific fact. Hence religion, which can thrive only upon realities, was fallen into decay.

Thus without openly proclaiming a revolution, Edwards effectively staged one. The object of his attack was what his society had hitherto assumed to be the relation of cause to effect, on which assumption it was constructed. If a ball that strikes another is called the cause of motion in the other, it then works the effect and determines the consequences; if, however, the first can be said only to transmit force to the second, it is but the first in a series of events determined by a law higher than itself. Puritanism all unwittingly had made the fatal mistake—it has proved equally disastrous for other cultures—of supposing that an event in one realm can cause effects in a totally other realm, that a man's act of belief can oblige the will of God. It had tried to make the transcendent conform to the finite, and pretended that it had succeeded. Edwards drew upon his study of Newton for a contradictory conception: "There is a difference between being justified by a thing, and that thing universally, and necessarily, and inseparably attending or going with justification." He went to physics for a cause that does not bind the effect by producing it; he found in the new science (few besides Newton himself understood that this was the hidden meaning of the *Principia*) the concept of an antecedent to a subsequent, in which the subsequent, when it does come to pass, proves to be whatever it is by itself and in itself, without determination by the precedent.

He never bewildered his auditors by expounding scientific analogies beyond their grasp, but he quietly took into the realm of theology the principles he had learned—or believed were obvious—in his inspired reading of Newton. Obviously his imagination had taken fire from such remarks of Newton's as, "It is not to be conceived that mere mechanical causes could give birth to so many regular motions." Thousands of Newtonians in the eighteenth and nineteenth centuries took this to mean only that "God" created the universe; Edwards took it to mean that cause in the realm of mechanics is merely a sequence of phenomena, with the inner connection of cause and effect still mysterious and terrifying. He interpreted the sequence of belief and regeneration by the same insight. His people, of course, were still ignorant of the "Notes on the Mind." Had they been permitted to take them from his desk, they might have comprehended how, in his view, the old Aristotelian array of causes—final, formal, and material—had been dissolved before the triumph of the now solitary efficient cause. Hence they might have understood that for him the secret of nature was no longer that an efficient cause of itself works such and such an effect, but is to be defined as "that after or upon the existence of which, or the existence of it after such a manner, the existence of another thing follows." All effects must therefore have their causes, but no effect is a "result" of what has gone before it.

The metaphysics of this idea were profound, but Edwards' statement is so enigmatic that we may rightly doubt whether many good burghers in Northampton had any notion what he was talking about. Still, the import was clear: a once harsh doctrine, which for over a century had been progressively rendered harmless and comfortable, was once more harsh. It was imperiously brought back to life. And there were many among the river gods, and in the counting houses of Boston, who were eager to let sleeping dogmas lie. What right had this grandson of Stoddard—whom the town had employed to carry on his grandfather's ecclesiastical organization—to raise again, and in so disturbing a form, theological issues which New England had settled long since? The society had learned how to live with Calvinism; why make it something with which men could no longer live, or at least could not live on the basis of a profit and loss economy? Edwards began quickly to make converts, but almost as rapidly he made enemies, and most promptly among his cousins.

In five or six compact pages of the sermons that later made up the discourse *Justification by Faith Alone*, pages marked by no rhetorical flourishes, uttered in the calm, impersonal manner that never stooped to the capacities of his audience but bore them down with imperturbable assertion, Edwards pointed out that if the loveliness of a person is what wins faith, if the human achievement is at all a "reward"—which to speculation divorced from the heart might seem, as we have heard, no more than reasonable—then faith is a cause that may or may not be put into action. Indeed, considering the general unloveliness of human beings, it is apt never to get started at all. Furthermore, if faith is an effect of merit, then it too becomes an event which in turn is the cause of still another event, and so on, *ad infinitum*. Every man can be a fresh cause every day of his life, as though he had never lived yesterday, and the universe will be the sum total of today's contingencies, which tomorrow will become still more contingent. Edwards might have called this heresy solely on the strength of the traditional creed or of the Bible, but he took a startling line: "Because the nature of things will not admit of it." By appealing to nature Edwards set up his thesis:

The wisdom of God in his constitutions doubtless appears much in the fitness and beauty of them, so that those things are established to be done that are fit to be done, and that those things are connected in his constitution that are agreeable one to another. . . . This is something different from faith's being the condition of justification, only so as to be inseparably connected with justification: . . . yet nothing in us but faith renders it meet that we should have justification assigned to us.

By this conception any act, either faith or lust, is not an instrument which works an effect, but is part of a sequence within a system of coherence. God is "a wise being, and delights in order and not in confusion, and that things should be together or asunder according to their nature." The connection between a subjective state and an objective fact is not the subject's conviction that his loveliness ought to be rewarded, but is "a natural suitableness," which means that the qualification and the circumstance go together. The difference is fundamental: in the theory of faith as an instrument—as in all "instrumentalism"—the world is supposedly so constituted that it regards the beauty or utility of acts committed by some Ebenezer or Jonathan; in the scientific conception, the ecstasy resides not in a "hypothetical proposition" but in the fact itself, in "the entire, active uniting of the soul." In the first scheme, God waits upon man, and if man elects to be worthy, a grateful cosmos yields to his virtues, or at least to his industry. In the order of the objective good, "Goodness or loveliness of the person in the acceptance of God, in any degree, is not to be considered prior but posterior in the order and method of God's proceeding in this affair." To the bewilderment of an energetic America, intent upon commerce and real estate, where an ounce of effort meant a pound of sterling, Edwards declared that "the nature of things will not admit of a man's having an interest given him in the merits or benefits of a Saviour, on the account of any thing as a righteousness, or virtue, or excellency in him."

If so, the nature of things must in fact be opposed to the

appearances of American society. There had always been in Calvinism a vague feeling that Protestant doctrine had a connection with the structure of the physical universe; Calvin himself, searching for metaphors, compared the light of grace to the rising sun that blots out the stars, or the persuasion of our own righteousness to a foolish eye that prides itself on its perspicacity in viewing adjacent objects and then is dazzled when it looks directly upon the sun. But Edwards, with Newton behind him, saw in the phenomena of nature, as employed in Christ's own discourse, not metaphors to adorn a discourse, but factual embodiments of eternal law. "These things," he confided to his notebooks, "are not merely mentioned as illustrations of his meaning, but as illustrations and evidences of the truth of what he says."

In Newton, Edwards found, as illustrations not of meaning but of the truth of what he would say, two primary conceptions: atoms and gravity. If there was a lion's mouth to be met with, Edwards would put his head in it. In ancient Greece, Democritus had laughed at the superstition of the senses that takes for reality the sweet or the bitter, the hot, the cold, or the purple, when "in truth there are atoms and a void." It is a startling fact about the rise of experimental science that, by the middle of the seventeenth century, scientists took the material universe to be made up of millions of particles which they had never seen, measured, or subjected to experiment, and in which they believed out of sheer faith. Thanks to Gassendi, Galileo, Boyle, and other physicists, this staggering assumption was one of the major premises of Newton:

> It seems probable to me, that God in the Beginning form'd Matter in solid, massy, hard, impenetrable, moveable Particles, of such Sizes and Figures, and with such other Properties, and in such Proportion to Space, as most conduced to the End for which he form'd them; and that these primitive Particles being Solids, are incomparably harder than any porous Bodies compounded of them; even so very hard, as never to wear or break in pieces; no ordinary Power being able to divide what God himself made one in the first Creation.

Newton knew that this doctrine raised the specter of Lucretius and of "materialism"; a major reason for the distrust of the new science which Johnson found active at Yale in 1714 was a fear of its atheistical atomism. But in 1721 Cotton Mather's *Christian Philosopher* laid New England's fears to rest by advertising that the Newtonian world, far from denying, actually proved the existence of God and of design in the cosmos; he invited New England "to avoid philosophical romances" by getting an insight "into the principles of our perpetual dictator, Sir Isaac Newton." Cotton Mather made out of Newton those generalities of law, order, and symmetry that were becoming the commonplaces of eighteenth-century optimism. His "insight" did not go deep, but Edwards' did, and it went to the crucial point: if atoms are so hard that they never break, how small is the smallest atom? And then, if they are massy, hard, and impenetrable, what holds them together?

These were annoying problems for Newton also, and he who boasted of making no hypotheses never gave an answer. Lucretian naturalism had supposed that the atoms were "hooked" and so got fastened together; Newton rejected this fantasy, but he did allow his mind to play with the possibility that some medium might pervade the interstices of bodies and act as a sort of glue to hold atoms together; yet all this, he agreed, was speculation, and the most he could say factually was, "I had rather infer from their Cohesion, that their Particles attract one another by some Force, which in immediate Contact is exceeding strong." When we get behind the brilliant façade of Newtonianism, the apparently rational system of which poets sang and which Cotton Mather embraced, we are brought more terribly face to face with the dark forces of nature than any Puritan had been while staring into the dazzling glare of predestination. That element in the early Newton which Lord Keynes calls necromancy, which was deliberately masked in his last years and was ignored in his panegyrics, was an intuition of pure magic.

> Matters that vexed the minds of ancient seers,
> And for our learned doctors often led
> To loud and vain contention, now are seen
> In reason's light, the clouds of ignorance
> Dispelled at last by science.

Behind the mathematical analysis which by its perfection of form inspired such hymns as this, concealed so carefully that only the most astute might catch a glimpse of it, moved a power that could not be seen by reason's light or dispelled by science, that hid itself in matter to hold the atoms in cohesion, and betrayed its existence by resisting the pressure of a finger. It was to Newton the necromancer that Edwards, who was of the same brotherhood, responded. This Newton, turning from his imaginings of a subtle medium that might give a rational explanation for the solidity of bodies, let slip the intelligence that just how primitive particles, which obviously touch each other only at a few points, "can stick together, and that so firmly as they do, without the assistance of something which causes them to be attracted or press'd towards one another, is very difficult to conceive." The best of Newton's popularizers, Colin Maclaurin, whose *Account* of 1748 was known to Edwards, admitted that while Newton had not quite explained everything, he "left valuable hints and intimations of what yet lies involved in obscurity." The best hint he could leave on this obscure but basic problem was that there must be some agents in nature able to make atoms hang together in bodies, "And it is the Business of experimental Philosophy to find them out." Edwards had the temerity, although he had no laboratory, to take him at his word.

The difficulty was that this problem was in reality a double problem, each aspect of which elusively played into the other: to think how atoms cohered soon became to wonder how large or how small the atom was. Imagine it to be as small as possible, it still occupies space: why cannot it be divided as a stone is split by a wedge? For a century Cartesians had challenged atomists, asserting that unless matter were conceived as completely indivisible, atheism would follow. Newton and his followers were devout men, but they hated Cartesians and believed passionately in atoms and the void. With dogged persistence Newton asserted again and again that the extension, hardness, impenetrability of all objects are founded upon the same qualities in each of the atoms, "and this is the foundation of all philosophy." If so, the Age of Enlightenment was founded on a mystery, but was incapable, except in a few Blakes or Edwardses, of recognizing it. Newton did not want to say that the atom could never be split, and he foresaw that if it could be, we should have to conclude that divided particles may be subdivided to infinity; but for the moment he called a halt before the irreducible minimum, the atom that cannot be shattered and is the stuff of bodies. "We have ground to believe," said his grateful followers, "that these subdivisions of matter have a termination." He warned them not to indulge in fancies nor "to recede from the analogy of Nature, which is wont to be simple, and always consonant to itself." On this basis we may occupy ourselves with formulae of velocity and prediction of comets, concealing even from ourselves that we do not know the size of the atom or how one atom hangs on to another, and above all keep well hidden from view that we suspect but dare not identify too closely some agent, some active "vis," who hides in the stone and makes for its resistance.

By the analogy of nature, this dark power might, of course, be the same that operates in gravity, but Newton would never say so. When he let his mind range over the possibilities of the subtle medium or ether, he saw that in addition to gluing atoms together it might exert pressure from the edges of the solar system and so impress centripetal force upon bodies within the gravitational field. In that case we should have a wholly mechanical explanation. The eighteenth century often had occasion to lament that Newton lent himself to such vagaries; in 1756 Edmund Burke was to deplore that this great man, "if in so great a man it be not impious to discover anything like a blemish," stooped from his mathematical eminence to such trivialities as "a subtle elastic ether," a subject which, Burke added, "leaves us with as many difficulties as it found us." But on the whole, Newton was faithful to Burke's notion of sublimity; he could not, or he would not, give a cause for gravity. He left his greatest discovery so wrapped in mystery that the only permissible conclusion was his "Scholium" to Book III: the one cause which can penetrate to the centers of the sun and planets, that can operate not according to the quantities of the surfaces of the particles (as do "mechanical" causes), but according to the quantity of the solid matter, must be God. Only He can be omnipresent both virtually and substantially, as the ultimate cause must be present for a world to exist at all; only He can suffer nothing from the motion of bodies and only in Him can bodies find no resistance. Since His inward substance is as inaccessible to us as the inward substance of stones, which speak to our senses only from outer surfaces, so "We know him only by his most wise and excellent contrivances of things, and final causes; we admire him for his perfections; but we reverence and adore him on account of his dominion." Newton's champions could present the Newtonian system as a method of approaching God, offering proof of His existence out of natural powers and laws "from the difficulty we find to account for them mechanically"—which was to say, out of the deficiencies of physics.

Thus Newton tried strenuously to say that it was enough, whatever the cause, that "gravity does really exist, and act according to the laws which we have explained, and abundantly serves to account for all the motions of the celestial bodies, and of our sea." But it is clear that this was actually not enough for Newton, and it certainly was not enough for Edwards. It was not enough because there were two problems, the cause of gravity and the cohesion of atoms, left unsolved, both of which threatened to yield up answers that Newton dreaded: he preferred leaving them as riddles to coming out with solutions that might prove the world Godless and mechanical. There could be no question that gravity was universal, but it simply could not be allowed to operate at a distance across the void, with no material intermediary. If there is no ether through which the force can be transmitted, then we had better leave unanswered the question of how the various solar systems are so wonderfully synchronized. All matter is subject to gravity, and every particle gravitates to every other, but under no circumstances could we allow ourselves to speak as though gravity were essential and inherent to matter: "Pray do not ascribe that notion to me." The way his popularizers elide the difficulty is a sign of their underlying anxiety: "From so many indications," wrote Maclaurin, "we may at length conclude, that all bodies in the solar system gravitate toward each other; and tho' we cannot consider gravity as essential to matter, we must allow that we have as much evidence, from the phænomena, for its universality, as for that of any other affection of bodies whatsoever."

The real motive for these maneuvers among the Newtonians is not far to seek, although recent studies have for the first time made clear its strength: Newton was a religious man first, and a scientist secondarily. What Newton wanted above all else was to give such an account of the cosmos as would make evident that God rules the world, in the words of Maclaurin, "not as its Soul but as its Lord, exercising an absolute sovereignty over the universe, not as over his own body but as over his work; and acting it according to his pleasure, without suffering any thing from it." Newton suffered an obscure nervous collapse in 1692-93, after which he abandoned natural philosophy and devoted himself to theology and prophecies. Perhaps he believed that the clues he was following would lead him through nature to God, but at the point where the certainty of approaching divinity grew shaky, he stopped. The Newtonian mechanics came to Edwards apparently a complete system of the world, but committed to two dogmatic presuppositions: that gravity at a distance is absurd, and that gravity is not synonymous with solidity. Gravity, said the Newtonians, is "an original and general Law of all Matter impressed upon it by God, and maintained in it by some efficient power, which penetrates the solid Substance of it." This result was all that Cotton Mather or most eighteenth-century theologues desired, and they betrayed little or no awareness that it was founded upon unprovable surmises and upon dogmatic evasions of mysteries. Edwards was the one man (or rather boy) in New England who refused to pretend that the questions of the cohesion of atoms and of the universality of gravity either were solved or were unimportant. He was prepared to venture in thought where Newton would not tread, into the hiding places of nature, to run down the force that was both the cohesion of atoms and the power of gravity, and to risk the possibility that could he find it or name it, the force might turn out to be simply monstrous.

Edwards was the forthright boy who knew no better than to use his eyes and cry that the emperor had no clothes. He asked what, after all, is an atom? Gassendi, Boyle, Newton had never held one in their hands nor even seen one in a microscope. Yet fervent apostles of experiment believed in this untested thing, and men who scorned hypotheses universally embraced this supposition. Of course, as a workable theory, atomism justified itself in Boyle's chemistry and Newton's physics; but it worked, Edwards made out, because it did not have to be proved: it was a way of thinking, not a thing. The scientists, talking exclusively in what Edwards called the "old way," did not listen to themselves long enough to catch on that their real difficulty was not in fixing the position of atoms in space or in measuring them, but in the confusions of their speech. If atomism was, as Newton declared, the foundation of philosophy, it was time that philosophy was taken in hand by a clear-headed theologian.

In all scientific discourse about the atom, the real point was its single oneness. So Edwards offered a succinct definition (he underscored it), *"a body which cannot be made less."* Therefore a body, no matter what its size, that cannot be lessened is all that scientists mean by an atom: "an Atom may be as big as the Universe; because any body, of whatsoever bigness, were an atom, if it were a perfect solid." This did not mean that Edwards took reality into the mind and treated matter as a dream; he was as thoroughgoing an atomist as any in the age, and commenced his thinking with Newton's definitions:

> God, in the beginning, created such a certain number of Atoms, of such a determinate bulk and figure, which they yet maintain and always will, and gave them such a motion, of such a direction, and of such a degree of velocity; from whence arise all the Natural changes in the Universe, forever, in a continued series.

What has been miscalled his idealism never meant to him that the world resides inside a man's head. Things are where they are, and Edwards had no intention of flouting "the science of the Causes or Reasons of corporeal changes." He was simply applying to the problem the method that was Newton's own, for Newton had once explained that he was not a genius except in so far as "when an idea first came to him, he pondered over it incessantly until its final results became apparent." Convinced that the "proportion of God's acting" would be the same, whether we suppose the world material or mental, Edwards set himself to ponder the nature of atoms and of gravity, an occupation which absorbed him for the rest of his life.

The first result was a group of the "Notes" to which he gave a title, "Of Atoms and of Perfectly Solid Bodies," which his editors believe to be among the earliest of his cogitations; the manuscript journals devote literally hundreds of pages to the same theme, and though many of these are possibly of greater literary interest, all confirm the first insight. Proposing that we cease to fool ourselves by taking an atom to be some small segment of space, as though we were speaking of a chair or a table, he said that all we mean by it is indivisibility. Therefore to talk of it as broken is to annihilate it. Hence it is evident that we really mean a point to which we can apply Newton's third law of motion: we are saying that an atom *resists*. Newton's stone, the farmer's stone, resists the pull of the horse, and by resistance stones have achieved the identity they so jealously guard. It would be easy to say, along with those who openly broached "schemes of a pernicious and fatal tendency," that God works from the outside and so compresses atoms together to form a stone. The danger of that position, as Newton had intimated, is that a more exact mathematical analysis of the inner structure of the nucleus may achieve a logic so sufficient unto itself that God will be relieved of the only work left for Him. It would also be easy to go to the other extreme of outright materialism, or at least of mechanism. When Newton toyed with the notion of a fluid that acts as glue among the atoms, he was trying to avoid the first extreme by veering in the direction of the second. Edwards instinctively rejected the subtle fluid, along with hooked atoms. The danger of the mechanistic extreme was not its atheism but its unscientific method: based on the fiction of the atom, it took the myth for a fact. Until it could isolate and draw a diagram of the atom, it was just as "speculative" as the rationalized theism of the optimists.

Both schemes were pernicious because both insisted upon treating atoms as pieces, as "particles," of existing substance. For Edwards, as for us, the whole question was altered as soon as he realized that the atom is a concept. It was useful in physics, not because it had spatial dimensions, but because it played only the one rôle, though an essential one, of providing a point on which resistance could be concentrated. It was, as Maclaurin put it, "a termination." It was what a more highly developed mathematics would call a "limit." And what resists is, by the act of resistance (not necessarily by substance), solid, because what else does solid mean? To speak of two atoms as *perfectly* joined is nonsense because the two, if absolutely united, must be "one and the same atom or perfect solid." Obviously no imaginable physical power can break up solidity; to split a stone into a thousand pieces, and each piece into another thousand, is not approaching termination.

It must needs be an Infinite power, which keeps the parts of atoms together; or, which with us is the same, which keeps two bodies touching by surfaces in being; for it must be infinite power, or bigger than any finite, which resists all finite power, how big soever, as we have proved these bodies to be.

Of the two dangers, optimistic theism or deterministic materialism, Edwards feared the second less than the first. Materialism, aside from its initial fallacy about the atom, gave a more truthful description of reality than was offered by "those modern divines." Edwards was mainly concerned to prove that the statement, "the constant exercise of the Infinite power of God is necessary, to preserve bodies in being," did not mean that God acts *ab externo* to press a million pieces of stone into the form of a rock. But it did mean that the principle of coherence is in the stone, because that principle is the being of the stone. Individuality is not merely the "hardness": it is "the immediate exercise of God's power." The substance of an object—a stone, a horse, a man—is a single event, "nothing but the Deity, acting in that particular manner, in those parts of space where he thinks fit." The grand, but to Calvinists the hitherto dangerous, conclusion was "that, speaking most strictly, there is no proper substance but God himself."

Edwards was apprehensive lest he sound like a Thomas Hobbes holding that God is matter, whereas what he intended was "that no matter is, in the most proper sense, matter." One may say that Edwards was making a distinction without a difference, that the world is one whether we call it all matter or all mind, and so he was actually a materialist. The charge has, I believe, more pertinence than the customary label of "idealist," but both labels are beside the point. He was trying to say something simpler than either, which modern students may find more intelligible than could his contemporaries or, for that matter, most readers in the last century—namely, that the corporeal universe results from concentrations of resistance at various centers in space, which have a power of communicating, through gravity and through collision, from one point to another, according to stated conditions which infinite wisdom perpetually observes. In such a cosmos there is no such thing as mechanism "if that word is intended to denote that, whereby bodies act, each upon the other, purely and properly by themselves," but there is a perpetual determination of sequences of events. The cohesion of thought makes possible both the idea of the atom and of bodies made of atoms joined together: "that Ideas shall be united forever, just so, and in such a manner, as is agreeable to such a series." If we hold the world to be composed of a number of atoms, ten millionths of an inch in diameter, and then try to deal with it as an assemblage of atoms, we can never be vigilant enough to keep every one under control; a few will slip loose and run wild through the system. But any experience with stones in a Connecticut field is enough to show that there are no wandering atoms. "The existence and motion of every Atom, has influence, more or less, on the motion of all other bodies in the Universe." No motion, either of the proud or of the contrite heart, is lost. Not that thinking makes the atoms law-abiding, for in that case thought might be only a kind of private vice, but that thinking, originating in the senses, is a true representation of what prevails. "The secret," cried the boy, trying at last to put it all into one searing paragraph, is that the true substance of all bodies "is the infinitely exact, and precise, and perfectly stable Idea, in God's mind, together with his stable Will, that the same shall gradually be communicated to us, and to other minds, according to certain fixed and exact established Methods and Laws."

A fixed and exact method was, according to Newton, a characterization of gravity. Therefore Edwards, having so read the riddle of the atom as to discover that every object is a continuing event, and God is within it and not outside it, plunged head-first into the thought which Newton most feared and avoided: gravity is a function of solidity and so inherent in matter. Edwards' religion differed fundamentally from Newton's in that he did not need to reserve to God the honor (he more than divined that it could easily become an empty title) of being the "immaterial" cause of gravity. He was never more clairvoyant than when he warned that gravity ought not any more "be attributed to the immediate operation of God, than everything else which indeed arises from it." To suppose God the creator of the world, and then over and above that the stage-manager of gravity, was a way of dispensing with God entirely. But by seeing the universe as a system of stable ideas, Edwards could see exactly why gravity should have the same proportions across the immensities of space without any material medium. This was why Newton's speculations on the ether seemed to him as frivolous as they did to Burke, "the folly," he called it, "of seeking for a mechanical cause of Gravity."

Nothing in Edwards' mind is more original or more exciting than this insight, but we need not wonder why, having reached it, he became cautious. Had he baldly proclaimed it, he would have been denounced in every corner of the land as a traitor to New England's Calvinism, by none more loudly than by those who long since had lost any real sympathy or understanding for the creed. They would have pounced upon him for identifying the laws of nature, not with the decrees of a transcendent sovereign situated somewhere above and outside the world, but with "a principle by which Matter acts on Matter"; by calling him the materialist and the Lucretian, they would have diverted attention from their own worldliness. I suspect Edwards would feel that most of the comment written about him since his time has been so motivated! But in the secrecy of the "Notes," Edwards could say what Newton dared not: "Solidity is gravity, so that, in some sense, the Essence of bodies is Gravity." Discretion was clearly advisable when speaking in public, but a thinker really should not handle the law of gravity quite so gingerly as did Sir Isaac; if body is a specification in one place rather than in another of a focus of resistance, then coördination among the several centers is to be expected. It is, in fact, the presupposition of there being any world at all, and the danger of atheism is infinitely greater if we pretend that it is not than if we frankly recognize it. To Edwards' clear eyes, Newton's fear, and still more the fear of his followers, that if gravity became a function of mass, science would become Godless, was what Bunyan called Little-faith; it was a failure to see what was written before their eyes.

> Therefore, we may infallibly conclude, that the very being, and the manner of being, and the whole, of bodies depends immediately on the Divine Being.—To show how that, if Gravity should be withdrawn, the whole Universe would in a moment vanish into nothing; so that not only the well-being of the world depends on it, but the very being.

The failure of Newton, and of the age, was a failure of intelligence. They were ready to call mobility a quality of matter without supposing themselves in danger of becoming atheists; but gravity, more than mobility, is essential in order for existence to exist, though for many reasons "the mind does not so intuitively see how." But actually, once Newton's laws are grasped, it seemed to Edwards logical, inescapable, that gravity does operate at a distance, for what is distance but, like time, a principle of stability for organizing a sequence of ideas?

Edwards could not know that a philosopher of the twentieth century, profoundly versed in a still more subtle and powerful physics, would deduce that cognition, having a unity of its own as an event, "knows the world as a system of mutual relevance, and thus sees itself as mirrored in other things." He would, I am sure, agree that Whitehead put thus simply the heart of his meaning, and he would agree further with Whitehead that men of thought, by virtue of this perception, are ultimately rulers of the world, but he knew more than Whitehead ever did of what is actually required for ruling a New England town. Though he was born to the purple, and though the society still bowed or curtseyed to the pulpit upon entering the meeting-house, a ruler could not tell them all his thought. Hence, could the good people (or those not so good) of Northampton be expected to comprehend that the young pastor they had chosen to be, like his grandfather, the administrator of their ecclestiastical foundation was inwardly and incessantly concerned with testing whether an assertion of *how* the universe acts can be made identical with the *why*? Could they comprehend that he had a new vision of the cosmos as a system of causes, atoms, and gravity, and that for the mind to achieve regeneration, it would need to strip itself of all verbal substitutes for physical reality, of all metaphor and similitude, and look squarely upon the purely factual? Could they understand that in this scientific version of grace, the perception of beauty is that which determines both value and reality, that only in such a perception can the natural world and the world of religious experience become one? Could they even begin to grasp that for him the sheer naked reality was enough?

We should claim too much did we call Edwards' metaphysical intuitions about gravity anticipations of Planck and Einstein. He was not, let me repeat, an experimental scientist, nor was he a trained mathematician, and he could never even have approximated the conception that laws may be formulated without reference to any particular space-time manifold. He was a man of his century, though his thought was in the forefront of it; he was a docile Newtonian, who believed in absolute and objective space, and he assumed absolute time; he accepted this very same space which we see and this daily time which we experience. Still, it is not extravagant to point out that, by his argument that an atom is not a thing but a way of speaking about a locus of attraction and repulsion, Edwards was divining the great line of the future. That he was predisposed to some such divination by his theology, and that he meant no more than would confirm his doctrines, cannot be doubted, but at least it is clear that he saw through the genial and obtuse rationalism which most of his contemporaries thought was the import of Newton.

In his sermons on justification, in 1734, he needed to draw upon the "Notes" for only one statement: the relation of event to event in a causal sequence, whether of atoms, planets, or of grace, flows "only from the natural concord or agreeableness there is between such qualifications and such circumstances." If atomic entities are really entities in enduring conception (and otherwise men can never know what they are), and are related one to another because God delights in order and not in confusion, then a cause is not one occurrence which is instrumental in producing the other, but properly speaking is "that, after or upon the existence of which, or the existence of it after such a manner, the existence of another thing follows." In this sense faith may be called a "cause" of justification, but not in the pernicious sense of that which brings it to pass. If the nature of things is a system of stable ideas which does not depend on the capricious goings or comings of atoms, why should the grace of God wait upon an uncaused achievement of virtue by this or that individual? Salvation, along with the atom and the law of gravity, can be only a manifestation of God's regard, not to the pretensions of individuals, but to "the beauty of that order that there is in uniting those things that have a natural agreement, and congruity, and unition the one with the other." For humanity this must mean, instead of a justification built upon the merit of our finite virtues, that "the acceptableness, and so the rewardableness of our virtue, is not antecedent to justification, but follows it, and is built entirely upon it." In the order of causation, a man is not a saint because he is good, but if he is a saint he is caused to be good. In more conventional language, he is elected.

Had Newton, or such of his disciples as Clark or Maclaurin, read Edwards' "Notes," they would not have been impressed as are we today. The scientists waged a hard fight to get their experimental, empirical method not only understood but even tolerated; they found that their chief enemies were those who "hastily," as they put it, resolve material motions "into immediate volitions of the supreme cause, without admitting any intermediate instruments," who thus "put an end to our enquiries at once." The physicists felt it essential for good science, and therefore they claimed for sound theology, that God be severely limited to governing the world not as His own body but as His work; in that sense alone, they would agree that God is "omnipotent." Persons who confounded God's lordship with His substance—the scientists said this in a hundred ways—"hurt those very interests which they would promote." Consequently, the majority of Newtonians, scientific and theological, would have called Edwards a brash boy who was perverting the incomparable Newton back to the obscurantism of immediate volitions of the supreme cause. They would not have appreciated that in fact Edwards gave over the material world to a chain of "intermediate" terms even more consistently than did the pious Newtonians.

Furthermore, they would not have understood that the sensitive Edwards was looking ahead to what they could only vaguely foresee; Maclaurin found himself stating, though with reluctance, a new problem which, in the very wake of Newton's success, appeared to be distracting the European mind. The intellectual world, he lamented, is becoming divided into two camps (where he thought they ought to be all one): those who from their fondness for explaining things by mechanism "have been led to exclude every thing but matter and motion out of the universe," and those with a contrary disposition, who will "admit nothing but perceptions, and things which they perceive," some of whom have gone to such extremes that "they have admitted nothing but their own perceptions." The majority of Newtonian rationalists were unable to figure out why these strange divisions had come about when it seemed that Newton had settled all such foolish arguments.

In the Boston lecture, Edwards exhibited the two orders, the objective and the inherent. The one, we find, forced us back to Newton and natural law, the other to Locke and perception. We cannot be certain how much was fully explicit in Edwards' mind, but considering how caution and reticence were thrust upon him, it appears that Edwards saw exactly where the modern problem is centered, upon this incompatibility of Newton and Locke, of the objective and the subjective, of the mechanical and the conscious. The effort of his life was to unite the two. The line of his speculation might well seem to less subtle Newtonians a slighting of "subordinate instruments and agents," but if so, they would again betray, as many in New England were soon to do, the shallow dogmatism which prevented them from comprehending what the age had really to grapple with, as it was to prevent Chauncy and his circle from ever seeing what Edwards was driving at.

His problem, then, was to get the two orders together— or else to confess that the modern world is incoherent. A stone transmits force to another by collision, and so is a "cause" of motion; in perception, there is a "fitness" of the antecedent sensation to the subsequent act. Is perception, then, just another form of collision, in which an object transmits motion through the senses? A moved stone receives what it must receive, no more, no less; but is man merely another kind of stone? Human perceptions notoriously vary in depth and width; is causality the same in either realm? In perception, may there not be a fitness between response and object that is still freedom of action? When the stone resists, is not the farmer at liberty either to curse or to pray? Does the tavern irresistibly attract the toper, does the woman inescapably arouse the lust of the adulterer? Are the principles of nature, the implacable sequences of things, applicable without change to human nature and society? If the inherent good is excellency and pleasure, while the objective good is the possession and enjoyment of that object which is good for the organism, is there not an incurable conflict between the two? Perception, either as pleasure or as beauty, is value, but if it is illusion, then reality is only the dance of atoms. The civilization of more than New England was at stake if the life of the spirit was henceforth to be a civil war between atoms and perceptions. Unless Edwards could merge, or at least reconcile, his objective good and his inherent, neither he nor, as he saw the predicament, anyone else would be able to locate the good where it might be of help to mankind.

"Very simply," replied the Superintendent. "You haven't once up till now come into real contact with our authorities. All those contacts of yours have been illusory, but owing to your ignorance of the circumstances you take them to be real. . . . There's no fixed connection with the Castle, no central exchange which transmits our calls further. When anybody calls up the Castle from here the instruments in all the subordinate departments ring, or rather they would all ring if practically all the departments—I know it for a certainty—didn't leave their receivers off. Now and then, however, a fatigued official may feel the need of a little distraction, especially in the evenings and at night, and may hang the receiver on. Then we get an answer, but an answer of course that's merely a practical joke. And that's very understandable too. For who would take the responsibility of interrupting, in the middle of the night, the extremely important work up there that goes on furiously the whole time, with a message about his own little private troubles? I can't comprehend how even a stranger can imagine that when he calls up Sordini, for example, it's really Sordini that answers. Far more probably it's a little copying clerk from an entirely different department. On the other hand, it may certainly happen once in a blue moon that when one calls up the little copying clerk Sordini will answer himself. Then finally the best thing is to fly from the telephone before the first sound comes through."

FRANZ KAFKA

Arminianism

I F CONTENTION be so evil a thing in a town among neighbors, how much more hateful is it between members of the same family." This is one of Edwards' classic understatements. Contention and party strife were "the old iniquity" of Northampton, and increased with the years; Edwards repeatedly castigated those who "have been on edge and their mouths open in evil speaking, in fierce and clamorous talk and backbitings and evil surmising." The Puritan character has unlovely aspects, and the struggle for power in a township can bring them all out. Yet Edwards could report to Colman, in his letter of 1736, that on the whole his people were as sober and orderly as any in New England; because they lived so far within land, away from seaports, they "have not been so much corrupted with vice, as most other parts," though, of course, a principal reason for their good order has been "owing to the great abilities, and eminent piety, of my venerable and honored grandfather Stoddard."

Thus the evil of strife could be mitigated when it was a matter of neighbors; despite open quarrels or secret intrigues, mostly over little things, sparks blown into flame by the bellows of unkind language, there was, as in every New England community, an invincible sense of the whole that took charge in emergencies. Furthermore, Puritan theology curiously bound these people together even in their vices, and welcomed them to the brotherhood of malice. Edwards spoke directly from the heart of Puritanism when he said that the dead, who once made a noise in the world, now lie quietly; those who have been warmly contending will presently be at peace: "Your dead bodies will probably lie quietly together in the same burying place." In New England the confraternity of the cemetery is the bond of a perverse solidarity.

But families are another story. In Edwards' case, an almost undecipherable story, for in accordance with immemorial custom, the infighting was done in the dark. External forms were respected, and few documents have been released from family coffers. Yet, in the manner of New England, everybody knew all about it. In his letter to Colman, Edwards said of his sermons on justification by faith in 1734, "great fault was found with meddling with the controversy in the pulpit, by such a person, at that time," and "it was ridiculed by many elsewhere." If Colman did not know who "the person" was and the location of "elsewhere," he had only to ask the first visitor from the Valley. When Edwards delivered his discourses on justification, the tension, long mounting between him and the Williamses of Hatfield, became open hostility, and there was joined that peculiarly New England struggle, a feud between cousins, than which nothing in the world is meaner, more bitter, or more unforgiving.

The code of New England, then and for a century thereafter, demanded certain amenities. When there is a disgrace or a deed that troubles the family conscience, a New England clan does not confess its shame; it closes ranks, never talks about the affair, but keeps the memory alive within the tribal system. The deeper the chagrin, the more resolute the silence, but the more persistent the legend. In the watches of the night, the children learn it; they keep their mouths grimly shut until the time comes to whisper it to their children, but awareness remains a daily condition of their lives. By an extension of courtesy—or a refinement of hatred—the neighbors, especially those who have suffered by the deed, wrap it in silence, yet for generations they too cherish the recollection. Consequently a vital portion of the social history is always suppressed, and can be made out only from the fragments which some inheritor of the legend half-remembers when at long last the original passions fade away. The families who conspired to drive Edwards out of Northampton in 1749-50 suffered the agony of remorse. They had to live with the knowledge that they had struck down New England's preeminent saint, as brutally as though they had stoned him. Among descendants, both of Edwards and of his enemies, it became a deed without a name, and reticence became an obsession.

There was only one exception. Rebekah, one of Stoddard's daughters and sister to Col. John, married Joseph Hawley, leading merchant among Northampton river gods, who sold the first knives and forks in the Valley; thrown into despondency by Edwards' preaching, on June 1, 1735, Hawley cut his throat. Rebekah was making cheese when they came to tell her, and "she did not leave the buttery until she had finished turning the cheeses." Her son Joseph was twelve; the next spring he saw a man fined 20s 6d and whipped with five stripes for saying, "Rev. Jonathan Edwards was as great an instrument as the devil had on this side of hell to bring souls to hell." Young Joseph came back from Yale in 1743; abetted by the Williamses, he got even with his father's destroyer, yet two years after Edwards' death, ten years after he had led the forces of expulsion, Hawley made public one of the most abject documents in New England literature, a complete recantation and self-condemnation. The church, he announced, should seriously examine whether its hard speeches against "so faithful and godly a minister as Mr. Edwards" were not great sins, and "whether ever God will hold us guiltless, till we cry to him for Christ's sake to pardon and save us from that judgment, which such ungodly deeds deserve." We injured the best of men, and persecuted Christ by persecuting His servant; we can expect no favor "until we shall be humble as in the dust on account of it, and till we openly, in full terms, and without baulking the matter, confess the same before the world, and most humbly and earnestly seek forgiveness of God, and do what we can to honour the memory of Mr. Edwards." Williamses were made of sterner stuff; no expression of regret is known to have passed their lips, not even after it had become clear to history that in expelling Mr. Edwards the town had come as near as they could, under the circumstances, to a crucifixion.

So, aside from Hawley's pitiful letter, the real story remains obscure. Edwards himself adhered to the conventions by refraining from speaking the names of his adversaries. If he had to explain to a foreigner, he would speak of "a number of Gentlemen belonging to other Towns, of a certain Family of considerable note in New England, which had long manifested a jealous and unfriendly spirit towards me," who in Northampton were "on the side of my Opposers, were their Chief Counsellors during the whole continuance of the controversy." In 1830, when Sereno Dwight wrote the life of his ancestor, with access to papers now destroyed, the legend was alive but so was the code; he hinted at more than he told by saying that the discourses on justification were resented by a family of wealth and influence, one of whom "somewhat categorically" commanded Edwards to preach on other topics, and found his refusal "an offense not to be forgiven." So there is no doubt, despite the dearth of evidence, of the identity of the main opponent and ultimate victor. When Edwards passed beyond the insinuations of his first two publications to an explicit attack upon "Arminians," even though he mentioned no names, he outraged all the Williamses, but chiefly Israel, son of Stoddard's daughter Christian, brother to Solomon Williams of Lebanon and half brother to Rector Elisha. The legend reaches back, though obscurely, to a conflict between Christian and Esther; in these matters, legends demand credence, but whatever the cause, in 1734 a civil war was declared among the posterity of Stoddard, with the most wealthy and most worldly—but not, so long as Col. John was alive, the most powerful—arrayed against the one who maintained that divine and supernatural light is reality.

That the Williamses were lax on certain doctrines was probably public knowledge; it is significant that Chauncy liked the head of the clan, William Williams, and thought him greater than Stoddard, though today he is the most shadowy figure in this misty tragedy. But one can understand why, when Edwards delivered the peroration of his lengthy disquisition, Williamses would think he was hitting below the belt. "I know that there are many that make as though this controversy was of no great importance, . . . and that more hurt is done by vain disputes about it than good." Of course, he conceded, with a generosity which to the townsmen was sarcasm, these people do not—or at least not yet—embrace "the Popish doctrine of merit," and perhaps what they believe in general they do not actually apply to themselves. It may be, said Edwards, adding insult to injury, that they have been led "by education, or cunning sophistry of others" into errors contrary to their hearts' true conviction, or perhaps they are merely awkward and express themselves badly, "using terms that are without a precisely fixed and determinate meaning." He would not, he gravely concluded, pass judgment, and would make allowance for frailty; nevertheless—he drove the point home!—teaching and propagating such doctrines springs from a pernicious and fatal tendency. We need no gloss on this passage to know why, when the shoe fit, Israel Williams was furious.

Arminius was a Dutch Calvinist condemned by the Calvinist international at the Synod of Dort in 1619 for deviating from the orthodox line on the article concerning enslavement of the will. Thereafter "Arminian" among Protestant nations was a smear word, and any and every effort to augment human responsibility by giving the natural will a power to act in some degree by itself was castigated as Arminianism. Arminius pled for no more than such ability as has the beggar who extends his hand when a rich man bestows alms, but even this scandalized the orthodox and started a civil war in Holland. In England, the Puritans found Arminianism an effective brand for their enemies in the Church. A court wit, being asked what the Arminians held, replied, "All the best benefices in England," thus suggesting that Laudian Anglicans did not stem directly from Dutch Remonstrants; but the bishops did share Arminius' objection against rigid or "supralapsarian" Calvinism. By this inhuman doctrine, Arminius remonstrated, God is represented as determining to condemn rational creatures; in order to have them to damn, He first creates them; in order to make it appear their fault, He creates them upright but ordains that they must sin. The whole scheme, said Arminius, who considered himself a Protestant and believed in salvation by faith, is a fraud: "In this process, I say, they ascribe far baser things to God than if they should simply say He created some creatures in order to damn them." Thus Arminianism may be most usefully defined for our purposes as a recurrent reaction among Calvinists that manifests itself whenever certain of them discover, or think they discover, that Calvinism "makes God the author of sin."

From the beginning, New England identified Arminianism with the Prelacy from which the founders fled, and it was traditionally the most reprehensible of heresies (or at least next to Antinomianism and Quakerism, which erred even more fatally by thinking that once a man has grace he is excused from all moral responsibility). In 1726 Cotton Mather boasted that there was not one Arminian in New England; yet here was Edwards in 1734 asserting, as though desperately rescuing the churches from imminent danger of this very heresy, that we are abominable creatures in the sight of God, that our righteousness is ten thousand times less than nothing, and that the majesty of God is more worthily exhibited if He delivers such vagabonds without any virtue on their part than if He should reward their righteousness. No "foolish exalting" opinion of themselves should sway divine judgment: as Edwards said this, he was not so much expounding a theological proposition as accusing American society of a foolish and exalting opinion of itself. Against its own increasing disposition, he attempted to rally it by raising a historic slogan.

Hence, if we would understand the situation, we must ask who in actual fact these subverters of true doctrine were. None in New England was an avowed follower of Arminius, and none but apostates like Cutler were prelatical. Israel and Elisha Williams, Samuel Whittelsey with his clear head, Edward Wigglesworth, President Wadsworth, Johnny Barnard, and Charles Chauncy were loyal Puritans; not one of them denied election and irresistible grace. True, they liked Tillotson, but that great conciliator was no high-flier, and they did not approve of Cutler. They saluted Newton, and a few of them were getting around to read Locke, who, as far as they could see, encouraged the free and catholic spirit. Why denounce them as "Arminians" and call them fatal and pernicious?

Edwards so arraigned them because he saw the cultural predicament of both England and New England—he thought of both together as "this nation"—in a light that modern historians and histories of literature make it difficult for us to recapture. We think of the early eighteenth century as consisting of Harley, Walpole, and Newcastle, its literature of Pope and Fielding, its philosophy of Berkeley and Hume; we think its radicals were Tindal and Toland or Mandeville. Edwards was aware, though mostly at second or third hand, of these people, but to him they were not important. What did count was the central core of "this nation," the essential Protestantism, call it low-church Anglican, Presbyterian, or Nonconformist, which had made England great by its adhesion to the Epistles of Paul. Deists and Socinians were symptomatic of the disease of the age, but they were incidental; the real issue of the times, viewed from the perspective of Northampton, was that not only had almost all divines in the Church of England become Arminians, "but Arminianism has greatly prevailed among the Dissenters, and has spread greatly in New England, as well as Old."

This insidious philosophy, though named after him, did not need to derive from Arminius; it had imperceptibly pervaded the nation, although the victims, as Edwards suggested, were not yet aware that they were infected. In other words, by redefining Arminianism in the context of the eighteenth century —which, from his mastery of Newton and Locke, Edwards was able to do more strikingly than any other in his time—he made it evident that many who considered themselves sound, though perhaps not fanatical, Protestants were no longer entitled to the name. He descended on New England as though he were a divinely commissioned physician equipped with a new technique of diagnosis, and told them they were leprous. Formally they professed the Westminster Confession and distrusted their own righteousness; but they insulated themselves against self-examination by a scorn of "nice speculation, depending on certain subtle distinctions" (whereas the essence of Puritanism was its subtle distinctions), or by discounting technical theological queries (which had been the delight of the founding fathers) as "not of such consequence as to be worth being zealous about." The Protestant tradition depended on blunt, honest men like Luther and Cromwell; in New England, congregations admired blunt, honest preachers, such men as Cooper or Shurtleff, who told off their sins and urged them to reform. But Edwards was honest in a fashion that blunt men took to be an instrument of the devil, and was blunt, when he set himself to it, with a vehemence that terrified the honest. Employing terms with a precisely fixed and determinate meaning—always the most dangerous of weapons—he demonstrated to New Englanders of 1734 that they had ceased to believe what they professed, and that as a result the society was sick. He did not merely call them hypocrites, he proved that they were.

To understand the workings of his mind, we must try to reconstruct what for him was the image of England. Properly to reproduce it we should require a yet unwritten chapter in English intellectual history, the story of dissent in the process of transformation from seventeenth-century Puritanism into what became Victorian respectability. When New Englanders like Colman and Prince visited London, they did not hobnob with Bolingbroke but with Watts; few in America were aware of Pope and none of Swift, but they read the pamphlets of some preacher of Bristol as the authentic voice of the great world. Bishop Butler was almost as far outside New England's ken (only in his last years did Edwards read Butler) as John Gay, and Berkeley as little prized as Matthew Prior. By colonial standards, *The Dunciad* was a silly book, whereas anything of Doddridge was worth reprinting in Boston.

Before we dismiss this correspondence as one of a province with provincials, let us remember that there was a profound reason for it, which is prerequisite to understanding the American Revolution and the course of American culture: what New England took to be the real England was lower-middle-class England, not the England on which *The Rape of the Lock* is a sociological report. The history of this level of English civilization is not yet adequately comprehended, although it challenges study by confronting us with at least two major artists, Defoe and Richardson, and is the link between the England of Cromwell and that of Cobden and Bright. Because it was this England that migrated to New England and then to the Middle West, and largely shaped American culture, it should be of the greatest interest to Americans; and Edwards was the pure, uncontaminated essence of the stock.

Therefore we must bethink us that in 1730, this plebeian, dissenting, serious-minded society was a world unto itself, accepting Newton, gradually absorbing Locke, approving Addison and adoring *Robinson Crusoe*, beginning to regard Bunyan as fit reading for apprentices and farm-hands, finding a slightly too ornate but still congenial expression in Young and Hervey, a perfect articulation in Richardson. It was ignorant of Shakespeare and the stage and of sculpture, and understood only the simplest music, but it loved Georgian architecture, fine crockery, and clean linen. It was troubled by Deism, but it was above all concerned with refashioning old Puritan doctrine into the language of such theologians as Daniel Whitby and John Taylor. For New Englanders, these two were the literary spokesmen of the age, and colonial Americans read them as Americans a century later received, let us say, Dickens. When we ask whom Edwards meant by Arminians, we have to consider first of all the steady influx of books from English Nonconformity which were accepted by his countrymen as the latest tidings from the capital, but which he judged little better than unwitting descents into Popery.

Whitby's *Discourse* of 1710 was the first work of the new theology to have a vogue in New England; organized as a commentary upon the "five points" of the Synod of Dort, it demonstrated for each that pure Calvinism is unscriptural, unreasonable, plays into the hands of atheists, and, most seriously, invalidates all moral effort. After 1738 John Taylor of Norwich became the rage with his *The Scripture Doctrine of Original Sin Proposed to a Free and Candid Examination.* Both these writers, who deserve to be better known, rephrased a question that had always bothered Calvinists, but in such a way that it now appeared unanswerable: if men are irresistibly predestined, how can you ask them to be good? You cannot exhort them to perform what you and they know cannot be accomplished. If God has an antecedent purpose to withhold the aid by which alone they can succeed, all your pleas are repugnant to the will of God. After two centuries of intense effort, this remained the unsolved riddle of Protestantism, and therefore it was high time, these theologians declared, to give over.

This dilemma was the real cause of the pervading spiritual

paralysis: the plea of insufficiency—"I could not help it, or I could not avoid it; I had no Means, and no Ability to do it"— was, by the enlightened standards of the eighteenth century, "an Excuse sufficient in the Judgment of all Mankind." This contradiction had also, Whitby pointed out, produced atheism, for all the atheist needs is that Christians stick fast in the absurdity that God acts by rules which, "according to the natural Notions and the natural Sense which we have of Justice," are utterly unjust. If the goodness and justice of God are not what men conceive to be good and just, we have no notion of God at all, and so no God! Here, in brief, was the crisis of English Protestantism which threatened to destroy the morality that was both the foundation and the safeguard of Protestant culture.

The focus of the problem was the human will. However it may have appeared to Calvin and Cromwell, it was now evident that if God moves the will by persuasion, " 'tis plain that his Motion may be frustrated, since the Regenerate too often act against the highest Motive and most powerful Persuasions" —an observation frequently confirmed in New England. But if, to avoid this alternative, we take the other, and suppose that God moves the will of man "by a Physical Influx which the Will cannot resist," then man becomes a stone or a wagon to be dragged passively about. If God "does thus unfrustrably interpose to determine the Will of Man before it determines itself, it is no more liable to an Account for acting, or not acting, than the Earth for standing still, or the Heavens for moving." There seemed only one way out: to grant that God proposes rational persuasions because men, in themselves and by themselves, being causes of their own effects, have the ability to accede or to refuse, and that heaven or hell depends on their own election.

The felicity of this inescapable conclusion was that it offered every prospect of reinvigorating piety and morality. A few English Dissenters, still faithful to Calvin, made a weak protest, and the Scots, who would have none of such heresy, objected vigorously, but Whitby and Taylor quickly became spokesmen for the dominant mood of English Puritans. Convinced that the will must be emancipated from the chain of causality in order that mankind may become capable of virtue or vice, that the race may reasonably be subjected to commands, to rewards or punishments, these theologians asserted anew "a self-determining power in the will," and all New England heeded, because the voice was not that of Prelacy, but of those to whom New England ever looked for guidance, the most pious and admired of Nonconformists.

However, had Edwards been confronted with no more than an invasion of fashionable Britishers, his problem would have been as simple as the Scots': he could have stoutly affirmed native doctrine. What made his situation complicated, and provoked the subtlety of his solution, was the fact that this imported Arminianism fell in with a home-grown variety. Edwards' problem, to phrase it exactly, was that he had to cope with two Arminianisms, the English and the domestic, and of the two, the American was even more the symptom of a growing, though at the moment incipient, social revolution. Interesting though Edwards' problem may be in itself, it has for us a representative value: it is an almost too neat example of what has repeatedly been a pattern of forces in American history, a convergence of the European and the local, out of which has come what the world considers distinctively American, although the world generally fails to comprehend either the struggle that went into the making of the synthesis or the instability of the result.

New England was caught off-guard by Edwards' onslaught upon its Arminianizing "tendency" because, as far as it could tell, it was speaking the language of the founders, the phraseology of the covenant. It assumed that as long as the words were the same, the thought was the same, not knowing that to every society there comes a time when meanings are perverted by the retention of old watchwords. A prejudice had arisen, said Edwards in one of those passages which, by their very density, bewildered his contemporaries and still deceive posterity into supposing him bereft of sociological wisdom, "through the insensible change of the use and meaning of such terms," and the concept of conditional faith thus degenerated into mere performance. Officially claiming no more than that the fulfillment of a condition conveyed assurance, the clergy of New England progressively developed inducements to incite the fulfillment. By 1734 community practice was utterly out of joint with theory; Edwards undertook, by the use of carefully fixed terms, to show his colleagues that their behavior was absurd: teaching that the will is enslaved, they were exhorting the citizens to take advantage of a bargain. The legalism of the seventeenth century, rigidified into a *quid pro quo*, had come to mean that the will of an unregenerate man, or woman, could be coaxed and wooed—even won—as though it were a self-determining power.

New England of 1730-40 is not the first or the last society to awake unexpectedly to the realization that its practice has become hopelessly sundered from its ethos. American history is a succession of such realizations. But in America or elsewhere, the lot of the analyst who calls attention to the inconsistency is not pleasant. When the economic and social order evolve of themselves into a system that contradicts the ideology, it takes courage to repudiate venerable formulae. This courage Jonathan Mayhew showed in the 1740's when he openly defied Calvinism and preached a theology compatible with rational and commercial Boston, although Boston was aghast when he did it; this courage Charles Chauncy somewhat tardily emulated by publishing, late in his long life, the news that God is benevolent and that all men can be saved. But it takes a still rarer courage not to go along with the tendency and so defy the old doctrine, but to subject both the tendency and the rationalization to an analysis so critical as to prove them equally fallacious. Men whose economic interests are identified with the process, as were those of the Williamses or the Boston merchants, forced to it, will compromise their inherited ethic, but they will fight to the death—as throughout American history they have fought—any accusation that they have been swayed by their interests, by education or the sophistry of others, into condoning practices contrary to their own hearts. Edwards is not an archeological curiosity: everything that America can do to a man, America tried to do to him. Long after the Williamses and Hawley had overcome him, he read the meaning of their plot: "From this secret delusion and prejudice they have almost all their advantages; it is the strength of their bulwarks, and the edge of their weapons. And this is the main ground of all the right they have to treat their neighbors in so assuming a manner, and to insult others, perhaps as wise and good as themselves."

Whitby and Taylor made the crisis acute, not only because they strengthened the secret delusion of a now debilitated federal theology, but because they relieved it from even ritualistic captivity by denying that there ever was any covenant or that God had ever dealt with men in legal contracts. Secret prejudice could take heart and, if it had sufficient courage, emerge under guise of rational enlightenment. Whitby pointed out that the covenant was only a way of postponing an unavoidable issue: even when God is supposedly encased in a contractual promise, men have no means of performing the condition without God's aid, and so what they gain by their federal device is only a means to increase their condemnation. If Christ must still supply both the promise and the condition, the so-called covenant is really "absolute"; a truly conditional offer would mean that the reward is promised "upon condition that I do something to obtain it," which would mean the freedom of the will to do or not to do.

Taylor delivered the final stroke: the theology of the covenant simply is not in the Bible! (It was like telling twentieth-century Americans that the profit motive is not in the Constitution.) Surely, Taylor appealed, if the covenant were a fundamental of faith, "it would have been affirmed directly, clearly, and positively," and we should not be left, as in all

New England literature up to this moment we were left, to grope for it "in the Darkness of Conjecture and Supposition." The edifice of American Puritanism rocked under Taylor's blows when, borrowing the language of Newton, he called the federal system "an Hypothesis." It is a sin to indulge our conjectures "beyond the Bounds of all Understanding into the Region of Fiction and Chimera, there form and settle our Schemes, and then turn to Scripture." It is worse than sinful. "This is Popery!"

Such language had a familiar sound in the Connecticut Valley. When the Mathers opposed Stoddard's reformulation of the ecclesiastical order on the grounds that in Scripture the only basis for a church was the covenant, Stoddard answered in tones that rang through every township, "There is no Syllable in the Word of God, intimating any such thing." Now Taylor was proclaiming that the Covenant of Grace, like the ecclesiastical, was a chimera. The choice was clear before the people: either they go back to unmitigated Calvinism, wherein the naked will of God decrees and compels every action, or they admit, as Stoddard had cheerfully admitted, that we can be embarrassed by the mistakes of our ancestors and that we should be criminal to continue mistaking with them. In the second case, we should obviously jettison the theology of election and predestination, bring ideology into line with social convention, and announce from every pulpit in the land that the will of an unregenerate American is a volition without a cause, and that contingency is essential to his freedom.

Edwards did not worship ancestors. He had cast off the "old Logick" in a day, as soon as he read Locke. Furthermore, he knew better than any man in Hatfield how utterly right Taylor was in calling the covenant theology an hypothesis. God had said, according to Alexander Pope, let Newton be, and all was light; legalism may have been plausible in a time when man's world was mainly political, but in a physical universe it was indeed chimera. In fact, the scandal of Edwards' discourses on justification, which reverberated through the

land even before they were published, was his rejection of the
covenant: no goodness or excellency of man, including what
is vulgarly called faith, "is the very fundamental condition of
the bestowment of that kindness on him, or of the distinguishing him from others by that benefit." Surely this was radical
enough! The student of Locke and Newton had approved his
masters; he had put aside legality for reality, passed from
feudalism to mechanics, from teleology to empiricism, from
status to intelligence. Edwards could have stopped at this
point, and have become—this is the fascination of his story—
the pioneer utilitarian in America, and all Williamses and
Whittelseys would have flocked to him. A Yankee printer,
temporarily down on his luck a few years before, had written
a short tract on necessity and freedom, in which he discovered
that a Newtonian world was, despite Newton, predetermined;
however, upon becoming prosperous, he eschewed all such
theorizing because it had no practical consequences, and in
accordance with the spirit of John Locke, devoted himself to
improving his own, and America's, welfare by issuing al-
manacs full of sound common sense, inventing stoves and
street lighting and lightning rods, and finally negotiating a
separate treaty of American independence. Why should not
Edwards, like Franklin, accept the mechanics of Newton, the
sensations of Locke, the free-will of Whitby, and so lead the
hinterland of New England to that economic exploitation of
the Berkshires to which it was obviously dedicated?

What held him up was a slight concession which Arminians
like Whitby were obliged to make, though generally as an
afterthought. Of course, God is omniscient as well as omnipotent, and so, while the will of man remains a self-determining
power which accepts or refuses moral exhortations, it must be
true that all the while God *knows* which way man will
choose. This foreknowledge of God, said Whitby, must somehow be compatible with the free-will of man, because otherwise man's actions are necessary, "tho' I know not how it is
so." True, the two seem inconsistent, but that must be merely

because of "my Ignorance of what this Foreknowledge of God is, or how he doth foreknow future Contingencies." Arminian theology, the counterpart in theory of Franklin's practicality, handled the historic problem by saying that it was insoluble, and that a man should rest content with the assurance that he commands as much freedom of will as if there were no such thing as divine foreknowledge, because he should "be satisfied with the like Experience."

Experience! It all came back, by every road, to this. The piety of New England, being "experimental," opposed the reality of experience to speculation; the inherent good was, according to Locke, experienced in sensation; the Newtonian system was derived from experience, not from hypotheses. The problem of reconciling the objective good, which was the irresistible sequence of law, with the inherent good, which was the perception of excellency or pleasure, was pressing. Obviously the intellectual framework of the covenant was no help. If there was an answer, experience must give it. But what is experience? Can experience be experienced by those who say, in effect, that they are ignorant of its basic terms? Can there be experience for those who make no sense out of it? Does one become a disciple of experience by obliterating nice speculations and subtle distinctions, thus abandoning himself to a fancied freedom which amounts to treating one's neighbors in an assuming manner and to answering the question of questions, in a universe where solidity itself means inexorable gravity, with an "I am not able to reconcile my Freewill to God's Foreknowledge"? Others might accept such intellectual bankruptcy; Franklin did, most Americans would, but Jonathan Edwards could not.

A historian needs little ingenuity to guess what forces dictated the Arminianism of Whitby and Taylor. Indeed, Whitby gives it all away by assuming what he feels no reader can deny, that the good God must act by such rules as impartial men naturally confess. Any alternative would be a practical joke on the race. The language is Whitby's, the

speaker is the eighteenth century. The problem of how ex-
hortation could apply to a predestined man was unanswerable
to him, not because of logical difficulties, but because the century had prejudged the question. Whitby and Taylor are now
forgotten, and historians regret that Edwards expended his
splendid dialectical powers on such ephemeral targets; this is
to lose the vital point that for Edwards, with his strong social
sense, these men were important as no Mandeville or Berkeley
ever could be, because they made articulate the average level.
He professed not to have read Hobbes (though he knew
about him at second hand), he never studied Berkeley, and
only in the last years, at the urging of his Scottish correspondents, did he look at Hume; and then commented that he was
glad to examine such corrupt books, "especially when written by men of considerable genius," in order to get an idea
of the notions prevailing in England. But Whitby, Taylor,
Dr. Samuel Clark, and even poor Mr. Chubb, although highly
"specious," were the writers who "lately made a mighty noise
in America." Among the masses where these authors now
made a noise, a century earlier Ironsides and pioneers had
emerged; but in this later day their darling theologians were
saying, in effect, that the Puritan stock could no longer face
the ineffable. The federal theology had tried to entice God
into the bonds of legality, but it had always retained the
decency to conceive of Him as stooping out of sovereign con-
descension; the new theology dispensed with the covenant
because it had the effrontery to tie God to the norms of human justice.

Whitby and Taylor were benevolent men, and they could
not allow the deity to be other than themselves. Hence their
hatred of nice speculations that might uncover their secret
delusion. "It is one great reason," said Edwards in his finest
vein, "why speculative points are thought to be of so little
importance, that the modern religion consists so little in respect to the divine Being, and almost wholly in benevolence
to men." The telling fact, to Edwards, was that a theology

which patently yielded to the temper of the times, which placed virtue in benevolence to men rather than in love to God, had emerged from the established centers of Puritanism, and was being welcomed, though still mainly in secret, by those whose tradition should have fortified them against so cheap a temptation.

Out of Edwards' work might be compiled an indictment of the eighteenth century that would rival Blake's and delight the heart of every Romantic. The tone of "the present fashionable divinity" assumed that boorish Calvinism was worth only "the greatest contempt of gentlemen possessed of that noble and generous freedom of thought, which happily prevails in this age of light and inquiry." In England especially "was there ever an age wherein strength and penetration of reason, extent of learning, exactness of distinction, correctness of style, and clearness of expression, did so abound?" And in New England, in the Valley, were not the results of the Enlightenment manifest? "God has greatly distinguished some of the inhabitants of New England from others, in the abundance that he has given them of the good things of this life."

Here was the point, as Edwards looked upon the river gods, where the appeal to experience became ambiguous. With all its glories, "was there ever an age, wherein there has been so little sense of the evil of sin, so little love to God, heavenly mindedness, and holiness of life, among the professors of true religion?" The Age of Reason came to New England, where it seemed to mean, along with a perfunctory admiration for the incomparable Mr. Newton, "frauds and trickishness in trade," oppression and extortion "in taking any advantage that men can by any means obtain, to get the utmost possible of their neighbor for what they have to dispose of, and their neighbor needs." The moral of Arminianism seemed to be that men might freely "take advantage of their neighbor's poverty to extort unreasonably from him those things that he is under a necessity of procuring," even that they might do it by falsely commending what they sell "above the true quality of it." Among children, it seemed to mean a liberty of "stealing fruit from their neighbor's trees or inclosures." Why? Was it because, as Arminians claimed, men who believe themselves incapable of doing what they are predestined not to do will have little sense of sin or little love to God? Or was it, perhaps, because even those elements in the age who still professed the living God were persuaded in their hearts that His justice must be similar to theirs, and that therefore the acquisition of profit justified the seller's techniques? Was this why, both in Whitehall and in Northampton, men behaved as though reward were to be obtained by merit, or even better, by a show of merit?

Edwards' excoriations of the century are often the preacher's conventional abuse of his times; there is a still more embarrassing note, a provincial querulousness. All New Englanders gave way to this vein when the occasion suited; Charles Chauncy, no less, could say that England was never more corrupt, that it disavowed the truths of God and violated all the commandments: "The Land of our Fore-fathers may justly be lamented over in the language of the Prophet Isaiah, Ah sinful Nation!" Yet, though Edwards could use oratorical stops, his attacks upon the century have a far different end in view from Chauncy's. Edwards really understood how tremendous were the scientific achievements: "the increase of learning in itself is a thing to be rejoiced in, because it is a good." He turned upon his century with a fury that is more than rural self-righteousness because out of this increase in learning it had manufactured a smug insensitiveness to the realities of that existence it claimed to comprehend. Liberals objected to predestination because it is "cruel"; yet the things we see and know of mortality—"the extreme sufferings of infants"—ought by the same token to be "objected mightily against, as inconsistent with God's moral perfections, not tending to amiable ideas of the Godhead."

Edwards most effectively assailed the Arminian theology (which was the Dissenters' way of accommodating to the century's arch-dogma that whatever is, is right) by calling it an insult to human suffering—a charge that echoes down the intervening centuries as the implacable comment upon the multitudinous forms of Protestant liberalism. The Arminians appealed to experience; very well, let them argue that the mercy of God being infinite, all misery must be reprehensible to His nature: "which we see to be contrary to fact; for we see that God in his providence, doth indeed inflict very great calamities on mankind even in this life." A strength of Puritanism from the beginning had been its ability to look on life as calamitous, though indeed it frequently therefore ran a danger that, out of contempt for others less tough-minded, it could lend itself to a multiplication of calamities.

His discourses of 1734 served notice that Edwards, accused of prostituting his pulpit to nice speculations, was appealing to fact, or to factual calamity, and that out of experience he, the supposed theorist, would disprove the shallow optimism of an Arminian century. Perhaps that is why he used the adroit device of quoting, for the first time in public by name, "a certain great man," John Locke, using him to confirm a thesis even while acknowledging that no one would call Locke "a likely person to be blinded by a prejudice in favor of the doctrine we are maintaining." Also, with a cunning that ought to have warned his opponents, he cited Tillotson to show that a certain position "was not thought unreasonable doctrine by one of the greatest divines on the other side of the question in hand." All this in a closely reasoned demonstration that in the realm of cause, where every effect must have its precedent event, justification follows the act of faith, not because faith is produced out of a self-determined choice, but because there is a congruity between salvation and faith, because the sequence is based upon the "divine establishment that it shall follow." It was, he might have said, the same sort of establishment that makes solidity congruent with gravity. Later he was to put it that no metaphysical necessity following from gravity compels a weight in the beam of a balance, at a greater distance from the fulcrum, to counterbalance a weight at a shorter distance on the other side, "but only as it contradicts that beautiful proportion and harmony which the author of nature observes in the laws of nature he has established."

Prepared to stake his career upon this as the correct reading of Newton, Edwards was telling Israel Williams and all his tribe that rugged individualists were operating on the mistaken notion that a cause is what "has a positive efficiency or influence to produce a thing, or bring it to pass," which was a disastrous misreading of science. The notion that a man can cause whatever results he happens to prefer was not only bad theology, it was perverted physics. The chain of causes cannot be broken, and man is not an original and sovereign instigator of anything he takes a fancy to. A cause, Edwards said, is whatever is antecedent, "either natural or moral" (that is, either objective or inherent), on which an event depends. "Having thus explained what I mean by Cause, I assert that nothing ever comes to pass without a Cause"—not even the wilfulness of Williamses. If they would not be convinced, he was prepared to appeal to what they naïvely supposed would be the refutation of Calvinism, to experience.

Still, in 1734 Edwards held himself in check. He was outspoken enough to anger his Hatfield cousins and many of his townsmen, but the thought in the back of his mind, his real critique of Arminianism, matured with the years. Eventually he found the formulation, which underlies all his work: if the will of man is a cause which is uncaused, then the acts of man must constantly defeat the purposes of God, who thereupon becomes guilty of want of foresight; God Himself must be subject to repentance, to changes of intention, and in the end "have little else to do, but to mind broken links as well as he can, and be rectifying his disjointed frame and disordered movements." Was this the lesson of experience? If so, those who made a cult of experience confessed that they could not reconcile their precious contingency with predictability, although Newton had predicted even tides and comets. Yes, the

problem was indeed to be settled in experience, but a redefi-
nition of experience was in order. From his first bout with the
spirit of his age, Edwards came to an unshakable conviction:
whatever or whoever God may be, He cannot be thought of
as uncertain of any event; there is somewhere a realm—into
which Newton had given us verifiable glimpses—in which
there is a predictability that governs even those who take advantage of their neighbor's need to raise the price of corn.
God "always sees things just as they are in truth," and "in
reality" nothing can be contingent. It was time to remind the
river gods and the small-time merchants, launched upon ca-
reers of gain by concealing the defects of what they had to
sell or by charging more than goods were worth, that the cer-
tainties of experience are not attained by sharp dealings, but
only by infallibility. It might be, supposing England corrupted beyond all hope, that in America—here was the dream
and the temptation—possibly right here in the Valley, a society could be modeled upon reality. Here, if anywhere, a
community could be brought to a public recognition that
God does not mend and patch.

To Edwards' mind, the lesson of the popular Arminianism
was central: the modern era was committing itself to the delusion that experience is a congeries of ill-matched pieces, of
disjointed frames and discontinuous moments. It made the
same mistake as did those who took atoms for things (indeed,
it was a logical consequence of the first mistake), and no
more than the naïve atomists could it join into coherent
wholes the particles isolated in its analysis. Already the age
was reduced, in the midst of progress, to confessing ignorance,
unable to understand how what comes about has to be. Edwards' reply to Arminianism took a form which no one seriously concerned over the predicament of modern man can
call anything but relevant: just as atoms are unitary concepts
of law, and just as bodies must henceforth be thought of as
foci of resistance, so experience becomes unified only when
coherently conceived. Experience is not meaningful or even

memorable when it is merely one thing producing another; the connection between a first and a second is not between means and end. Diligence and industry are connected with riches and prosperity by "congruity"; when God decrees summer, at the same "moment," so to speak, He decrees the growing of plants and orchards, and "things do unavoidably go fatally and necessarily." God is not a distressed ship captain guiding His vessel by skill, steering it so as to escape as many dangers as the case will allow, but threatened with wreck despite His best efforts. The agonies of experience are not just cross-winds, tempests and currents, which God is forced to suffer; they are real agonies. What belongs together goes together, though the connection be not always "benevolent." In our own day, Sherwood Anderson put the Edwardsean thesis in a sentence: "The tale of perfect balance, all the elements of the tale understood."

At the end of life, every man knows this, or he knows it in rare moments when he can hold it all suspended in his mind, but in the daily doing of it, a radical propensity fights against the recognition, and cries out, "I am my own cause." This lust for selfhood insists that men are good or bad according as they do, and wants them praised or blamed proportionably; it objects to the possibility that "a man may have been a bad man, and yet it may be a good thing that there has been such a man." Arminian rationalism—we would call it liberalism— tries to haggle with life, to purchase life piecemeal; it has no resources for coping with the prospect that God may "incline to suffer that which is unharmonious in itself, for the promotion of universal harmony," and when it can no longer ignore the unharmonious, its fabric of experience is shattered. This is sin, the *original* sin. Only in the perception of what things go unavoidably and fatally together has suffering any dignity or experience any harvest; the ignorance that Whitby professed was sin, not because man is finite and so cannot know everything, not because it was the kind of ignorance to which Newton confessed, but because it invited the finite to accept itself with all its deficiencies as adequate. It declared that a man loves what he decides to love, and could not understand that he can love only what he knows how to love.

In 1741, William Williams died. As the only figure in the Valley who could at all measure up to Stoddard, he had preached Stoddard's funeral sermon and delivered the charge to the successor; so now Williams' nephew-by-marriage preached the sermon at Hatfield. This nephew, as we know, had qualified himself upon the subject of spiders that use their wings "to go with the wind," and had found that at the year's end they are "swept away into the sea, and buried in the ocean, and leave nothing behind them but their eggs, for a new stock the next year." He had also resolved in 1724, "Remember to act according to Prov. xii, 23, *A prudent man concealeth knowledge*," and counseled himself before undertaking a treatise on causation, "let there be much compliance with the reader's weakness." In the ceremonial manner, the orator saluted the survivors: to the "honored relict," to Christian, sister of his mother, he bowed: "Suffer me, honored madam, in your great affliction, to exhibit to you a compassionate Redeemer." Then he came to "the afflicted children" and permitted himself one of his sardonic touches. "I would particularly, in humility, address myself to my honored fathers, the sons of the deceased," both to those engaged in the work of the ministry (meaning Solomon of Lebanon) and to those "in other public business for the service of their generation" (meaning Elisha the Rector, but chiefly Israel the real-estate promoter). It would, Edwards continued, be more proper that he seek instruction from them than that he presume to exhort them: "And while you go to Jesus, honored sirs, on this occasion, for yourselves, I humbly desire your requests to him for us the surviving ministers of this country, that he would be with us, now he has taken from us him that was as a father amongst us."

It was, all told, one of those dramas of controlled passion and barely perceptible irony of which New England has been compacted, but an appreciation of its fine shadings is necessary for getting inside the work of Edwards. Behind the show of harsh logic and polemic is hidden a delicate manipulation of innuendo. But then, this particularly sly passage must be read in the light of that year, 1741. Edwards defied the Williamses and preached against Arminianism in such a fashion that everybody in the Valley knew they were his targets. But he thereby committed himself to a warfare in which even the most precisely fixed and determinate terms could not, by themselves, decide the outcome. If he could not make good his case in fact as well as in metaphysics, they would beat him. Shortly after the sermons of 1734, in part as it seemed because of them, he succeeded: he got up a revival that silenced his critics, attracted the notice of the Protestant world, and made Edwards famous in London and Glasgow. For a while the issue then hung in the balance, but in 1740 success came overwhelmingly. When Edwards deftly insulted the sons of William Williams at Hatfield, he was riding high. He had precipitated the Great Awakening, was master of New England's soul, had vindicated in experience, in the shrieks and groans of repentant Americans, the laws of causality and of perception, and was destroying Arminianism root and branch.

THE EXTERNAL BIOGRAPHY II

In the last years of his college life, probably around 1720, Edwards stitched together forty-four sheets of foolscap into a blank folio book, and wrote at the top of the first page an observation under the title "Of holiness." He numbered it 1, drew a line across the page, and commenced a second meditation, "Of Christ's mediation and satisfaction." By the time he died, in 1758, this manuscript, which he called "Miscellanies" or "Miscellaneous Observations," had become nine volumes containing 1360 entries, some of them elaborate treatises. He gave each a title, and kept an index. He was to draw upon these journals for his later publications (sometimes taking whole passages intact), but most of these thoughts he kept back, intending ultimately to put them into a monumental book which he provisionally entitled, "Rational Account of the Main Doctrines of the Christian Religion Attempted."

He also took a King James version of the Bible that had belonged to Sarah's father—probably this project was begun after his marriage—and interleaved it with blank folio pages. He started to annotate crucial passages. Eventually he filled up his pages, and then three more manuscript volumes. These "Notes on the Scriptures" were also meticulously indexed.

The real life of Jonathan Edwards at Northampton and Stockbridge was the continuous interior monologue of which these as yet unpublished journals are the partial record. Manuscripts, or at least manuscript outlines, for about a thousand sermons also survive, as do various drafts of attempted works, but into the meditations he poured the full intensity of his thought, and so absorbed was he in this interior logic that it may truthfully be said that his external biography was virtually an adjunct to his subjective.

He rose at four on summer mornings and by five in the winter; he scrupulously regulated his diet so that his mind would be most active, and he averaged thirteen hours a day in his study. For exercise he chopped wood or rode horseback, but even then his mind was at work. After dinner (as everywhere in New England, this was at midday), he would ride to some solitary place in the woods, carrying pen and ink with him; he would dismount and walk, jotting down thoughts that were then reworked at night into the "Miscellanies." On long rides he would carry with him papers and pins, and, having thought through an idea, would pin a paper on his coat, charging himself to associate it with the theme of his cogitation. The legend is that he would reach his door with leaves pinned all over his coat, and that Sarah would help to unpin him.

By the terms of his settlement, the town paid Edwards £300 for the purchase of a homestead (with which he bought the lot on King Street, where he lived until 1750), and £100 a year as salary, and gave him two pasture lots, one of ten and the other of forty acres. In 1729 his salary was increased to £200.

In that year, while he was seriously ill, the townspeople built him "a Good Large Barn." The congregation numbered about 600. Edwards preached on Sundays and gave a "Lecture" on Thursdays. He catechised the children in public on Sunday afternoons, and often summoned them individually or in groups to his house, to talk and pray with them in private. He refused to follow the custom, generally observed by his colleagues, of making regular visits to all his people in their homes, because, he said, he had no talent for entertaining them or for profiting himself by their entertainment. He felt he could do most good by preaching and writing, or by conversing with the people in his study. Still, he always went when he was sent for by the sick or when he heard of persons under affliction, and he preached frequently at small private meetings. Ministers and other dignitaries traveling from Connecticut to Boston stayed at his house, and he usually rode out with them for a few miles as they resumed their journey.

His third child, Esther, was born in February 1732, and his fourth, Mary, in April 1734. At the end of 1733 he preached with success against the habit, that had grown up over the past years, of visiting and relaxing on Sunday evenings. His sermons, delivered slowly, distinctly, and with dignity, in a low, moderate voice, with "habitual and great solemnity, looking and speaking as in the presence of God," began to have an increasing effect upon the people in 1734. For sermon notes he cut up foolscap into booklets 3⅞ by 4⅛ inches, or else used any paper available, such as the backs of official proclamations and Yale commencement programs, or even the ends of Sarah's fan papers. In later years, especially after 1740, he wrote out only the topic headings and trusted to habitude for the body of his discourse.

A particularly effective series of sermons in the last months of 1734 were followed by sudden and violent conversions, most notably on the part of a young woman of the town who had been one of the greatest "company-keepers." Through the winter and spring Edwards led the most spectacular revival that New England had yet beheld. Over 300 persons were seized upon, and practically the whole town became communicants. Strife, backbiting, and gossip disappeared. The suicide of his uncle-by-marriage, the merchant Joseph Hawley, in May 1735, commenced a reaction, and by the end of the year the revival was over, the town not knowing quite what had happened and remembering with mingled feelings the ecstasies of the first months.

A new church structure was begun in the summer of 1736. On March 13, 1737, the gallery of the old meeting-house fell during the service, but none was seriously hurt. The spire of the new building was raised "with good success" on July 21, and in November a committee of the church arranged the plan of seating, strictly according to social status.

In 1735 the church of Springfield elected Robert Breck as pastor. He was reputed to be an Arminian, and the Hampshire Association refused to concur in his ordination. The church called a council of ministers from Boston; when Breck attempted to speak, the local authorities, instigated by the Hampshire clergy, arrested him. The Boston delegates protested, and the General Court of Massachusetts Bay censured the Association, thus effectually denying its legality and intimating that Western Massachusetts was not Connecticut. Breck was finally ordained in January 1736. Edwards, although not present at the sessions, drew up and published a defense of the Hampshire Association, apparently at the request of his uncle-by-marriage, William Williams, who was moderator of the meetings. Edwards thereby made an enemy of Breck, who published a rebuttal, as well as of those who had supported Breck. The lines of a contest between the Connecticut Valley and the metropolis can clearly be made out in this otherwise trivial event.

Edwards' fifth child, Lucy, was born in August 1736, and his sixth, his first son, Timothy, in July 1738. His sermons dated between 1736 and 1740 show him struggling terribly to revive the spirit of 1735. In 1739 he wrote the *Personal Narrative*, and in that year, as part of his effort to arouse the people, he gave the thirty sermons that constitute the draft of his *History of Redemption*.

In 1738 Joseph Bellamy came to study with Edwards and resided for some months in the family. The seventh child, Susannah, was born in June 1740. On Friday, October 17, George Whitefield arrived from Boston and spent three days as Edwards' guest in Northampton.

What is the matter, that, with all his ill usage of me, I cannot hate him? To be sure, I am not like other people! He has certainly done enough to make me hate him; but yet, when I heard his danger, which was very great, I could not in my heart forbear rejoicing for his safety; though his death would have ended my afflictions. . . .

Good Sirs! good Sirs! What will become of me? Here is my master come in his fine chariot! Indeed he is!—What shall I do? Where shall I hide myself?—O! What shall I do? Pray for me! But O! you will not see this! Now, good God of Heaven, preserve me! if it is thy blessed will. . . .

And then I heard his voice on the stairs, as he was coming up to me. It was about his supper; for he said, "I shall choose a boiled chicken with butter and parsley." And up he came. . . .

And so he went out of the room; and I was quite sick at heart. "Surely," said I, "I am the wickedest creature that ever breathed!" . . .

"Ah!" said she, "thou art a pretty creature, it's true; but so obstinate! so full of spirit! if thy strength was but answerable to that, thou wouldest run away with us all, and this great house too, on thy back! But undress, undress, I tell you." . . .

I was so weak all day on Monday that I could not get out of my bed. My master shewed great tenderness for me; and I hope he is really sorry, and that this will be his last attempt: but he does not say so.

SAMUEL RICHARDSON

Revivalism

IN 1740, the lid blew off New England. It also blew off other colonies, as it had shortly before blown, or at least risen, in Europe. The mysterious phenomenon known in Germany as Pietism, in England as evangelicalism and Methodism, in America as the Great Awakening, presents everywhere a curious uniformity, as though each people had been searching for the same thing, and suddenly, in the heyday of the Enlightenment, found it. Whatever it was, it was always a rejection, a violent rejection, of the free and catholic spirit. In September of 1740 George Whitefield came to Boston; a more repulsive individual never influenced history, but his voice could reach thousands and set them wailing for their sins. Garrick, who should be an authority, said that Whitefield could throw an audience into paroxysms by pronouncing "Mesopotamia." Converted by the Wesleys, whom he outdid in the strenuousness of his devotions, and ordained in 1736, he immediately became a sensation, addressing crowds of twenty or thirty thousand, all of them "affected and drenched in tears." In cold print his sermons are bombast, but when delivered out of his mighty lungs, they gathered up the anguish and the cravings of the masses, who thereupon fell into weepings and convulsions, "like persons that were hungering and thirsting after righteousness."

Whatever the explanation elsewhere, Whitefield's success in New England can be accounted for: he stepped into a situation prepared for him, he touched off a powder-keg that had long been building up to an explosion. Or, to speak more accurately, Jonathan Edwards had already put a match to the fuse, and Whitefield blew it into flame. In New England the Awakening was the culmination of a smoldering process that had long been consuming the Puritan churches, a process that developed out of the ceremony called "owning the covenant." The primitive Congregational system assumed that an individual encounters the crisis of conversion alone, in the closet or in the fields; after wrestling with the Lord, he reports to the congregation, and out of his hard-won liberty swears to the church covenant. It further assumed, because the Bible promises grace to the "seed," that the saint's children would one by one repeat the behavior; but as early as 1650 it became evident that the New England system was started upon an unexpected evolution when fewer and fewer children were receiving the experience. An accommodation was made in 1662, entitled the "Half-Way Covenant," permitting these children to bring their own infants to baptism upon "owning the covenant." This acknowledgment gave them no right to membership, to the title of saint, or to the Lord's Supper, but it treated them as presumptive saints and kept them and their children under church government. By 1700 the majority of members were but halfway participants, and communities consisted of three concentric circles: the small body of professing members known as the "church," the larger body of halfway professors called the "congregation," and then the town, which paid for the church and was legally required to attend, though neither saints nor half-saints.

The story is an object lesson in the way artificial distinctions can, before any perceive it, alter the character of a society. Inevitably the ministers put pressure upon the people to own—or to reown—the covenant. Gradually the ritual confession became a community affair; the congregation would observe a fast by reaffirming their corporate allegiance. After the clergy lost direct control of the government, they steadily developed the oath into periodic demonstrations, and days of communal owning became catharses of social anxieties. Thus emerged an utterly new phenomenon, a confession in unison and a public purgation of conscience, something totally foreign to the private soul-searching of Puritanism, a mass expression which in American history is called a revival.

The device circumvented without openly violating Congregational theory; its advantages were, first, as Cotton Mather said, that the duty of owning could be pressed upon everybody, even upon the unbaptized, since it did not require the ardors of actual faith; it could be urged upon those who "apprehend themselves not attained unto such comfortable degrees of Experience as may imbolden them immediately to approach unto the other table." Secondly, once these had owned a covenant, they could legitimately be exhorted to extend themselves. Although God alone gives the enabling grace for profession, halfway members could still be dealt with as in a hopeful state, and be thus addressed: "You will also carefully and sincerely labour after those more positive and increased evidences of regeneration, which may further encourage you to seek an admission unto the table of the Lord." By 1730, a type of sermon designed for communal response was an almost perfected literary form, waiting only for someone to take it in hand, just as the novel was ready for the touch of Richardson. New England had fallen into a rhythm of periodic revivals, and the beat was accelerating; if all local outbursts could be synchronized, an awakening could be organized that would attain "great" heights of confession—or depths of contrition.

The apathy of the people prevented it, over which they themselves sorrowed. As Colman observed in 1707, they stopped short with the halfway status because it obtained baptism for their children, "which when they have gained, we hear no more of 'em." So the clergy held more and more festivals of renewal, attempting to provide the incentive which the system did not offer. Cotton Mather reported that the innovation of owning the covenant had become such a public parade that there was "a vast confluence of other neighbors usually present." Finally, the incongruity between these spectacles and the theory decided Stoddard, a man of decision, to scrap the theory and to take the confluence of spectators into the performance. He pragmatically justified his throwing over the covenant, with its effort to limit membership according to a rule that could no longer delimit, by staging New England's most elaborate revivals. Offering all sacraments, now openly called "converting ordinances," to all the people, he reaped five "harvests"; in 1679, 1683, 1696, 1712, and 1718 he so worked up his flock that "the bigger Part of the Young People in the Town, seemed mainly concerned for their eternal salvation," and thus won Northampton the honor—in some circles, especially Cambridge, the dubious honor—of being the most "enthusiastical" town in the colonies. When Edwards stood beside the bier of Stoddard in 1729, and heard William Williams say that a great work was "rowl'd" upon him, he knew what was required: he had to produce a Stoddardean harvest. In the spring of 1735 he more than made good; his revival was spectacular, but more importantly, he gave to it such literary expression that it became the exemplar of what New England had been obscurely tending toward for a hundred years.

Like his fellows, Benjamin Colman was calling for a re-kindling of piety, and inquired for news from Northampton. On May 30, 1735, Edwards wrote him an account. To the eternal credit of Colman (these things are relative to time and to the culture), he recognized a work of genius. He had the letter printed, and sent copies to his friends in England, to great pundits among the Dissenters, like Isaac Watts, and they too recognized the accent of authority. Edwards was persuaded, evidently by Colman, to rework the letter, and so, under the date of November 6, 1736, was published in London and in Boston Edwards' first masterpiece, *A Faithful Narrative of the Surprising Work of God in the Conversion of Many Hundred Souls in Northampton, and the Neighboring Towns and Villages.* It went through three editions and twenty printings by 1739, and a hundred years later was still a handbook of revivalism in Illinois and in Wales. Without exaggeration one may say that the *Narrative* did for bewildered English Nonconformists of 1736 what Goethe's *Werther* did for young German romantics: it perfected a formula for escape from an intellectual dilemma by opening an avenue into emotion and sensibility.

The success of the *Narrative* with a public that could take Pamela or (even more) Clarissa to its bosom owed much to two novelettes that Edwards interpolated in order "to give a clearer idea of the nature and manner of the operations of God's spirit." He used "idea" in the Lockean sense, and reported these biographies as case histories; but the heroine of the first, Abigail Hutchinson, was a virgin who died prematurely, and of the second the protagonist was Phebe Bartlet, a child of four. Thus sentimentalism came to New England and triumphed, but it came, let us note, through the empirical psychology. Abigail was "a still, quiet, reserved person," infirm of body, first awakened by the terrors of hell, and then so ravished by the love of God that she no longer found pleasure in the midst of the busy town, but preferred "to sit and see the wind blowing the trees, and to behold in the country what God has made." Edwards agreed that her health had something to do with the story, yet indubitably she had discoveries of Christ greater "than the present frail state did well consist with." The story of Abigail carries us forward to Edgar Poe's Annie, but Phebe anticipates the stereotype of little Eva, except that Phebe did not die and Edwards did not write her up as a stereotype. Edwards belonged to a society which assumed that children, far from being insulated with innocence, are in the midst of life from the beginning; if a progressive era finds this brutal, it should acknowledge that there was some compensation, that the emotions of four were treated with as much respect as those of twenty-four. Phebe went through the cycle, crying "and wreathing her body to and fro, like one in anguish of spirit," until she found surcease; then she smiled as she cried, "Mother, the kingdom of heaven is come to me!" She loved her minister, and babbled among the children when he returned from a journey, "Mr. Edwards is come home! Mr. Edwards is come home!" In 1736, Mr. Edwards could report that occasionally she seemed doubtful whether she was prepared for death, but that generally "when asked, replies yes, without hesitation."

This study is not, as I trust is evident, an apology for Jonathan Edwards. The problem he poses is fundamental for American civilization; so much nonsense has been written about the "fiery Puritan" that precision of statement is imperative, and yet so much has also been penned by historians incapable of understanding Abigail and Phebe that the student must make an especially vigorous effort to strike a balance among the historical factors. These events did happen, but more importantly, the most profound student of Newton and Locke in all America took them seriously; he so shaped them in literature that Abigail and Phebe are enduring prototypes of American experience. Nothing is gained in exoneration of Edwards by pleading the standards of the age; certain of his contemporaries, Mandeville, Voltaire, Franklin—and Charles Chauncy—would have handled Abigail and Phebe differently, but they were not grandsons of Solomon Stoddard or pastors of inland Puritan communities, and none of them had resolved in his youth, "Never to do anything, which, I should be afraid to do, if I expected it would not be above an hour, before I should hear the last trump."

The literary charm of these little romances in the key of Richardson should not distract attention from the radical achievement of the *Narrative:* no anthropologist ever reported more objectively on the fertility rites of a jungle tribe, for Protestantism had not yet seen, though it had often aspired to, so perfect a union of the hot heart and the cool head. Edwards made no secret of why he could maintain detachment from events in which he was deeply implicated: he had a technique for analysis, the Lockean psychology. He was as empirical as Boyle or Huygens, and wrote the *Narrative* as though for the *Transactions* of the Royal Society. The experiment certainly demonstrated that God does not confine Himself to a standard procedure; the variety of observed behavior was immense, "perhaps as manifold as the subjects of the operation." Still, taking all cases together, and not accepting "every religious pang, and enthusiastic conceit, for saving conversion," in all verifiable instances there was "a great analogy."

Investigation demonstrated, first of all, that the preaching of God's absolute sovereignty and "a conviction of the justice of God in their condemnation" were essential links in most conversions. So much for Arminians! Secondly, the Lockean psychology proved an accurate prognosis of how the psyche works: before the revival, many had "very imperfect ideas what conversion was," but as it got under way, the people were able to show by their use ·of words that they really had acquired "those special and distinct ideas" which the words properly signify. Obviously the Arminians were using an obsolete psychology when they said that conversion had to be either a reasonable persuasion or a physical influx; the Northampton experiment proved that grace comes not as argumentation or as interposition, but as idea. Conversion is a perception, a form of apprehension, derived exactly as Locke said mankind gets all simple ideas, out of sensory experience. Furthermore, the event supplied a sound empirical test for certifying the stigmata: an ability cogently and exactly to put the idea into words. Clearly then, when words are used only as sounds, disconnected from special and distinct ideas, they are signs (perhaps even "causes"?) of a dead and lifeless frame.

One other result of the experiment should be noted, which comes out more clearly in the first and more spontaneous version of the *Narrative*: in the heat of the revival, the old iniquity of Northampton, the party strife of a generation, disappeared; the people were united in love, and not only forgave enemies, but prayed for their salvation. "This Town," wrote Edwards in one of his most poignant sentences, "never was so full of Love, nor so full of Joy, nor so full of distress as it has Lately been."

The first letter came to an abrupt halt with the intelligence of Joseph Hawley's suicide; when he wrote the second, Edwards had digested this reverse. By May of 1735, he could say, it "began to be very sensible that the Spirit of God was gradually withdrawing from us." As should be expected, Satan began to rage, and a gentleman who came "of a family that are exceeding prone to the disease of melancholy," being kept awake so many nights "that he had scarce any sleep at all," cut his throat, whereupon many heard voices crying, "*Cut your own throat, now is a good opportunity.* Now! Now!" This passage stands near the close of a controlled work, written by one who always knew what he was saying: hovering over the last pages of the *Narrative* is the half-formed shape of a new thought: that these occurrences are in time and run a course. Therefore analysis must not only employ psychological and spatial terms, but become aware of the temporal morphology. An outpouring of the divine spirit is implicated in causes and perceptions, but it also has a tempo, a rise and a fall. Edwards left Yale equipped with an entire philosophy of the mind and the cosmos; experience gradually forced upon him one major addition, a concept of the career of things in time. He was beginning, out of the revival of 1735 and the suicide of Hawley, to confront the problem of history.

In spite of Satan, Edwards was confident. A religious disposition was still, in 1736, evident in the town; no young person—the crucial test—had returned to extravagance, and "God has evidently made us a new people." Experience vindicated psychology; allowing everything for natural or mechanical causes, for the peculiarities of the town or for Abigail's consumption, the experience had been real, and after discounting all "distempers," the scientist could declare "this amazing work, as it appeared to me, to be indeed divine." Undoubtedly, by merely physiological stimuli, many imaginations were too much inflamed, and this natural propensity is, he warned, a danger to be watched lest false "impressions" be taken for real experiences. Such workings of the brain are mysterious, "and I have been at a loss about them." Yet, if caution be observed, each case can be unraveled, and the certain guide will be the propriety of language; if the longings and the words of the convert arise "from nothing but a sense of the superlative excellency of divine things," and excellency be understood in the Edwardsean definition, the experience is genuine. Here was the responsibility of the leader, who must exercise both caution and power; in the ecstatic period, the town gathered to worship, "every hearer eager to drink in the words of the minister as they came from his mouth."

One thing all New England knew by now: during these months, Northampton drank in the words of Edwards. His fame as a preacher, not as the cold theoretician of the Boston lecture, but as one who spoke in a new way, directly to emotions, whose words were tangible to the senses, who made language one with experience, this fame he now acquired, never to lose. The curiosity of New England was so great that in 1738 he published four of his revival sermons, together with his treatise on justification, under the title, *Discourses on Various Important Subjects, Nearly concerning the great Affair of the Soul's Eternal Salvation.* When Whitefield relit the conflagration and it spread through the land as through dry timber, New England already had an orator greater than Whitefield, and a model for the revival sermon, although few yet realized the peril to mere mortals of daring to handle Jove's thunderbolt.

By October of 1740, Prince could report that the face of Boston, cleansed with four weeks of Whitefield's torrent, was altered. Negroes and boys ceased to be rude, taverns were occupied only by legitimate lodgers, and at Harvard, the report ran, prayer and praise filled students' chambers. Prince, Cooper, Sewall, Shurtleff at Portsmouth, and Joshua Gee (aroused from indolence) joined in the chase, their great moment come at last; Foxcroft did what he could despite the paralytic stroke he had suffered in 1736; and the now magisterial Colman blessed the work. Then Whitefield rode across Massachusetts, preaching at Concord, Sudbury, Marlborough, Leicester, to crowds that "were sweetly melted." We must go to such analogies as Peter the Hermit or Savonarola, or possibly the Pied Piper, to grasp what this triumphal progress was like: a whole society was stricken and convulsed. On Friday, October 17, 1740, he arrived in Northampton.

He preached four times from Edwards' pulpit, held a session with the children, and went with Edwards to Hatfield (I suspect Edwards arranged that!). Whitefield reminded Northampton of its experience in 1735, and, along with his people, "dear Mr. Edwards wept during almost the whole time of the exercise." Whitefield put into his diary—"confided" would not be the word since he was publishing it serially and thousands were buying it—that he never had a more gracious meeting. He also was impressed by Sarah Pierrepont Edwards, who talked so solidly of the things of God and was such a helpmeet to her husband that Whitefield pondered whether his duty did not call him to marriage, betraying no suspicion that his exceedingly crossed eyes might make him less attractive as a lover than as an evangelist.

Within the fold of revivalism, there are no personalities more uncongenial than Whitefield and Edwards. Whitefield did not use the rigorous mold of the Puritan sermon; instead he improvised dramatically. He did not stare unmoved at the bell-rope; he gesticulated, shouted, sang, wept. Above all he wept. He was reckless and irresponsible, whining and sanctimonious. Jonathan Mayhew said his performance was "low, confused, puerile, conceited, ill-natured, enthusiastic," which can be taken for accurate reporting. Since we still lack a precise terminology for social analysis, we must content ourselves with recognizing that this performance made explicit a dark cry for satisfactions which, in the Puritan tradition, had not been recognized and certainly not provided for. Cooper and Sewall and Prince had not found the formula nor sprung the lock; Whitefield, a child of English sentimentalism, was too shallow to respect and too facile to understand a severe form; he exploded the sermon structure in which the mounting emotionalism of a hard-working society had been bottled up.

The most damning word of Mayhew's scorn is "enthusiastic." This was an old term of reproach in Puritan theology, generally applied to Antinomians and Quakers; historically, it denotes those who mistake some mechanical or psychological disturbance for the voice of God. The victim of enthusiasm believes that by a direct communication with the deity, he is a moral absolute, freed of restraint, incapable of sin. The enthusiast heeds "impulses," and in them receives the content of theology, instead of submitting, as does the true saint, to logical propositions already worked out in systematic divinity. The Enlightenment (which in England drew upon Puritan sources) even more heartily condemned enthusiasm; in the fourth edition of the *Essay*, Locke was obliged to insert a chapter upon it lest any suppose that by placing truth in perception, he condoned subjectivity. Because ideas derive from experience, a proposition is true only so far as it can be proved; what a man believes by "immediate revelation" is nothing but "the conceits of a warmed or overweening brain." Such fancies are insidious because, "freed from all restraint of reason and check of reflection," they carry the whole man with them. The enthusiast supposes that ideas acquired in experience are valid apart from experience, and since an idea is a perception which preconditions how a man shall see and how react, to suppose ideas inwardly given is to behave in a way dangerous to society. The true light of the mind, said Locke, is an idea conformed to objective reality, and no idea (unless, of course, it be "a self-evident proposition," in which case it is entirely one with the thing) can have any more light than comes from the clearness and distinctness of the proofs.

In the crowded weekend, Edwards asked if his guest did not give too much credit to impulses, and conveyed his dislike of Whitefield's readiness to pronounce other people unconverted without meticulous examination. He also questioned Whitefield's wisdom in insinuating that the people ought to forsake "unconverted ministers." Stoddard had been explicit that as long as a minister's docrine was sound, he was a means of grace, regardless of his inner condition. The clergy and not the people were judges of conversion, and if the rabble of New England ever got it into their heads that they could forsake settled pastors and run after any enthusiast who pleased them, New England society would become chaos. Edwards says that Whitefield answered with kindness, but, obtuse though he could be to merely human reactions, Edwards made out that Whitefield did not treat him quite as an intimate. However, Edwards never questioned that God could use any instrument He chose, and on Monday rode with Whitefield to East Windsor, where the evangelist mowed down his father's congregation. At Suffield, someone said that ministers need not be converted; whereupon, Edwards having returned to Northampton, Whitefield devoted his discourse to the topic, honoring Stoddard, but excoriating him for this error. At Wethersfield he met and at once embraced as intimates Wheelock and Pomeroy, members of David Ferris' little band which a few years before had made an enthusiastical noise among Yale undergraduates; as he continued his march through New Haven to New York, he said kind things about the most conspicuous of their associates, James Davenport: he "never knew one keep so close a walk with God as Mr. Davenport." Thus he sowed the wind, and then decamped, leaving Edwards to reap the whirlwind.

The wind of revival now blew through the entire Valley. All the ministers joined in, but Edwards preached up and down the region. The phenomena of the first awakening were repeated in the second, except, Edwards noted, that now "conversions were frequently wrought more sensibly and visibly," which confirmed the sensational thesis; the transition from one state to another, being more sensible, "might in many instances be, as it were, seen by by-standers." Well into 1741, Edwards was persuaded, "the work seemed to be much more pure, having less of a corrupt mixture, than in the former great outpouring of the Spirit in 1735 and 1736." On July 8, ten years to a day after the Boston lecture, at the request of the minister in Enfield, who found his town peculiarly stubborn, Edwards delivered the one work by which, if he be remembered at all, he is likely to be known forever. Legend has exaggerated what happened, but the facts themselves, recorded by a reliable witness, are impressive: there were moanings and cryings, until the shrieks became so "amazing" that Edwards (his eyes fixed on the bell-rope) had to pause. Considering how distasteful or incomprehensible these rituals have become, we should notice that the witness was struck with how many were hopefully wrought upon that night, and with the cheerfulness and pleasantness of their countenances.

Sinners in the Hands of an Angry God, as the Enfield sermon is called, slowly, with implacable slowness, coils a monstrous accusation against mankind, until the bow of God's wrath is bent and the arrow justifiably aimed at the entrails of the race. The climactic image is, as we might expect, the spider:

The God that holds you over the pit of hell, much as one holds a spider, or some loathsome insect, over the fire, abhors you, and is dreadfully provoked; his wrath towards you burns like fire; he looks upon you as worthy of nothing else, but to be cast into the fire; he is of purer eyes than to bear to have you in his sight; you are ten thousand times so abominable in his eyes, as the most hateful and venomous serpent is in ours. You have offended him infinitely more than ever a stubborn rebel did his prince: and yet it is nothing but his hand that holds you from falling into the fire every moment: it is ascribed to nothing else, that you did not go to hell the last night; that you was suffered to awake again in this world, after you closed your eyes to sleep; and there is no other reason to be given, why you have not dropped into hell since you arose in the morning, but that God's hand has held you up: there is no other reason to be given why you have not gone to hell, since you have sat here in the house of God, provoking his pure eyes by your sinful wicked manner of attending his solemn worship: yea, there is nothing else that is to be given as a reason why you do not this very moment drop down into hell.

Enduring images are given early, anterior to thought, previous to love. Edwards told his people that they, like him, had seen the spider thrown on the kitchen fire: "There is no long struggle, no fighting against the fire, no strength exerted to oppose the heat, or to fly from it; but it immediately stretches forth itself and yields; and the fire takes possession of it, and at once it becomes full of fire, and is burned into a bright coal." A sensitive boy fixes instinctively upon his emblem, and is transfixed by it; the artist catches his glimpse, and is forever caught by it.

> But after I had seen
> That spectacle, for many days, my brain
> Worked with a dim and undetermined sense
> Of unknown modes of being.

Was this the recoil of a sensibility that could not endure the spectacle of agony, that was given, in the ethos of East Windsor, only one explanation? Was then and there engendered a dread of soul that could be assuaged only by being shared? Or was the final expression, though fed from subterranean sources, more calculated? My point is that whatever it owed to impulse, it was also conscious design. Conditioned by New England, Edwards found the route from Locke's sensationalism to the burning spider inescapable. Locke confirmed what the spider taught, that the life of the soul is the life of the senses. Edwards scientifically, deliberately, committed Puritanism, which had been a fervent rationalism of the covenant, to a pure passion of the senses, and the terror he imparted was the terror of modern man, the terror of insecurity. He overthrew the kind of religious philosophy that had dominated Western Europe since the fall of Rome, the system wherein there was always—whether in terms of the City of God, or of the Mass and absolution, or of final causes and substantial forms, or, at the last, in terms of the Puritan covenant—an ascertainable basis for human safety. Now there was none:

> Unconverted men walk over the pit of hell on a rotten covering, and there are innumerable places in this covering so weak that they will not bear their weight, and these places are not seen. The arrows of death fly unseen at noonday; the sharpest sight cannot discern them.

In the moment of triumph, Edwards threw off disguises and exposed the secret long nurtured; the last remnant of scholasticism was discarded, and God was no longer bound by any promise, whether of metaphysics or of law. Edwards brought mankind, as Protestantism must always bring them, without mitigation, protection, or indulgence, face to face with a cosmos fundamentally inhuman: "There are no means within reach that can be any security to them." They are without any refuge, and "all that preserves them every moment is the mere arbitrary will, and uncovenanted, unobliged forbearance of an incensed God." Edwards' preaching was America's sudden leap into modernity.

The modern student must, if he wishes to comprehend, free himself of certain ultra modern prejudices. Even among the devout, torments are generally considered, in Edwards' word, "bugbears." Were Edwards only a shouting evangelist who drummed up hysteria with hell-fire and brimstone, he would pertain to social history along with Asbury and Peter Cartwright, but not to literature and not to philosophy. By supplying a vehicle which ignorance and crudity soon adopted, Edwards wrought incalculable harm, though we must remember that the main current of American revivalism flows from Whitefield and the Methodists rather than from him, and that among revivalists he is a peculiar figure. Edwards was primarily concerned with the problem of communication. By the time of Channing, Emerson, and Horace Bushnell, the terms of this problem were so different from those of the early eighteenth century that they could not understand him; today, the terms forced upon us, albeit more complex, are essentially those that confronted him: a behavioristic psychology and a universe of a-moral forces. Far from being street-corner evangelism, Edwards' sermons are immense and concentrated efforts to get across, in the simplest language, the meaning of the religious life, of the life of consciousness, after physics has reduced nature to a series of irreversible equations, after analysis of the mind has reduced intelligence to sensory conditioning. They are, we may say, explorations of the meaning of meaning.

Not that they are systematic expositions. The terms of art are concealed, and they attempt to solve the problem not by metaphysics but by action. Edwards strove to work so upon his listeners that in the act of comprehension they could not help knowing the answer. They are direct, frontal attacks upon epistemological doubt. Locke condemned enthusiasm for holding ideas without regard to objective fact, and pled for their control by reason; yet he had to confess that by his philosophy no ideas in the mind could ever be "exactly the images and resemblances of something inherent in the subject." How, then, can an idea be called true? How can a perception have moral or passionate value if the sequence of causes is implacably fixed without regard to values? In parrying these questions, Locke hit upon a significant analogy:

sensations bear no more likeness to things existing without us "than the names that stand for them are the likeness of our ideas, which yet upon hearing they are apt to excite in us." To his surprise, Locke stumbled upon the discovery that the problem of language is one with the problem of knowledge. Thereupon, further embarrassing questions disclosed themselves: how can language be anything but the chance accumulation of conditioned reflexes? How, in a scientific cosmos, can words be used to regenerate or to unite a society? Edwards' sermons must be read as an effort to meet these questions head-on. They are experimental wrestlings with the two gigantic issues of modern philosophy: of the link between the objective and the subjective; and of semantics itself—of how words can be manipulated so that, despite their radical unlikeness to concepts, they will convey trustworthy ideas.

Of course, Edwards never doubted that a hell exists to which sinners go after death, but that consideration was a footnote. Pervading all his oratory was his conviction, learned out of Newton, that truth is indifferent to past, present, or future, "for all are alike to God." As gravity is a corollary of solidity, time is a mode of the finite. The certainty of connection between sinfulness and misery rests not upon anything in the cause which will, in some future, engineer the effect, but upon an "inviolable sequence" which is independent of time. It does not wait upon the contingency of anyone's behavior: to say that God will not certainly fulfill His threats is to suppose Him obliged to use a "fallacy" in governing the world, to imagine that because the fear of punishment is a device of great utility in restraining men from sin, God utters insincere threats to assist social regulations, and then finds Himself compelled, regretfully, to punish those who still persist in sinning. As everywhere, the fallacy of Arminians was not so much their theology as their physics; they thought themselves so cunning that "they can discern the cheat, and defeat the design." But God's threats do not hang upon suppositions; they rest upon "what He knew would be future in execution." God speaks truth, and truth is not conditioned by time, and so God cannot speak "contrary to what He knows and contrary to what He intends." Thus for Edwards, the futurity of torment was of less interest than the eternity and the certainty—the timelessness—of agony. Newton was as little concerned about the precise dates of a comet's rotation, but as much concerned with the laws of acceleration and the inviolability of the orbit. Whether future or past, pain has a law, and Edwards' contention was that the law is given in the mechanism of physical sensation.

Even the "future life" will conform to the model of this one: it will be "sensible." In fact, the sense of the soul will be all the stronger, because the "impression of eternity" will be greater, though any man's sense of it would be as strong, here and now, could he just once apprehend what the spider knows in the fire. The pattern of perception is the pattern of the universe; the punishment of the wicked must be "an abiding sensible punishment," not because God is gratuitously cruel, but because only out of experience can false judgment be rectified. That which "senseless" sinners will not learn—there is no more revealing argument in Edwards than his equating of obtuseness to sense impression with sin—must be taught "by briers and thorns, and by the flames of hell." If we whimper that the judgment is barbarous, we show only that we have no "idea" of the sin; in comfort we read of the brutalities that men inflict upon each other, in torture-chambers and concentration camps, and "we have a sense of the evil of them," but not enough sense, not an "ideal sense," to make us understand the congruity of vengeance with evil. We object that it is shocking that God should sink the sinner into an abyss of misery: "is it not at all shocking to thee, that thou shouldst be so utterly regardless as thou hast been of the honour and glory of the infinite God?" If once we perceived the justness of the proportion, in the Lockean meaning of perception (as Newton perceived the justness of relation among previously supposed discrete phenomena within the field of gravitation), "all objections against this doctrine would vanish at once."

But if we refuse to perceive, then only in experience can a wrong judgment be brought to a right judgment: "They will be convinced of the *reality* of those things which they would not be convinced of here."

Edwards underscored reality. "At the end, the vision will speak and not lie." The new problem, the hitherto unappreciated problem, was time. All things are in sequences, and there must be a nexus of one with another. Among inanimate objects, such as the stones in the pastures, the nexus is collision and their identity is resistance; likewise among planets and cosmogonies, and the farmer's wisdom is cosmic wisdom. But for sentient beings, the nexus is sensation, and their identity is consent; thus the wisdom of both saints and adulterers is also cosmic. By sensation the body moves in adjustment to external fact, but in perception, unlike simple collision or the bare reflex, the direction of the response depends, not upon the force imparted by the object, but upon the manner of perceiving, upon the idea that the mind forms out of the seeing. Stimulus and response constitute an inviolable sequence no less than collision; but consciousness has a further responsibility, of perceiving and responding to reality and not to enthusiastical phantasies. If the organism refuses consent to what must be, it is still incapable of interrupting the sequence or of defeating the design (why can we not know this?); yet it must pay the cost of learning, sooner or later, that it failed to agree to what was and to what is. Sense is life's method, and life's error is not in the senses but in its own transmitting of force from object to deed. The regenerate sense consents, not to conditional contracts, but to a chain of efficient causes. And in Northampton, in 1740, there was the opportunity for consent: otherwise, "you will believe it when the event shall prove it, when it shall be too late to profit by the belief."

In his sermons Edwards began to distinguish the two orders under names he henceforth employed, the "natural" and the "moral." The natural order, as the 1734 discourses declared, is "the natural concord or agreeableness there is between such qualification and such circumstances," the suitableness, for example, that four should come after three, and five after four. The moral order is that fitness of relationship which depends upon the fashion in which an object "affects" the perceiver. Because it reveals the state of the soul, it is the realm of values. Stones and planets fulfill the natural order ineluctably according to the laws of motion, and react upon each other through gravity or collision; and even "brute creatures," through some "degree of perception and perfection given them," are without defect. An essential element in the terror Edwards evoked at Enfield was the categorical statement: "God's creatures are good, and were made for men to serve God with, and do not willingly subserve to any other purpose, and groan when they are abused to purposes so directly contrary to their nature and end." Man, too, has natural appetites which, left to themselves, would insure faithful adherence to natural law: "Man has a natural craving and thirst after happiness," and happiness, in so far as it is pleasure, is coequal with excellency. In the realm of nature, in the logic of causes, there is no such thing as "chance, or mere contingence." The very notion of it is "a gross absurdity." Satan himself, "educated in the best divinity school in the universe," has been a spectator of the "series of these works," and knows what Arminians will not confess, that the tissue of nature is no cheat and cannot be rent. The conduct of the universe is a "train" of events, a "course" of dispensations, and no enormity of human prejudice can alter the path of a single atom.

Still, while atoms follow their courses, human experience is moral. Side by side with the collision of bodies, perception has its logic: man perceives the object, receives an impression, forms an idea, and acts by his conception. This train of events is as irresistible as that of spring and the flowering of trees. If sense be purely sensual, "if man have no other end but to gratify his senses," he reacts to fact as does the brute, and "reason is nothing but an impediment." But a man is affected by—that is, he loves or he hates—not things as they are in themselves, but things as he perceives them. We are "capable of rationally determining for ourselves." That part of the creation which understands is indeed subject to the same government as the sun, moon, and stars, as "even the motes of dust which fly in the air"; but, because it is intelligent, it is aware of what it ought to be as well as of what it is. Hence the necessity, as strong as gravity, "that there should be a judge of reasonable creatures." In both orders, in the natural and the moral, the link is perception through the senses, and thus God "doth maintain his dominion in the moral as well as the natural world." When, in the configurations of nature, there comes a time (as in Northampton in 1740) that especially imparts to perception both "a sense of the great importance and necessity of the mercy sought," and also "a sense of opportunity to obtain it," then is the moment when, deep in his moral being, a man must answer with "the disposition of the heart to do what is resolved to be done." The difficulty of reconciling natural necessity with humanity's freedom to perceive in various ways disappears, or can be made to disappear, in the certainty that the newness and freshness of these things will affect the mind and work a free consent to reality.

The sight of a person writhing in conversion was "found by experience to have an excellent and durable effect" on bystanders. So it should have, according to the sensational doctrine: it was the transfer of an idea from one mind through a sensible medium to the mind of a perceiver. The mechanism was the same as when the significance of an object is conveyed, through eye and ear, to a brain, from the red thing to the idea of redness, from honey to the taste of honey, from the glowing spider to the apprehension of infinite pain. Countless theologians had declared that the "contrivance" of redemption by the God-man was too ingenious to have been devised through human cunning; they addressed this commonplace of Protestantism to speculation, whereas, said Edwards, it was designed by its very ingenuity to astound the senses. The intellect, thanks to Newton, could no longer be astounded. The argument persuades by a sensible impact; conviction comes not by proof but by "abundant experience," and once lodged in the mind as an "ideal apprehension," it becomes a mold of perception, and so a "motive." Grasped in simplicity, not as a collegiate thesis, the Christian insight is what Locke called a simple idea, an irreducible unit of experience, one in kind with redness, with the taste of honey, and with pain. It is not a content, but a frame of conception; it is a consent, not to a syllogism or to a covenant, but to an experienced "taste" or "relish" which cannot be gainsaid. Regeneration is the convergence of the two orders upon a single perception, of the order of causes along with the order of morality, so that simultaneously there is given "union to a proper object—and a relish of the object." Redemption is a flash of experience, forever abiding, in which natural good and moral good merge in a sense of the real good.

Man must attain a complex response, and that it may be started, he needs a sense of the newness and freshness of the object for which he must entertain a relish. It was up to the leadership of New England, with the golden opportunity now in their hands, to furnish that sense. The crisis in nature and in history was literally the heaven-sent possibility of resolving the moral crisis. The difference between saving grace and the experience of devils was a sense—a "sense of the divine beauty and amiableness of the scheme of doctrine there exhibited, that savingly convinces the mind that it is indeed divine." The ministers had the responsibility of providing this sense, not by flourishing such big words as would, in the vulgar notion, cause it, but by such words as it would follow, through inviolable connection. If the people were to get the idea of Christianity, the language of their pastors had to be changed from speculation into the objects of Christian experience. Now, if ever, the clergy were obligated to supply the phrases from which sensitive minds might receive—from which they could not avoid perceiving—the annexed ideas.

For a generation the clergy had packed their sermons, especially at renewals of the covenant, with threats. Contrary to the accepted belief, the founders of New England, even preachers like Shepard and Hooker, whom Edwards most venerated, did not preach hell-fire; instead, their works were rich and intricate analyses of the stages on the way to conversion, filled out by their use of the subtle psychology of Aristotelian physics. Only with the turn of the century did the clergy begin to employ the fear of hell as a whip and a goad. In 1699 Increase Mather urged:

> Now tho' this earth is a miserable place to some, Hell is infinitely worse. Hell is the pit wherein is no water; fire, but no water. The souls there have not a drop of comfort to mitigate their sorrows.

In 1702 the eminently unexciting Wadsworth preached that when a person was a million years in this inconceivable misery, he would be no nearer the end of it than when he began. We have seen how, in 1731, so enlightened a gentleman as Samuel Whittelsey painted the terrors of the damned, and Cooper dwelt upon them constantly.

Again, however, Stoddard had led the way. As he wiped out the covenant, so he also announced that whispering would not awaken the people: "the threatnings of God had need ring in their ears." Rhetorical strains suitable to the schools—Stoddard was not an admirer of Harvard—may scratch itching ears, but "the word is an Hammer, and we should use it to break the rocky hearts of men." Stoddard characteristically blurted out what others were hesitant to admit. The Mathers, though they were drifting with the tide, were shocked when he announced, "If men be thoroughly scared with the danger of damnation, they will readily improve their possibility, and not stand for assurance of success." Stoddard justified his frankness by his five harvests, and declared, in words that his grandson never forgot, "Experience fits men to teach others." Nevertheless, great though his successes were, they were local.

and temporary, and other preachers of terror, Cooper or Fox-croft, got even more meager results.

With his 1735 revival behind him, Edwards saw why: their preaching was all in the vein of Whittelsey, and who would ever get a "sense" from a depiction of sarcasms and insults? Whittelsey addressed speculation and made hell unpleasant, but he gave nobody the experience of living in hell; he was descriptive, not factual; he appealed to the moral system, but he had no conception of the natural. Like him, the clergy of New England were, even for a people who believed in hell, unconvincing. They uttered "great big sounding words," which did not reach the heart of old soldiers "too much used to the roaring of heaven's cannon, to be frighted at it." If a sermon was to work an effect, it had to impart the sensible idea in all immediacy; in the new psychology, it must become, not a traveler's report nor an astrologer's prediction, but an actual descent into hell.

By this road Edwards led New England toward the semantic problem that, in one form or another, challenged everyone around the beginning of the century, and still challenges us. Locke himself only belatedly became aware that it existed, and midway through the *Essay* had to turn aside from his argument to spend Book III on "Words." At first the answer seemed to him simple enough: language in the sensational psychology is wholly artificial; in themselves words are merely noises, and either "pain" or "bread" may signify the staff of life, depending on the convention established in the society. There is absolutely no "natural connexion" between a particular sound and a specific thing; a word has meaning, conveys an idea, only "by a perfect voluntary imposition." Imposition is an act of will, of the corporate will, which is often capricious and subject to fashion. A word is merely "annexed" to reality.

But precisely here difficulties began to accumulate. In the hypothetical state of nature, words might stand for the signs of basic realities, but as society grew more complex, the words would become separated from their objects and lead a life of their own. This was psychologically explicable: the tongue can say the word when no idea is in the mind; the mind itself can take the idea for granted and retain the word after the perception is utterly forgotten. Instead of being annexed to an object, the word itself becomes an object, a pallid object as compared with the thing it stands for, but the only object the mind any longer knows. Children and whole societies—New England for one—can learn the words before they have the experience, and their knowing the words will preclude the experience; thus they drag on for generations, like virgins reading of love in romances, without ever knowing the meanings. The leadership of New England would never arouse virgin souls from formality until it jolted them into a new awareness—a fresh perception—of the primordial oneness of word and idea. Otherwise the orators would induce an ecstasy which is, at best, verbal, which leaves the emotions untouched and gives the listener no more than a pattern of words—sarcasms, insults, derisions—in which the fitting of phrase to phrase proves to be only meticulousness, from which all ulterior reference has vanished. They would scratch men's ears, but never scare their hearts.

By his dissertation on language, Locke had no intention of assisting theologians; instead, he hoped to silence them once and for all. If he could prove that the controversies "which have so laid waste the intellectual world" were nothing but ill-use of words, mere haggling about "mixed modes" (which are not imprints of real things but constructions "put together in the mind, independent from any original patterns in nature"), he could call a halt to "wrangling, without improvement or information." Edwards saw that Locke's satire on the language of theologians—"the voluntary and unsteady signs of their own ideas"—applied to his colleagues, but his admiration for Locke was thereby increased, and Locke was still "a certain great man" despite his hostility to Calvinism because he showed Edwards, if no one else, that New England's problem was primarily linguistic. Edwards read more deeply into Locke than did Locke himself; he put the substance of his penetration into an early resolution: "To extricate all questions from least confusion or ambiguity of words, so that the ideas shall be left naked." Again, the resolution was concealed in the performance, but occasionally he showed his hand: "Sounds and letters are external things," he let slip, "that are the objects of the external senses of seeing and hearing." Hence Edwards' pulpit oratory was a consuming effort to make sounds become objects, to control and discipline his utterance so that words would immediately be registered on the senses not as noises but as ideas. To use the term in its technical rather than its debased sense, his was truly "sensational" preaching, which wrought an overwhelming effect by extraordinary simplicity.

The problem given him by New England society was to make words once more represent a reality other than themselves, but he formulated it out of Locke: if language is inherently conventional, and if in a particular culture it has become wholly conventionalized, how can one employ a convention to shatter conventionality? It could be done only by freeing language from stale associations, by forcing words so to function in the chain of natural causes that out of the shock upon the senses would come apprehension of the idea. Only then could the meaning of meanings be carried to the heart of listeners. Committed by Locke to an environmentalism in which not the nature of the shock but the nature of the recipient determined the kind of effect, Edwards further committed himself to administering the kind of shock that would transform the recipient, by psychological processes, into the kind of person who would absorb the shock in only one way. He was emboldened to this improvement upon his master by Locke's hint that subjective perception is true in so far as it is also perception of reality. The source of human error is not the senses, which never deceive, but an inability or a wanton refusal to comprehend the evidence of the senses. Preaching should address the real culprit: "I am not afraid to tell sinners, that are most sensible of their misery, that their case is indeed miserable as they think it to be, and a thousand times more so; for this is the truth."

To teach, said Kierkegaard, requires that the teacher give the learner not only the truth but the conditions for understanding it: the student must be recreated before he can learn. By working out his thesis that an idea is the fashion in which the heart apprehends an idea and so acts toward the object, Edwards anticipated Kierkegaard. In the midst of the Awakening, he could see that "the main benefit that is obtained by preaching, is by impression made upon the mind in the time of it, and not by any effect that arises afterwards by a remembrance of what was delivered," because an after-remembrance "is from an impression the words made." The verbal impression is not "ideal," because an idea is born of the senses, not of empty sounds. "And nothing is called sensible knowledge upon any other account but the sense, or kind of inward tasting or feeling, of sweetness or pleasure, bitterness or pain, that is implied in it, or arises from it." The doctrine first adumbrated in *A Divine and Supernatural Light*, tested in two social crises, was assured: "so that perhaps this distribution of the kinds of our knowledge into speculative and sensible, if duly weighed, will be found most important of all." Most important, because the sensible relates to the will and emotions; it is the sort of knowledge that considers things in the respects "they bear to our happiness or misery." Heaven might thus be defined as knowledge in respect to happiness; and hell—here or hereafter—is no longer a "place" but is knowledge of things as they tend to our misery.

Gradually taking shape in this analysis was a radically new definition of the religious man, not as right-thinking, but as "influenced by some affection, either love or hatred, desire, hope, fear." Multitudes may hear the word, none will be altered except those that are affected; good commentaries and

rhetorically perfect essays will give men speculative understanding, but make no real impression: "God hath appointed
a particular and lively application of his word to men in the
preaching of it, as a fit means to affect sinners with the importance of the things of religion, and their own misery, and
necessity of a remedy, and the glory and sufficiency of a
remedy provided." The parting between heaven and hell is
located not in the regions of the sky or under the earth, not
even in the Last Judgment, but in the human perception; the
function of art is to make the distinction unmistakable. This
requires of the artist a stupendous assertion of will: he must
make words convey the idea of heaven, he must *force* them to
give the idea of hell.

The great moments in Edwards' apocalyptic sermons are
such efforts of will. Let us consider another passage, as suc-
cessful as any in the Enfield sermon, this time without the
image of the spider:

> We can conceive but little of the matter: we cannot conceive
> what that sinking of the soul in such a case is. But to help
> your conception, imagine yourself to be cast into a fiery oven,
> all of a glowing heat, or into the midst of a glowing brick-kiln,
> or of a great furnace, where your pain would be as much
> greater than that occasioned by accidentally touching a coal of
> fire, as the heat is greater. Imagine also that your body were to
> lie there for a quarter of an hour, full of fire, as full within
> and without as a bright coal of fire, all the while full of quick
> sense; what horror would you feel at the entrance of such a
> furnace! And how long would that quarter of an hour seem
> to you! If it were to be measured by a glass, how long would
> the glass seem to be running! And after you had endured it
> for one minute, how overbearing would it be to you to think
> that you had it to endure the other fourteen!
> But what would be the effect on your soul, if you knew you
> must lie there enduring that torment to the full for twenty-
> four hours! And how much greater would be the effect, if
> you knew you must endure it for a whole year; and how vastly
> greater still, if you knew you must endure it for a thousand
> years! O then, how would your heart sink, if you thought,
> if you knew, that you must bear it forever and ever! That

there would be no end! That after millions of millions of ages, your torment would be no nearer to an end, than ever it was; and that you never, never should be delivered!

The achievement of this passage is the nakedness of the idea. There is no figure of speech (the blunt command to imagine yourself in a brick-kiln is literally the thing, not a simile or a metaphor), nothing pejorative; it is as bare as experience itself, as it would be to the sense that suffers. It is, I take it, what Hermann Broch calls the style of old age, a phrase applicable to Edwards' earliest as to his latest writing, a style reduced to a few prime concepts, that relies on the syntax: the artist who has reached this point, says Broch, is beyond art, "his attitude approximates that of the scientist with whom he shares the concern for expressing the universe." When critics objected that the shrieks and exclamations of his auditors were not signs of the presence of the spirit, Edwards replied from the lofty height of his linguistic science: "Cryings out, . . . as I have seen them from time to time, is as much an evidence to me, of the general cause it proceeds from, as language: I have learned the meaning of it, the same way that persons learn the meaning of language, viz., by use and experience."

Thus language could become the vehicle of an idea without pretending to be itself the "general cause." In 1740-41, even more than in 1735, the general cause was an outpouring, which meant a series of events within the natural order so interconnected that a moral awakening followed inside the order of perception. Here and now, Edwards cried, is the opportunity; seize it while you can. "Improve the present season of the pouring out of the Spirit of God on this town." "Now is the accepted time! Now is the day of salvation!" He exulted in the tide of success and could not conceal his pride that Northampton had seized the leadership of New England: "You who live here, where this work first began." "You that have long lived under Mr. Stoddard's ministry," he declared, at last entering fully upon his inheritance, "consider what a happy opportunity you have in your hands now." Now he could exhort everyone, regardless of decrees of predestination; once this is over, there will be no hope for those who refuse. "The wonders that we have seen among us of late, have been of a more glorious nature than those that the children of Israel saw in Egypt and in the Wilderness." Edwards' preaching fitted in with the design of physics and psychology, and also of history; now God was come again, "the same great God who so wonderfully appeared among us some years ago," and "Now, now, then, is the time, now is the blessed opportunity to escape those everlasting burnings."

In the summer of 1741 Edwards was at the height of his career and influence. Every house in town was full of outcries, faintings, and convulsions; but if there was distress, there was also admiration and joy. He could recite the transformations: young people forsaking frolicking, impure language, and lewd songs; reform in dress and avoidance of taverns; beaux and fine ladies become serious and mortified; throughout New England the Bible in esteem, the Lord's day observed, differences reconciled and faults confessed; old grudges and long-continued breaches made up in entire amity. In Northampton, party spirit so far ceased that town meetings were no longer disfigured by unchristian heats, and, almost too amazing to relate, they came to an agreement about the common lands! If more evidence were needed, the divine power had supported many hearts under great trials, the death of children and extreme pain of body; and finally, proof beyond all proof, under its influence some "have, in such a calm, bright and joyful frame of mind, been carried through the valley of the shadow of death." This indubitably was the work of a general, not of a particular cause, not of mechanics but of reality. "That which is lovely in itself, is lovely when it appears." Such effects could not be wrought by words, but only by ideas; these were not mass hysterias or mob frenzies, but universal subjective conformations, among an entire people, to the objective fact. They were inviolable sequences arising out of a sense of newness and freshness. They were not enthusiasm. If any still doubted—all that winter and spring there was no sign of life from Charles Chauncy—let them face the facts. This was the day of God's visitation. "Experience shows it."

In Freud's mentality, the mystical gift of the seer is continually at war with the need for mechanical description. . . . He is afraid of his own supreme talents, and throughout all his life as an investigator he has been imposing a curb on himself. One who by temperament is a seer, has been ardently devoting himself to the study of exact science, by the ordinary methods of scientific investigation.

FRITZ WITTELS

Naturalism

AFTER APOPLEXY disabled Foxcroft, Charles Chauncy directed the First Church. He published occasional lectures or funeral sermons—solid, dignified works, one of which considered human life under the similitude of a vapor. In 1739 came his first philosophical essay, a discourse on the only compulsion proper in religious matters: "As Men are rational, free Agents, they can't be religious but with the free Consent of their Wills; and this can be gain'd in no Way, but that of Reason and Persuasion." Thereafter, for two years, he published nothing; neither did President Holyoke, Professor Wigglesworth, Appleton, Gay, Barnard, or any Whittelsey. Whatever they said in their pulpits, while crowds were shouting and swooning with Whitefield, they were always men of discretion.

In these months, Cooper, Foxcroft (despite his stroke), Prince, Sewall, Shurtleff, were prolific. In April 1740, Cooper published a tract on predestination, with a preface by Sewall and Prince and by his great colleague Colman, which was an open manifesto of the party that soon called Whitefield to their aid; while it may be hard, Cooper said, to reconcile divine foreordination with human liberty, nevertheless conversion is the fruit of God's purpose and not of men's reason "excited by those rational arguments that have been set before them." By autumn, the Boston press was turning out thousands of Whitefield's journals and tracts, including a sermon on *The Marks of a New-Birth,* in which he dared affirm that whoever, upon impartial examination, can find in himself a spirit of supplication, an aversion to sin, conquest over the world, and love toward others, "may be as certain, as tho' an Angel was to tell him, that his Pardon is sealed in Heaven." For decades the New England churches, wandering among the hesitations and contradictions of the Half-Way Covenant, had lost their confidence, so much so that Stoddard gave up as hopeless all effort to determine the identity of even visible saints. Now the wondrous evangelist made it all easy. As multitudes wept and sang, everybody seemed to have the marks, and every pardon was sealed.

In December, invited by the revivalist leaders, Gilbert Tennent arrived to cap Whitefield's climax. He had agitated a revival in the Jerseys, and in history is linked with Edwards as an American forerunner of Whitefield; he was a burly, salty, downright man, whose works, unlike Whitefield's, are still alive. He was totally without polish, but, says Prince, had been through deep and terrible convictions; a less charitable auditor says he preached "like a Boatswain of a Ship, calling the Sailors to come to Prayers and be damned." He had just delivered at Nottingham *The Danger of an Unconverted Ministry,* wherein he underscored Whitefield's argument that the people have every right to forsake formalist ministers: the sermons of natural men "are cold and sapless, and as it were freeze between their Lips"; people can get nothing from "the sapless Discourses of such dead Drones." Tennent had split the Presbyterians, so that Cooper and Sewall were fairly warned, but they needed help, and Tennent had, he boasted, the courage and honesty to thrust the nail of terror into sleeping souls. He made the boast good; when he left Boston, in March 1741, in addition to the "ancient lecture at the Old Church" (Chauncy's), four weekly lectures were going strong, along with countless private meetings; all ministers except Chauncy were besieged by applicants for communion, among whom, cried the delighted Colman, "were many of the rich and polite of our sons and daughters." Four years later, Wigglesworth regarded this period as a time for which he and his friends should humble themselves before God and man, "that they suffered themselves, at first, to be governed more by plausible Appearance, than by the unerring Oracles of God." But in the spring of 1741 they kept their mouths shut, at least in public, and that summer, *Sinners in the Hands of an Angry God* was published.

However, their mouths opened wide enough for a few whispers to reach Northampton, and soon Chauncy, whose disapproval was an open secret, made his voice audible. One of his congregation opportunely dying, he saw through the press her funeral oration. During these months, the heroine of New England was Abigail Hutchinson, who even on her agonized death-bed begged an unconverted friend to stay away because the sight "so wrought on her compassion, that it overcame her nature." Mrs. Lucy Waldo of Boston, said Chauncy, "had a good Understanding, a Wit that was sprightly, yet conjoin'd with solidity of Judgment, and a becoming Tho'tfulness, the effect whereof was, her being chearful and pleasant, yet serious and grave; free and open, yet prudently cautious and reserv'd." She lived happily in the middle of town, and had no strange yearnings to watch the wind blow the trees in the country. On June 4, encouraged by the thought of Mrs. Waldo, Chauncy preached upon the raging issue, *The New Creature*, and offered "seasonable advice" to the new creatures now everywhere abounding. If Edwards' watchword was "sensible," Chauncy's was ever "seasonable." With the appearance of this work on the book-stalls, along with Cooper's latest on the sin and danger of quenching the spirit and Shurtleff's on the obligation of all Christians to get converted, President Holyoke was emboldened to print his convention sermon concerning the duty of ministers to guard against "the Pharisaism and Sadducism of

the present day," and Appleton, considering "the late powerful and awakening preaching of the Rev'd Whitefield," published an admonition that God and not ministers be given the
glory.

Thus the counterattack was mounted. Yet the opposers remained men of tact, students of the free and catholic spirit.
Holyoke saluted "those two pious and valuable Men of God,
who have been lately labouring more abundantly among us,"
and only then cautioned against enthusiasm and Antinomianism. Chauncy did his level best to show himself a Calvinist:
"You hang, as it were, over the bottomless pit, by the slender
thread of life: and the moment *that* snaps asunder, you sink
down into perdition." (Another month, and all could compare:
"It is nothing but the mere pleasure of God, and that of an angry
God, without any promise or obligation at all, that keeps the
arrow one moment from being made drunk with your
blood.") However, Chauncy quickly added, the real mark of
a new creature is not his terrors but his manner of life; if you
have not been terrified, do not fret, because many are redeemed by the love rather than by the fear of God; positive
assurance is seldom obtained, and many who have "a sudden
flash only, a meer sensitive passion," are guilty of spiritual
pride. And finally, the new creature must never suppose that
because he is new he is thereby qualified to unravel "the
knots of school-divinity." Thus a challenge, guarded but resolute, was laid down: Whitefield said that conversion was easy
to recognize, and the people were drunk with assurance, but
Chauncy opposed Lucy Waldo to Abigail and Phebe, the
knots of school-divinity to the ecstasies of Enfield. He insinuated that most new births were not in fact excited by the
spirit, but by the corporeal frenzies of Whitefield and Tennent.

In the struggle with his Hatfield cousins, Edwards learned
that the best defense is attack. Eight days after he buried William Williams, he went to Commencement at New Haven,
and on September 10 preached before many ministers and

other gentlemen, who desired that he publish his discourse. It was the last time that Edwards was even semiofficially honored by Yale, for which neglect restitution has lately been offered in the form of an architecturally splendid college, whose athletic teams court disaster by calling themselves "the Spiders." *The Distinguishing Marks of a Work of the Spirit of God,* advertised on the title page as dealing with the uncommon operation lately appearing "on the minds of many of the people of this land," with particular consideration of the extraordinary circumstances, is a scientific anatomy of the group psychosis; it appeared in Boston with a preface by Cooper, was reprinted in Philadelphia by Benjamin Franklin, in London with a recommendation by Isaac Watts, in Glasgow and Edinburgh with an epistle "to the Scots Reader," and again in London, 1744 and 1745, with an endorsement by John Wesley. Letters now began to flow from Great Britain to Northampton bearing the signatures of the greatest of Dissenters, and addressed to a recognized master.

Edwards challenged Chauncy (though not by name) to face the basic issue, whether "this is the work of God, or not." Maintaining the affirmative, he laid down five distinguishing marks to certify the authenticity of a divine work; within the next year he had intensely to rethink them, but what is remarkable in this sermon is the list of manifestations which, he argued, would inevitably accompany any disturbance, either natural or divine, which are psychologically explicable, and therefore prove nothing. Imagine the bewilderment of Chauncy, just as he was about to suggest that the entire commotion was a natural or sociological phenomenon, at having the arch-revivalist make a free concession to nature and to social circumstance of almost everything in the revival that Chauncy hated! At having him, actually, extend the capabilities of nature beyond anything Chauncy thought possible, and then to dismiss *that* argument as inconclusive. Bodily effects, for instance, on either supposition, "are easily accounted for, from what we know of the nature of man"; or again, if people are affected, can they be kept from making noises? "The nature of man will not allow it." Of course, many have their heads full of imaginations, but that "does not prove that they have nothing else." "Such is our nature, that we cannot think of things invisible, without a degree of imagination." If we are able to understand anything of "human nature, under these intense exercises and affections," we may understand why the mind often fails to distinguish "between that which is imaginary and that which is intellectual and spiritual." At this point, Edwards was employing one of his devices: he sardonically withheld any mention of Locke. However, Chauncy was supposed to be a scholar; so Edwards blandly asserted that experience confirmed revivalist theory, though he remarked that since many New Englanders, "especially elderly persons," had lived all their days in a time of decadence, they would not have the background of experience to understand how human nature behaves when intensely affected! As for terror preaching, he epitomized, again without expounding, the sensational thesis: "words are of no use any otherwise than as they convey our own ideas to others," and so he justified example as "a language in actions." The minister who preaches hell in a frigid manner—here was his defiance—though he may say in words that it is infinitely terrible, defeats himself, "for the language of his actions, in such a case, is much more effectual than the bare signification of his words." The proof? "Nature teaches men."

The sermon closed, or at least the published version closes, on a different note. Edwards later said that about September 1741 he first noticed signs of a change in Northampton. One can sympathize with, even while pitying, Edwards' contention that "we were infected from abroad." His townsmen, Stoddard's people, hearing of towns where there were greater commotions and more extraordinary appearances, where converts surpassed them in raptures, "looked little in their own eyes." Jealous for the honor of Northampton, they began to raise bigger commotions, to cultivate raptures, and to say (as in other towns new creatures were saying) that they had seen "that Light shine, come along, enter in at their Mouth, and went into their Heart." In the reworking of his New Haven sermon, Edwards was obliged to turn his conclusion, not against Chauncy, but toward his own supporters, to warn them against errors and absurdities which, even when construed as the concomitants of grace, were still dangerous. Do not listen to impulses, he said, overcome your impressions; prophetical visions are no assurances of revelations, and they who follow them "leave the guidance of the polar star, to follow a Jack with a lantern." In public sermons, saints should not forsake "method," and it is the height of folly for any to determine whether other souls are sincere. "Experience has taught me that this is an error." Edwards ruled out prophetic visions, but his sentences are many times prophecies; nine years before he was expelled from Northampton, even while the town was as clay to his hands, he declared, "I once did not imagine that the heart of man had been so unsearchable as it is. I am less charitable, and less uncharitable than once I was."

In that September, abuses or extravagances were minor distractions; he thought he could afford to rebuke them without giving ammunition to the enemy because he thus showed himself no enthusiast or Antinomian. At New Haven he uttered a proud thought, which by implication was an assertion of his royal prerogative among the Connecticut divines: Providence had settled him, he reminded them, for two years with the great Stoddard, and so he could assure them that the work now going on throughout the Valley was the same that had distinguished Northampton in Stoddard's reign, "though attended with some new circumstances." It was Edwards' greatest moment; the God of Calvinism prevented him from realizing that he was putting into the hands of his foes the one instrument by which they could undo him.

By the next summer, the Great Awakening was a shambles. Commotion, rapture, and vision ran riot; Wheelock and

Pomeroy got out of control, and in June, James Davenport, after a career on Long Island and in Connecticut that recalls some of the more extravagant legends of the Middle Ages, came to Boston, denounced all the ministers as unconverted, and addressed seething crowds on the Common in defiance of ecclesiastical and civil authority. To our reading, Davenport was insane, but to Chauncy he was only slightly more so than Whitefield and Tennent. He had a habit of stalking into ministers' studies and demanding point-blank if they were saved, a challenge he delivered not only to Chauncy but to Colman, whose ardor for the Awakening thereupon perceptibly began to cool. In August Davenport was brought before a Grand Jury on the charge of having said that the Boston ministers were leading the people blindfold to hell; Colman and Sewall begged that he be let off, and a verdict was returned of *non compos mentis.*

Davenport symbolizes what by 1742 became the bane of New England, self-appointed "itinerants." Yokels and charlatans felt the call and took to the roads. The land was filled with enthusiasm, not just the faintings of 1740, and orgies too fantastic to be credible mounted, while the bastardy rate began to rise. The ancient order of New England had no way to cope with itinerants; it was constructed on the expectation that the church should coincide with the political unit, with the town or the precinct, and that no visitor had a right to invade the bailiwick of a settled pastor without an invitation, as Whitefield and Tennent had been invited. Churches were split, and ultrarevivalists hurled accusations of formality, legalism, and Arminianism, until "censoriousness" became the new, and more terrible, iniquity of infuriated towns. Davenport finally passed into the hands of Solomon Williams at Lebanon, who extorted from him a *Retraction*, but the damage was done. Colman wrote in gratitude to Williams a letter which is an oblique effort of a man who has made a bad mistake to pretend he has not: if only, he prayed, Davenport's repentance may have some effect upon the "many poor and miserable Exhorters who have sprung up under 'em, like Mushrooms in a Night, and in the Morning tho't themselves accomplished Teachers." Colman loved poetry and tender sentiments, but not delirium, and that he should live to see people going about "singing Hymns or Psalms in Ferryboats and through the Streets" was more than he bargained for. He still insisted that at first the work had been good, but now he begged New England to look with humility upon that time, "and not be ashamed to confess our Inadvertence and Impudence in not being more aware of the Tendency of those Extraordinaries and Irregularities, unto these Errors and Extravagances of others." With Colman deserting, the movement was doomed.

The prestige of Chauncy, the one man who from the first was never swept off his feet, increased daily as he rallied the counterreaction in a series of able pamphlets, such as his blast at the Harvard Commencement against enthusiasm or his letter to George Wishart in Edinburgh, which told all Europe of New England's chaos. In town after town, he wrote, people who have screamed themselves into what they suppose is conversion are so delighted with screaming that they keep it up "on the account of others." I assure you, he declared, this is "no romantick Representation of Things." There may have been a kernel of grace in the first weeks of the revival, but now it is sheer insanity. The enthusiast mistakes the working of his own passions for divine communications, "when all the while, he is under no other influence than that of an overheated imagination"; he is the victim of a "bad temperament of the blood and spirits; 'tis properly a disease, a sort of madness." Its infallible symptom is hostility to reason. Most of the so-called new creatures, he could now openly proclaim, were simply deranged. As the tide turned in his favor, he more energetically reviewed the history of enthusiasm, and scored with the sons of the rich and polite, who twelve months before had been overwhelmed with a sense of sin, by telling them: "It has made strong attempts to destroy all property, to make all things common, wives as well as goods." Firmly

planted against all enthusiasm and communism is the Bible—
"but then," Chauncy added, "you must use your reason in
order to understand the Bible."

With Chauncy in the lead, the free and catholic gentlemen,
whose tendency, as we have seen, had been evident as early
as 1731, rallied their forces, and joined their voices to his. At
elections, orators called for the suppression of "bare-faced
extravagances." From Lebanon, Solomon Williams, who for a
time went along with the revival, now published two sermons. The first proved that the ordinary graces of the spirit
are more excellent than extraordinary gifts; the second, on
the surprising variety of God's ways to man, showed that in
that variety God definitely does not include filling men "with
a Slavish fear and dread of him, that it should drive to
Despair." (Young Hawley was now returning from Yale,
where Chauncy Whittelsey had been his tutor.) Early in 1743
Chauncy figured that he could strike at last at the root of the
evil. In *The Late Religious Commotions in New England
Considered*, he went after Edwards' New Haven sermon,
point by point. Edwards can give no incontestable evidence
of the presence of God; many factors have been at work
"which had a Tendency in a natural Way to work upon the
Passions of the People." Phebe Bartlet is no miracle: "Imitation is natural to Children." Edwards' doctrine of example
would be more persuasive if the persons moved were not always excited by persons who shrieked, and as for his marks
of a divine work, they "seem to me in general to proceed
from some other Causes." The Apostles always spoke to men
as to rational beings; all that Chauncy could make out of Edwards' psychological theory was this: false teachers have "always been very shy of close Reasoning, chusing rather to
have their Scheme admitted by the Affections." And then
Chauncy struck the blow that would most hurt Edwards:
Satan can delude people through sensations and imagination,
"and if Mr. Edwards doubts of this, let him consult his venerable Predecessor."

Even as Chauncy was composing this work, Edwards was bringing out, at the end of 1742 but too late for Chauncy to notice it in this discussion, a 378-page reworking of the New Haven sermon, *Some Thoughts Concerning the Present Revival of Religion in New England*, "humbly offered to the publick." On May 25, 1743, a majority of the Massachusetts clergy, in convention assembled, passed so many resolutions against errors and abuses as to amount to a condemnation of the Awakening; a rump session on July 7 tried to rally the revivalists, but the heart was going out of them. Then Chauncy exploded his biggest bomb, a major work in American literature or in the century, *Seasonable Thoughts on the State of Religion*. Half of it was directly, and all of it by implication, trained against Edwards' *Thoughts*.

If one desires a roster of antirevivalists and also a social register for New England in 1743, he need only consult the list of subscribers to *Seasonable Thoughts*. Gay, Appleton, Barnard are there; Holyoke took four copies and Samuel Whittelsey six. At New Haven, Edwards committed the tactical blunder of telling opponents that, instead of ignorant denunciation, they ought to come where the evidences were to be seen, "narrowly observing and diligently inquiring into them." Chauncy went, and he narrowly observed; he made a three-hundred-mile tour and gathered accounts from eye-witnesses; he undermined his health, but he assembled such descriptions as this:

> The Meeting was carried on with what appeared to me great Confusion; some screaming out in Distress and Anguish; some praying; others singing; some again jumping up and down the House, while others were exhorting; some lying along on the Floor, and others walking and talking: The whole with a very great Noise, to be heard at a Mile's Distance, and continued almost the whole Night.

The Book is a massive, Johnsonian, indignant work, a source-book for American communal behavior; learned and dignified, it is monumentally honest. Scholarly to the point of pedantry, and formally Calvinist, it is a classic of hard-headed, dogmatic rationalism. On all rational grounds, it decides, "We have seen enough to convince us, that Man may not be trusted in"; but still, with all the confidence of the Enlightenment, it concludes that we cannot be too solicitous, "so far as we are able, to see with our own Eyes, and believe with our own Understandings." The argument is marshaled for 400 pages to demonstrate that the Awakening is nothing more "than a mechanical impression on animal Nature." One may have a "just idea" (Chauncy does not say "clear and distinct") of conversion without reliance on screaming, shrieking, swoonings, or "extatic raptures," and one may legitimately conclude that terror has "been heaped upon Persons already distracted almost with Terror, in a Manner that justly deserves to be blamed." One clear reflection emerges from contemplating New England's disorders: "The plain Truth is, an enlightened Mind, not raised Affections, ought always to be the Guide of those who call themselves Men"; the effect of exhibiting divine truth to the understanding should be "a reasonable Solicitude," not censoriousness, separations, itinerants, and frenzies.

The subsequent history of the Awakening no longer concerns the Edwards story. On his fact-finding tour, Chauncy visited the west, and no doubt received help from such men as the Whittelseys; by 1743 Edwards was beaten, an awesome but discredited figure. Harvard and Yale, infuriated by charges in Whitefield's journals, published testimonies that they did not prefer Tillotson to Shepard, but that they did not approve identifying the operations of the spirit with "the swelling of their Breasts and Stomachs," and condemned extravagance, which meant that they had no more to do with Edwards. When Whitefield returned in 1744, the opposition was organized and kept him out of most pulpits; only diehards, like Cooper and Shurtleff, stood by him. Chauncy was the great man; hundreds of churches were split, the people were exhausted, and the solidarity of New England society in the preceding century had been sundered as by a knife. Attention was absorbed in the new war with France, returning prosperity, and the campaign against Louisburg. To judge by appearances, Edwards had been overwhelmed by a barrage of highly *Seasonable Thoughts.*

In the winter of 1742-43, when he knew the Awakening was lost, he gave a series of lectures which, as was his habit, he reworked. The market for revivalistic apologies was diminished, and not until 1746 did he publish his ultimate philosophy of the revival, *A Treatise Concerning Religious Affections.* Only one edition appeared in Edwards' lifetime, and it had no effect on the situation. Chauncy never bothered to reply, and went to his death, three decades after Edwards', convinced that Edwards was "a visionary enthusiast, and not to be minded in anything he says." It was left for those who came after to mind, if they can, the most profound exploration of the religious psychology in all American literature.

Chauncy's and Edwards' publications between 1740 and 1746 constitute a great debate, which exhibits several peculiarities. For one, Edwards refused throughout to name Chauncy or to recognize his existence; this was simply studied insult. Secondly, Chauncy persisted in arguing the whole case on the grounds of the scholastic psychology. We know from his election sermon of 1747 that he read Locke's treatise on government, and in a volume of 1765 he ultimately expounded Locke's psychology of ideas, sensations, mixed modes, like a veteran; but in the 1740's he wrote as though everybody in Christendom assumed that reason, imagination, and will were distinct "faculties" and the affections a separate and autonomous power. He used perception as meaning only to see, and sense was only the register of the phantasms. Thus he conceived the psychological problem as it had been conceived since the Middle Ages, that of controlling the imagination and the will by reason, and of subduing the emotions to the will; hence all intelligible address must be directed to the reason, through which decisions are always given to the will. Any appeal directly to the passions, which attempts to bypass speculation, was demonstrably immoral. Whether this affectation was ignorance or a debater's trick, I cannot say, but it put Edwards under an immense handicap: in order to make himself understood he had first to expound a radical and foreign psychology, which few in New England were prepared to grasp. The irony is that the theological liberal, who in every trait stands for the rational Enlightenment, spoke in the language of outmoded science, and the defender of Calvinism put his case upon a modern, dynamic, analytical psychology in which the human organism was viewed, not as a system of gears, but as a living unit.

Thirdly, to follow Edwards' argument, we must appreciate the shift in orientation that develops through the sequence of his books. At New Haven in 1741, Chauncy is the target, and the caution to his own followers is incidental; in the *Thoughts* his attention is equally divided between Chauncy and the extremists in his own camp; in the *Religious Affections*, Chauncy and Boston are almost ignored, and the major effort is directed against the visionaries who have made a travesty of the Awakening. The real test of his doctrine and his psychology became not their ability to withstand rationalism, but to cope with enthusiasm. Edwards fought Chauncy with only one hand; with the other he contended against his own people, and by the end of the ordeal, they and no longer Boston were his antagonists. There would be no escaping 1750.

His studies of the revival are great, one may say, because greatness of theme was thrust upon him. New England in the eighteenth century was a laboratory for America, and it divided itself in two, into "new lights" and "old lights." The split was the measure of this community's encounter with the parting of the ways in modern culture. There was Davenport with all his passion; and there was Chauncy with all his rationalism. Out of his genius for definition, Edwards wrote a sentence that is applicable, in its recognition of ultimate significance, far beyond the borders of New England, far deeper into time than the eighteenth century: "Such distinguishing names of reproach, do as it were divide us into two armies, separated, and drawn up in battle array, ready to fight one with another; which greatly hinders the work of God."

Furthermore, there is a striking metamorphosis to be traced in the New England literature of this crucial decade: the debate began as an argument concerning a work of God; it became, on both sides, contention about the nature of man. The bitter-end revivalists, like Cooper, were driven at last to pleading that Whitefield's kind of oratory was justified, not by Scripture, but by the constitution of man; while Chauncy maintained that it was pernicious, not by the authority of the church, but by the construction of the human organism.

Neither side knew exactly what they were doing, or realized for decades what they had done, but Edwards knew at once. For that reason he centered his studies upon definitions of the human species, and pled with both camps not to cling to fragmentary, half-formed conceptions. He besought them to enter fully into the complete vision that modern thought made possible. There must be light in the understanding, for heat without light is not heavenly; yet "where there is a kind of light without heat, a head stored with notions and speculations, with a cold and unaffected heart, there can be nothing divine in that light." These are not two opposites to be played off against each other: they can be made one in single perception: "if the great things of religion are rightly understood, they will affect the heart." The alteration of New England from the extreme of high affections in 1741 to the collapse of 1743, the rejection of all emotions without distinction, was the masterpiece of Satan in a land "not versed in such things," in a nation too constricted in experience to comprehend the vocabulary of passion. A product of American society at its most starved and narrow, Edwards tried to teach it the language of affection. He was not only a child of America, but, as such, is one of its supreme critics.

He cannot be reproached because he failed to persuade his

countrymen, he can hardly be reproached that he failed with himself. I would not claim that his formulations are still usable, though I would contend that every sentient being struggles still with the same antinomy, now grown unbearably severe. In the highest sense of the word, Edwards was a prophet. Put upon him was the task of becoming, the first in our history, what Paul Tillich calls a "theologian of mediation" between the pure understanding, which was reason and Chauncy, and the mystery, which was terror and the spider. Generalizing from the specific configurations of his society, he was able to comprehend those who could not comprehend each other; more deeply passionate than Davenport and more finely intelligent than Chauncy, he was accused by the one of being too intellectual and by the other of being too emotional. That he failed is not the point. A more serious question is, who yet has succeeded?

In structure, the *Religious Affections* follows the scheme laid out in the *Distinguishing Marks*, a classification of those psychological symptoms that are experimentally indifferent, followed by those with intelligible meaning. Each series is completely "natural" in that the same interior mechanism produces both according to ascertainable laws, but the first are "false signs," while the second distinguish the significant from the mechanical. All experience, in the realm of nature, is valid, but not all experience is true. Undoubtedly there are difficulties in applying the rules to specific persons, even to oneself, but that is a matter of technique. The fundamental question is whether any such rules exist: "The rules in themselves," answered Edwards, "are certain and infallible." Man does not escape the religious problem by shifting the focus from a teleological universe, a universal church, or a covenant, to his own nature and destiny; instead, it is precisely there, in consciousness itself, that he requires mediation between knowledge and faith, science and ethics, intellect and the heart.

In Charles Chauncy's philosophy, the affections are conceived as different from and independent of the will, and are rated "the meanest principles" of the soul: "these gentlemen labor under great mistakes, both in their philosophy and divinity." Edwards appears at what, to this present age, must be his most sympathetic when in the *Thoughts* he contends that the emotions are one and the same with whatever is meant by the will: "all acts of the affections of the soul are in some sense acts of the will, and all acts of the will are acts of the affections." When Chauncy betrayed by his replies that for all such gentlemen understood, he might as well have said that black is white, Edwards had to amplify his definition. Chauncy persisted in accusing Edwards of overstimulating the emotions; none among those called opposers, Chauncy claimed, deny that "the Passions were planted in the human Constitution for very valuable uses" or "that it was reasonable they should be excited"; but they objected to raising them so high as to unfit men for the exercise "of their reasonable powers." Edwards saw that under the plea of controlling the emotions they were seeking to negate them, and countered this blundering argument with his new definition: "The affections are no other than the more vigorous and sensible exercises of the inclination and will of the soul." If he supposed he could convince Chauncy by introducing "inclination," he was mistaken; probably nothing ever made less sense to Chauncy, but the addition tells in a word what the hammering of the Awakening had done to Edwards' thinking.

Unhappily, Edwards was limited by his vocabulary; all he had to work with was what Locke gave him. Locke started one of the great revolutionary movements of modern times when he rejected the scholastic psychology, with its theory that each "faculty" is a separate province or a power capable of acting like a distinct being, as "a confused notion of so many distinct agents in us." If it were reasonable, he said, to talk of faculties as entities, then we should speak of a walking faculty or a dancing faculty; but walking and dancing are "modes of motion." In the same respect, what we call willing and understanding are not independent centers in the brain, but are "several modes of thinking." Chauncy and Edwards could never meet on common ground so long as Chauncy refused to comprehend this statement of Locke's: "We may as properly say that it is the singing faculty sings, and the dancing faculty dances, as that . . . the will directs the understanding, or the understanding obeys or obeys not the will: it being altogether as proper and intelligible to say that the power of speaking directs the power of singing."

Yet, even after discarding the faculties, Locke called understanding and will "faculties." No other term was available. His disciples crystallized his manner of speaking into a new faculty psychology that lost the original power, and which, by 1765, proved acceptable to Chauncy, but Edwards kept the fresh insight. He did not intend that will and understanding be considered "agents"; he used them as names for the ways in which a soul functions. "Nor can there be a clear distinction made between the two faculties of understanding and will, as acting distinctly and separately, in this matter." Yet he, too, called them faculties, and the "New England theology," professing to derive from him, enchained itself for a century to a psychological thesis he never intended. By the understanding he conceived the soul as it perceives, and by the will he meant the soul perceiving as a sentient, passionate being, with hopes and fears, and therefore perceiving according to its vital inclination. The coherence of a person is not the mathematical sum of his faculties, but his abiding disposition, of which his reason and will are expressions—are, as he called them in his notebooks, a person's "image." There is, in fact, only one faculty: "it is our inclination that governs us in our actions."

Edwards could not quite reach the explicit formula of a monistic organism because he knew no biology, and because he was still gripped by the Puritan worship of operations of the mind carried on in logical abstraction, apart from all self-interest or anxiety. He had no method for interpreting even the most rigorous dialectic, contrasted with mere opinion, as a "rationalization," and this lack of a biological, or of a psycho-

somatic, insight is what probably makes much of Edwards'
thought seem archaic today. Yet, though he defeated himself
by employing the very term he repudiated, his thought was
tending, as fast as any in the eightenth century could, toward
conceiving reason itself, or even logic, as an image of temperament; it would have taken him about an hour's reading in William James, and two hours in Freud, to catch up completely.
Hence he pictured the supreme faculty by which the mind beholds things when it is not "an indifferent, unaffected spectator," but when it loves or hates what it sees, in a way that
makes clear how profoundly he had penetrated even indifference itself, and found it no less a "disposition." What determines in advance the nature of a mind's perceptions is that
mind's previous inclination:

> This faculty is called by various names; it is sometimes called
> the *inclination*: and, as it has respect to the actions that are
> determined and governed by it, is called the *will*: and the mind,
> with regard to the exercises of this faculty, is often called the
> *heart*.

As a corollary, there follows the position which Edwards
made resonantly clear, the absolute identity of the will and the
emotions: affections are not separate from the will, "nor do
they differ from the mere actings of the will, and inclination
of the soul, but only in liveliness and sensibleness of exercise."
His effort at mediation failed historically because neither the
Davenports nor the Chauncys of the world can understand
this: to the Davenports, emotions are irresistible seizures, like
love in popular balladry, and man is their victim; to the
Chauncys, emotion is something to be measured out in judicious quantities upon suitable occasions, and at other times
stored in the refrigerator.

However, it would be gross misrepresentation of Edwards
to present him as a classicist preaching the mean between extremes; he was no Latin, no Stoic—he was a Puritan, an American, and a barbarian. By identifying the will with the affections, and by striving to unite the understanding to the will,

he came in the end to declare the supremacy of passion. Even in abstract reasoning the mind is "sensible" of the beauty and amiableness of things, and in the presence of the idea of them, experiences sweetness and delight. This delight, not any bare conception, reaches the heart, even the heart of a Chauncy. A perception "carries in the very nature of it the sense of the heart." By maintaining a sharp distinction between "mere notional understanding" and the sense of the heart, Edwards fully intended to subordinate understanding to feeling. When a man knows the stench or the sweetness of a thing, he has a more accurate knowledge than that "by which he knows what a triangle is." "More than the mere intellect is concerned, . . . as he that has perceived the sweet taste of honey, knows much more about it, than he who has only looked upon, and felt of it." We must make no mistake about Edwards: he did not propose, by combining the reason and the emotions, to form a whole man. He dismissed that kind of thinking as hopelessly schematic, and asserted the radical conception of man as an active, interested, passionate being, whose relation to objective reality is factual to the extent that he is concerned about it, whose anxieties and not his clear thinking make his destiny.

Edwards' problem, therefore, was to distinguish, scientifically, between emotions which are mechanical reflexes, one in kind with collision among stones, and those which signify something other than the juices of the glands. His psychology prepared him, as he believed, perfectly to understand why a terrific upheaval like the revival would generate emotional excesses. "How little do they consider human nature, who look upon it as so insuperable a stumbling-block, when such multitudes of all kinds of capacities, natural tempers, educations, customs and manners of life, are so greatly and variously affected, that imprudences and irregularities of conduct should abound." After nature has been shut up in the winter, and spring returns, along with the heat of the sun comes "very dirty and tempestuous weather," before nature can rejoice in beauty. (Edwards is always refreshingly realistic about the New England spring!) Edwards needed no Freud to suggest that the ganglion of religious excitement lies close to the sexual: "yea, through a mixture of a natural love to the opposite sex, may degenerate more and more, until it issues in that which is criminal and gross." Consequently, the enlargement of his list of inconclusive manifestations from the *Distinguishing Marks* into the inventory of the *Religious Affections* is an index, not only of how the Awakening exploded into perversion, but of how Edwards' thought, keeping pace with the phenomena, took stock of the manifold forms in which nature, of and by itself, under intense strain, simulates grace. By 1743 he could analyze and reduce to natural or clinical history such "counterfeit" behavior as high affections, bodily jerks, fluent talking, involuntary compulsions, mottoes and texts falling into the mind, zeal, transports of love or joy, fears of hell, confident assurance, or such noble deeds as win the approbation of the godly.

Again he insisted that if these actions prove nothing, neither do they disprove anything, since the will is emotion, and a conversion of the will could produce any or all of these reflexes as by-products. But the point was that, as by-products of a true work, in themselves they still are "false." (To show Chauncy and the Williamses that he appreciated their tactics, he quoted Stoddard, "Common affections are sometimes stronger than saving"; to make clear his tradition, he studded his footnotes with quotations from Shepard and Hooker—but none from John Cotton or the Mathers.) What counts finally is not the quantity and range of experience, but the kind. The various principles of human nature are channels; if the water is poisonous, a poisonous stream will flow through them: "the great difference will lie in the nature of the water." Because Edwards took account of elements in human nature which Chauncy, the self-confessed rationalist, excluded, Edwards could comprehend human pathology, and exhibit what was utterly lacking in Chauncy, namely, compassion. Yet precisely because he could explain aberration scientifically, he was subjected to an ordeal against which Chauncy was protected by his ignorance of the soul: loving nature, Edwards was condemned to war upon it. He could not sneer, but he had to cure, in the name of a standard wholly compatible with nature, yet without which nature itself, in all its beauty, would be no more than a nightmare, a mere grinding of atoms.

In the *Religious Affections* he could no longer wrap his meaning in a cryptogram. Now or never, he had to specify precisely what kind of water flows through regenerate channels. At New Haven his first list of the marks of redemption was conventional: esteem of Christ, hatred of Satan, belief in the Bible, love of God. The twelve signs which he now formulated bespeak an entirely different conception of religion, and his discussion of the first four is the very heart of Jonathan Edwards. Here the inherent good and the objective come at last together. The primary tests of a true affection, he declared, are: its origin, its relation to external reality, its relation to excellency, and finally—that which binds together all relationships—its arising from a mind that "richly and spiritually" apprehends the pattern of divine things.

Yet even here, Edwards could not be entirely candid. He said, as flatly as any Calvinist could wish, that a gracious emotion comes from a supernatural influence, but he then offered such a description of the operation of the supernatural as was, and remains, so highly naturalistic that neither new lights nor old lights would have anything of it. Western culture has never been uncomfortable when living with the out-and-out supernatural: the mystery of the Mass is frankly mysterious; if grace is an influx of spirit, the people pray for grace as parched counties pray for rain. On the other hand, when conversion is defined as a rational persuasion, those who have the education and the wit manage it, and the others bow to a superiority they cannot understand. But Edwards wove the supernatural into the natural, the rational into the emotional, and thus made the mystery so nearly comprehensible that it became terrifying. He called it a form of perception, and from his description everybody would seem to be capable of it— except that not everybody is. His supernaturalism was naturalized, or if you will, he supernaturalized nature, and introduced the divine element into the world, not as a substance or a quantity, not as a compound of already existing things or an addition to them, but as "what some metaphysicians call a new simple idea."

He wanted desperately to conceal the terms of art, and not bewilder simple people by parading great names like Newton and Locke; but more desperately he needed a vocabulary, and so published grace as a simple idea, an irreducible pellet of experience which has no tangible being and yet is the principle of the organization of being, as light is an organization of color and sweetness an organization of honeys. This new principle, "in a mind, that is a perceiving, thinking conscious thing," being a sensation, is at once a perception, and so "a principle of a new kind of perception or spiritual sensation," without which "all other principles of perception, and all our faculties are useless and vain." This evanescent, universally accessible, and yet seldom seized-upon power—in Edwards' packed statement, it is practically one with consciousness aware of the conscious—he substituted for that which Christianity had hitherto treated as an eternal decree within the economy of the Godhead.

No matter how much he called the new simple idea supernatural, the suspicion then and now is that he meant only that it was not unnatural. He fascinated a few, but outraged more, when he insisted that the idea is no addition to knowledge, no increase in the number of atoms in the universe, no injection of a divine fluid into human veins, not even (except metaphorically) a light. It "is not a new faculty of understanding," it is a new principle of coherence in the soul which immediately becomes the foundation "for a new kind of exercises of the same faculty of understanding." Even "principle" is a dangerous word, which he used "for want of a word of a more determinate signification." It usually connotes something added to the previous store, a new substance materialized out of nowhere, but Edwards' point was that for the truly perceptive there has been no more, possibly even less, of a fund of experience than for others, only that into such natures, "either old or new," is laid a method of making coherent what before was incoherent. Though it is always available to the natural man, he can no more employ it than "a man without the sense of hearing can conceive of the melody of a tune." It is, said Edwards in a sentence that proved as enigmatic to his followers as to his enemies, "a natural habit or foundation for action." It is inward, supernatural, mysterious—and also scientifically explicable, empirically verifiable: it gives "a personal ability and disposition to exert the faculties in exercise of such a certain kind," it is activity itself, "a new kind of exercises of the same faculty of the will."

Edwards' insistence upon "same" and "natural," upon the fact that no measurable substance is changed, is a confession of how deeply his thought had been formed by Newton; it is a magnificent acknowledgment that modern physics has made the tissue of nature a self-sufficient materialism, which is indifferent to the comparative worth or virtue of one man over another. No pounds of matter or ounces of spirit can be added to the creation for the saints to draw upon. Ideas are not embodied in things, as the Puritan technologia believed; there are no intelligible forms, there are only atoms and the void. A simpler way for us to say it might be to fall back upon modern textbook jargon and call Edwards' definition of grace "subjective," which would leave the external world to conduct itself by the laws of motion, and the drama of salvation, which the centuries had regarded as the central event in creation, to go on inside the heads of those who elect, or are elected, to worry about it. In one sense Edwards was, as we have seen, so much a materialist that he could join hands with Spinoza, and his insistence that the data of experience are extrinsically the same for either the natural or the regenerate man amounts to saying that the grinding of the atoms takes no cognizance of inward fluctuations. "Natural men may have conceptions of many things about spiritual affections; but there is something in them which is as it were the nucleus, or kernel of them, that they have no more conception of, than one born blind, has of colors."

Hence it is not technically a misstatement to call Edwards a subjectivist. The boy had written it clearly: "How large is that thing in the Mind which they call Thought? Is Love square, or round? Is the surface of Hatred rough, or smooth? Is Joy an inch, or a foot, in diameter?" Yet to call this subjectivity in the usual sense is to miss Edwards' conception entirely; it is to leap with Chauncy to the facile conclusion that he was only a jesuitical sort of enthusiast, when all the time he was one of the few men who understood that Locke had performed a surgical operation from which few of us shall recover. Locke (or rather the whole investigation of which he was the most influential spokesman) amputated consciousness from things, and though Locke was a judicious man with no intention of encouraging enthusiasts, still when some back-country yokel, excited by a revival, fastened upon an external image in his mind, "when that thing is not present in reality, nor anything like it," he had every right, according to Locke and a thousand modern poets, to call that thing a spiritual discovery. Since spiritual things are "not things that can be pointed forth with the finger," we are obliged, being material bodies and the children of sensation, to borrow names to signify them "from external and sensible objects"; yet if we are eternally cut off from those objects, knowing them not as they are in themselves, the impressions are a part of our experience and not of reality. So Edwards saw—his defining of issues is everywhere his genius—that in a scientific cosmos man's mortal need is some principle of discrimination more comprehensive than Chauncy's "enlightened mind" and more cognizant of human nature to explain how these external ideas "through man's make and frame" inevitably attend our moment of illumination, yet are no more part of it—cannot at the risk of sanity be permitted to be a part of it—"than the motion of the blood, and beating of the pulse, that attend experiences, are a part of spiritual experience."

So Edwards added to his thesis that grace is a simple idea, the antithesis of his second test of authentic emotion, that it has reference to things "as they are themselves; and not any conceived relation they bear to self, or self-interest." Each of the fallacies, Davenport's and Chauncy's, conceives of man as immediately under the instigation of a principle that pretends to give him freedom, but in effect relieves him of responsibility: either the rule of reason (until Hume destroys it) or the flood of intuition (until Nietzsche goes insane). Edwards proposed a simple paradox which is only an extension of the sensational calculus. A man "necessarily seeks his interest and happiness." No one understood better than Edwards that an individual is an ego, but he reached into the heart of egoism and brought it (and the id), through self-centered perception, to recognize an order wherein, precious though it may be to itself, it exists along with stones and planets. Man can readily give worship—or what he fancies to be worship—to a universe in which whatever is can be proved to be right, even if the proof demands that certain partial evils be shown as tactical maneuvers in the strategy of the universal good. As against this Arminian and optimistic solution (which Hume and Kant were to show is no solution), Edwards asserted that the sensual man can come through the senses to apprehend the nature of God as He is in Himself, "prior to all considerations of his own interest and happiness." This would be a trite moralism had Edwards believed that man can escape into such apprehension by some uncaused transformation, but his way offered no easy release into the supernatural, for he held that men are enmeshed in the system of things. He gave them no other redemption than their own appreciation of the system that holds them.

"How can that be true love of beauty and brightness, which is not for beauty and brightness' sake?" Edwards was not here introducing, out of the transcendent, "Platonic ideas" of beauty and brightness. He was simply saying that in a universe where the organism calculates its motions on the basis of pleasure and pain, those who love God for the pleasure they get out of it love the profit and not God. Those who avoid crimes for the fear of pain know nothing of the fear of God. The basis of the self is a cluster of sensations around a point; as he had said in the "Notes," "The soul may be said to be *in the brain;* because ideas, that come by the body, immediately ensue, only on alterations that are made there; and the soul most immediately produces effects no where else." Because the source of ideas is external, and yet every idea is a self's manner of conceiving, there must come a time when the redeemed self realizes that a sensation cannot be clutched to his bosom as a private luxury, but belongs to a system of impressions that has a logic deeper and more beautiful than any incidental advantages (or disadvantages) that accrue to him. If the self goes through time without this realization, it is lost, damned before it starts; it is predestined. In the sequence of sensations, there will—or there may—come a moment when it is truly "a diversion and loss" for the self to survey his own experience and to congratulate himself "what a high attainment this is, and what a good story I now have to tell others." Instead, he will be able to think, out of the new simple idea, without regard to his own qualifications or graces, only of the beauty of that which lies in his direct view, "which sweetly entertains, and strongly holds his mind."

The third and fourth qualifications, therefore, constitute a synthesis of the thesis and antithesis, of the subjective idea and of the order of things in themselves; it is love of the order, of divine things for their beauty and sweetness, arising out of a perception of their "moral excellency." Not the perception of excellency within the soul, or of the idea of excellency suspended before philosophical contemplation, but of the excellency of the cosmic method, which contains cholera, burning tigers, the evil deeds of men, and death. Here Edwards expounded the distinction between moral and natural excellency, and demonstrated how completely he had perceived that in the realm of nature, out of the premises of Locke there follow inevitably the ethics of pure utilitarianism. "Pleasure is a natural good." But a conception of the good framed solely in terms of pleasure and pain is soon lost in an infinite, unending calculation; the calculus may or may not have a respect for divine things as they are in their own nature, but it has meaning only when it also sees that all things are beautiful. The supreme test, then, is a sense of the beauty of the universe, and because this is a sense and not an imagination, it is a sense of reality. This is "that thing in spiritual and divine things which is perceived by this spiritual sense, that is so diverse from all that natural men perceive in them; this kind of beauty is the quality that is the immediate object of this spiritual sense." The sense of the heart enables the sight; without the sight, the universe remains the same universe, but "unless this is seen, nothing is seen that is worth the seeing; for there is no other true excellency or beauty." If this is not understood—Edwards was here at his most defiant—nothing is understood that deserves to be understood. "This is the beauty of the Godhead, and the divinity of divinity (if I may so speak), the good of the infinite fountain of good; without which, God himself (if that were possible) would be an infinite evil; without which we ourselves had better never have been; and without which there had better have been no being."

"If that were possible!" Is it possible? Without the insight, evil is the only possibility. Without it, there is only the good of pleasure and the evil of pain, "that which perfects or suits nature, considering nature abstractly from any holy or unholy qualifications, and without any relation to any rule or measure of right or wrong." Nature so considered, the nature of pure scientific description and unrelieved human nature, is the nature of pestilence and disease, of torture and tyranny. Considered only within itself, nature, either cosmic or human, is indeed evil. Again and again, Edwards said, experience shows it. The rationalist and the enthusiast alike are in the machine, and sooner or later, when their schemes prove incapable of coping with the multiplying accidents and the torments of existence, when their intoxication wears off and they are left with nothing but the dead, dull frame of exhaustion, then the real terror comes, not the terror of hell and of flames, but the emptiness of the soul that has seen nothing worth seeing, has understood nothing worth understanding.

Edwards' peculiar analysis of the emotions makes evident, I believe, how utterly incorrect it is to call him, as he is often called, a "mystic." At least, in any sense that would imply the merging of the finite individual with a distinctionless divine. By redefining the historic Christian concept of grace as "a new simple idea"—acquired through sensation and entirely dependent upon sensation—Edwards was asserting in the language of Locke the indestructible particularity of the individual experience. Hence, in its ultimate signification, the point of his critique of both rationalism and enthusiasm was that each of these emergent monstrosities, though in different ways, would absorb the individual into a pretended universal, into a scheme of abstraction, or into a rush of inspiration. Both Chauncy and Davenport laid claim to possessing a principle of comprehension which in itself was all too comprehensible. By it they could see men and judge them from a vantage point outside the world of finite fact, or of cause and effect. But if the grace of God comes through sense experience, in the form of an idea, in the form of a perception which requires a stimulus, which all may receive but not all do, it is then itself a part of the collocation of finites which we call the world and which we seek to comprehend, being involved therein. Though the mechanism of the perception submits to description, and can be documented by case histories, the idea nevertheless remains a mystery, a given, an incomprehensible fact, exactly as the divine predetermination of election and reprobation was first declared to be in primitive Protestantism. The new simple idea becomes a principle of comprehension beyond the capabilities of man, but since it always pertains to the economy of the human psyche, it is capable of dealing with men and with objects. It brings the individual face to face with the divine, but it maintains his individuality in all its imperfection, and particularly in all its passion. For this reason the central thesis of the book has immense implications: "True religion, in great part, consists in holy affections," because, as he further elaborates, these emotions "do not only necessarily belong to the human nature, but are a very great part of it." To assert that beauty guarantees reality was radical enough, but to assert further that only the emotional sanction guarantees the beauty was to pose a proposition with which the modern phase of European culture still contends. If it cannot be defended, Edwards declared, the insight that redeems the universe from evil may indeed dwell with God and with angels, but it will be useless to particular men, who must cope with solid stones or with specific vocabularies.

Many definitions of Puritanism have been offered by historians. For the student of American culture, I suspect that the most useful would be simply that Puritanism is what Edwards is. This must be qualified, as we have seen, by the historical consideration that Edwards rejected the metaphysics and psychology of original Puritanism, and substituted Newton and Locke; but he used science and sensation, not to erect a new system of theology, but to bring men face to face with what Puritanism always demands that they face, the divinity of divinity. As the Great Awakening subsided, leaving in both camps men who had taken their eyes off the ravishing object of contemplation and had fixed them upon either rational persuasion or hysterical stimulants, Edwards calmly, resolutely forced upon them a prediction of their fate. Out of the turmoil and confusion, he extracted the essence of Puritanism, and told modern civilization, both the river gods and the milling herd, that without the sense of the heart they are befuddled and lost. In the spirit of essential Puritanism, he would allow no mercy, no extenuation, no forgiveness. One has to look directly into the blinding sun; otherwise, all becomes infinite evil.

THE EXTERNAL BIOGRAPHY III

In the spring of 1740, as a result of Edwards' efforts, there had already been "stirrings" at Northampton, but the movement became general throughout the area after the visit of Whitefield in October. Edwards' preaching wrought its greatest effects during 1741. He was then in correspondence with the revivalist preachers of the west, and was in effect a sort of director-general of the attack.

At the end of 1740 his children had the measles. Samuel Hopkins, then a Yale senior, heard him preach the *Distinguishing Marks* on September 10, 1741, and thereupon resolved to go and study with Edwards, "though he lived about eighty miles from my father's house." In December 1741 and January 1742, Edwards made an extended tour through western Massachusetts and into Connecticut, preaching in many pulpits; in February and March he preached at Leicester, during which time his own pulpit was occupied by one Buell, who rekindled the languishing fervor of Northampton. Under his preaching, Sarah Edwards attained the heights of religious ecstasy about which she wrote, at Edwards' request, the account he utilized in *Some Thoughts*. When Edwards returned in March 1742, he found the people tending toward the excesses he feared, and on the 16th he swore them to his new "covenant." He preached the sermons that make up the *Religious Affections* in the winter of 1742-43.

By 1743 Edwards was in frequent correspondence with a number of Scottish ministers who, like him, were Calvinist evangelicals, to whom he gave voluminous reports on New England and with whom he discussed abstruse points in theology. These friends spread his fame in Great Britain. In May he wrote to one of them, "I live upon the brink of the grave, in great infirmity of body, and nothing is more uncertain, than whether I shall live to see it: but I believe God will revive this work again before long, and that it will not wholly cease till it has subdued the whole earth." In this month his eighth child, Eunice, was born. Samuel Hopkins became an intimate of the household, and as close a friend as any man could become to Edwards.

In September Edwards met David Brainerd at the Yale commencement. Brainerd came for the graduation of his class, and petitioned to be given his degree along with them; Edwards was deeply impressed by the calmness and humility with which he received the faculty's decision to refuse him.

In May of 1743 Edwards went to Boston for the annual convention of the Massachusetts clergy, his daughter Sarah riding on a pillion. (There is no record that he ever again came to Boston.) At Brookfield they fell in with Thomas Clap, the Rector of Yale and successor of Elisha Williams. A year later Clap returned for the Harvard commencement, and there told a number of persons that while riding through Leicester in 1743 Edwards had told him of a scheme plotted by Whitefield for bringing in zealous young ministers from England in order to turn out of their pulpits the antirevivalist clergy of New England. Edwards denied that he had said anything of the sort; Clap repeated the charge and published it. Edwards printed two pamphlets in refutation. Thereafter Edwards appears to have had no connection with Yale. He was isolated in the back-country, and his hope lay in the new college that was being planned in the hinterland of New Jersey.

His relations with the town and with his church began to deteriorate in 1742-43 as he asked for salary increases; certain of the townspeople responded by criticising the extravagance of his scale of living, and particularly said cruel things about Sarah's clothes. By March 1744, Edwards lamented to a Scottish correspondent that the Awakening was dead and that the state of affairs in New England was truly melancholy. In this same month he assumed the interrogation, and then the prosecution, of the children accused of reading the "bad book"; he thus alienated a large and powerful faction of the community. About this time he evidently began to doubt the wisdom of Stoddard's practice of admitting candidates to membership without at least some semblance of public profession, but after 1744 no applicant appeared and for four years the issue did not come into the open.

His ninth child and second son, Jonathan, was born in May 1745. Sermon notes for these years show that he preached much on themes relating to the war with France and to political events in the colony and in England. He strove incessantly to rekindle the flames of 1735 and of 1741; when the people did not respond, he berated them, recalling their past glories, celebrating the reputation of Northampton as the leader of the revival, denouncing the present lassitude and factional strife. "No town in America is so much like a city set on a hill, to which God has in so great a degree entrusted the honor of religion."

A group of Scottish ministers organized a movement to devote regular hours every week to concerted prayers for a revival of religion; Edwards joined in their program and in 1747 published a piece of propaganda for it, *An Humble Attempt to Promote Explicit Agreement and Visible Union of God's People in Extraordinary Prayer for the Revival of Religion and Advancement of Christ's Kingdom on Earth.* The booklet gives further hints of the fascination he found in the doctrine of the millennium, which he had already expounded in the sermons of 1739. The emphasis is remarkably strong upon the triumph to be achieved "on earth."

In 1747 his friend Bellamy, now minister in Bethlehem, Connecticut, purchased sheep for Edwards, spending £90. Edwards' tenth child, Elizabeth, was born in May; that month David Brainerd came to live in Edwards' house, and died there on October 4. His betrothed, Edwards' daughter Jerusha, died the following February. Edwards wrote to Bellamy, "I have great satisfaction concerning her state, from what I know of her in Life, & what appeared in her at Death." He preached the funeral sermon for Brainerd and began preparation of the biography, which was published in 1749.

Col. John Stoddard died on June 19, 1748; Edwards preached the funeral sermon on the 26th. His correspondence with the Scottish ministers was immense during these years. He corresponded with Governor Belcher of New Jersey about the college in that colony, and informed his Scottish friends of all developments.

Your thoughts have more power than kings to compel you.
You have also thought, sometimes at your prayers,
Sometimes hesitating at the angles of stairs,
And between sleep and waking, early in the morning,
When the bird cries, have thought of further scorning.
That nothing lasts, but the wheel turns,
The nest is rifled, and the bird mourns;
That the shrine shall be pillaged, and the gold spent,
The jewels gone for light ladies' ornament,
The sanctuary broken, and its stores
Swept into the laps of parasites and whores.
When miracles cease, and the faithful desert you,
And men shall only do their best to forget you.
And later is worse, when men will not hate you
Enough to defame or to execrate you,
But pondering the qualities that you lacked
Will only try to find the historical fact.
When men shall declare that there was no mystery
About this man who played a certain part in history.

T. S. ELIOT

Hubris

I
N 1723, according to legend, after Edwards returned from New York, when he was twenty and Sarah Pierrepont was thirteen, upon the blank page of a book he was reading he wrote her a hymn, which, next to the Enfield sermon, is the most widely known of his writings. There is justice in posterity's selection, for between this and the sermon lies his story. Familiar though it may be, it must here be repeated:

They say there is a young lady in [New Haven] who is beloved of that Great Being, who made and rules the world, and that there are certain seasons in which this Great Being, in some way or other invisible, comes to her and fills her mind with exceeding sweet delight, and that she hardly cares for any thing, except to meditate on him—that she expects after a while to be received up where he is, to be raised up out of the world and caught up into heaven; being assured that he loves her too well to let her remain at a distance from him always. There she is to dwell with him, and to be ravished with his love and delight forever. Therefore, if you present all the world before her, with the richest of its treasures, she disregards it and cares not for it, and is unmindful of any pain or affliction. She has a strange sweetness in her mind, and singular purity in her affections; is most just and conscientious in all her conduct; and you could not persuade her to do any thing wrong or sinful, if you would give her all the world, lest she should offend this Great Being. She is of a wonderful sweetness, calmness and universal benevolence of mind; especially after this Great God has manifested himself to her mind. She will sometimes go about from place to place, singing sweetly; and seems to be always full of joy and pleasure; and no one knows for what. She loves to be alone, walking in the fields and groves, and seems to have some one invisible always conversing with her.

On July 28, 1727, five months after he was ordained at Northampton, he and Sarah were married. There still circulate in western Massachusetts fantastic rumors about their life, vestigial remains of his enemies' whispering campaign in the 1740's. The marriage was a true and a deep one; with eleven children, they were an affectionate family, where a preponderance of girls made for strain, but where Edwards was lord of the household and utterly adored. Sarah, the eldest, developed an unhappy disposition and became the occasion of the only witticism reported of her father: Elihu Parsons asked to marry her, and Edwards "plainly disclosed to him the unpleasant temper of his daughter" (one can imagine with what directness he would do it!). "But she has grace, I trust?" asked Mr. Parsons, and Edwards replied, "I hope she has, but grace can live where you cannot." Jerusha, the second daughter, loved David Brainerd, and nursed him on his deathbed. "Dear Jerusha," he said at the end, "are you willing to part with me?—I am quite willing to part with you. . . . But we shall spend a happy eternity together." Five months later, aged eighteen, she died, and Edwards noted, "She was a person of much the same spirit with Brainerd." Neither he nor anyone else in Northampton knew that Brainerd had tuberculosis or that it was contagious, though Edwards described the symptoms so accurately that the modern physician can make the diagnosis at once. In April 1758, as she was preparing to move the household to Princeton, Sarah Pierrepont Edwards received the news of her husband's death. "What shall I say! A holy and good God has covered us with a dark cloud. O that we may kiss the rod and lay our hands on our mouths! The

Lord has done it. He has made me adore his goodness, that we had him so long." She died seven months later. I believe one may safely conclude that passion was something the Edwards family knew at first hand.

In the summer of 1742, as James Davenport was wrecking the Awakening, there appeared in Boston one of the most effective pieces of propaganda the counterreaction hit upon: *The Wonderful Narrative, or a Faithful Account of the French Prophets, their agitations, extasies, and inspirations.* It told of a band of French fanatics who fled to London and in 1706 started a scare about the end of the world; it exposed a pattern of enthusiasm, which spreads like "a kind of Infection" among the lower classes. To support the thesis, it cited Mahomet, John of Leyden, and that "virago" Anne Hutchinson, all of whom acted "from a Heat." Bibliographers doubt that Chauncy wrote it, but Edwards thought he did; it was clearly a work of the free and catholic cabal. Throughout the debate, Edwards never stooped to recognize by name any of his opponents or their works with this sole exception. But to counter this, the cheapest of all attacks, Edwards employed a means as astonishing and as revelatory as any in modern literature.

She was "ravished with his love and delight forever." She had experiences of "an uncommon discovery of God's excellency," but in 1742 a shattering one. Her husband had written of spiders and rainbows and understood the nature of the controlled experiment; he asked Sarah for an "exact" statement. Her uneasiness, which she took for a wrestling with God, commenced on a morning in January, "at Mr. Edwards' suggesting, that he thought I had failed in some measure in point of prudence, in some conversation I had with Mr. Williams of Hadley, the day before." She fell into loud tears, then felt an inexpressible peace, and was lifted above earth and hell, until the troubles of the world were as nothing, until even the threats she most feared—"the ill treatment of the town, and the ill will of my husband"—were so comparatively nothing that she could contemplate with serenity being chased from town into the deep snow. Edwards went to Leicester, leaving his pulpit to one Buell, and Sarah was able to resign herself to Buell's having a greater success than had recently favored Edwards. Verses of Dr. Watts' *Hosannas* came to her, with such a sense of Christ's presence "that I could with difficulty refrain from rising from my seat, and leaping for joy." Her strength failed, "when they took me up and laid me on the bed, where I lay for considerable time, faint with joy, while contemplating the glories of the heavenly world," where she became resigned "that God should employ some other instrument than Mr. Edwards, in advancing the work of grace in Northampton." Her soul was in Elysium, and, as far as she could make a comparison, each minute was worth more than all she had heretofore enjoyed put together: "It was pure delight which fed and satisfied the soul. It was pleasure, without the least sting, or any interruption. . . . There was but little difference, whether I was asleep or awake, so deep was the impression made on my soul; but if there was any difference, the sweetness was greatest and most uninterrupted while I was asleep." She achieved the assurance that were she to be cast off by her nearest friends, "if the feelings and conduct of my husband were to be changed from tenderness and affection, to extreme hatred and cruelty," she would still with alacrity perform every act of duty.

In *Some Thoughts*, at the end of 1742, Edwards marveled that in this orthodox country, where for decades every minister had prayed for reformation, there should be so many at a loss whether the Awakening was of God or the devil. He had immortalized Abigail and Phebe; the opposition still contended that this work was devilish because of its "high transports of religious affection." He needed another case history to confute both Chauncy and the enthusiasts, and so he published the confession of "a person." Suppressing every indication of sex, he excised all mention of Williamses or of the possible ill-will of a husband, but he faithfully reprinted the ecstasies, and claimed everything for them, because this person was not "in the giddy age of youth," was a convert of twenty-seven years' standing, "and neither converted, nor educated in that enthusiastical town of Northampton."

He retold Sarah's narrative word for word, except for the change of "I" to "the person" and a few insertions to emphasize the absence of impulses or prophetical visions. It was a blanket assertion of the absolute validity of transports, even when accompanied by "great agitations of body, and an unavoidable leaping for joy." The person's readiness to renounce the "lives of dearest earthly friends for the love of God" was cited with approval, as also the person's attaining to the riches of full assurance.

> These things have been attended with a constant sweet peace and calm and serenity of soul, without any cloud to interrupt it; a continual rejoicing in all the works of God's hands, the works of nature, and God's daily works of providence, all appearing with a sweet smile upon them; . . . Oh how good, said the person once, is it to work for God in the day time, and at night to lie down under his smiles.

None of this, he noted in conclusion, altered the person's disposition to attend to the business of a secular calling, or induced the person "to show humility and devotion by a mean habit, or a demure and melancholy countenance, or any thing singular and superstitious." For pages Edwards subordinated himself to the narrative, and then came the cry, the only personal cry he ever let escape:

> Now if such things are enthusiasm, and the fruits of a distempered brain, let my brain be evermore possessed of that happy distemper! If this be distraction, I pray God that the world of mankind may be all seized with this benign, sweet, beneficent, beatifical, glorious distraction.

As against the evidence of this person, what will it advantage the opponents "if agitations of body were found in the French prophets, and ten thousand prophets more"? Against Chauncy and against Boston, when at last he needed the ultimate symbol, Jonathan Edwards flung the image of her who loved to be alone in the fields, with someone invisible conversing with her.

There was, however, one case history still unreported. During the Awakening, apparently about 1740 but possibly later, Edwards finally subjected himself to the technique of the certain and infallible rules. The *Personal Narrative* is perhaps as astonishing a piece of clinical dissection as the history of analysis affords. It has been called "mystical" and "charming." It is not charming, and as for the much-abused word mysticism, one may, if he wishes, apply it to the description of the calm, sweet abstraction that followed his reading of the Song of Solomon: "a kind of vision, of fixed ideas and imaginations, of being alone in the mountains, or some solitary wilderness, far from all mankind, sweetly conversing with Christ, and wrapt and swallowed up in God." What really applies to the *Personal Narrative* is the apparatus of psychological investigation formulated in the *Religious Affections*, of which the later and larger part is devoted, not to the defense of emotion against reason, but to a winnowing out of the one pure spiritual emotion from the horde of imitations.

The *Personal Narrative* must be read, not as autobiography or as reminiscence of early Connecticut, but as a revelation of the point at which Edwards turned from asserting his doctrine of causality against the Arminians to an examination of those who took him at his word, who conceived grace as emotional, and then ran riot. When the supreme sacrifice was necessary, he sacrificed himself, even while celebrating Sarah's certain redemption. Upon his youthful reading of "I am the Rose of Sharon," there followed a sweet burning in his heart, which, to his mature gaze, was an explicable natural effect. Here was the dual necessity, on which he was impaled, of being both more charitable and less charitable; here was the fine line between reality and its counterfeits. He could study hundreds throughout the Valley, and guided by Sarah's criteria, pronounce a "uniformity observable" which assured them their salvation, but the perfect analysis must be close, and the analyst must know his patient thoroughly. "It is easy to be accounted for, from mere principles of nature, that a person's heart, on such an occasion, should be raised up to the skies with transports of joy." It was, for instance, a transport, but no proof of an influence of God, that a boy with a mind full of objections against the idea that God chooses and rejects persons at His mere pleasure should suddenly apprehend the justice of the doctrine; this was the work of speculation alone, and sensationalism explained why, once the idea of God's absolute sovereignty was thus formed in his mind, it became pleasant, bright, and sweet. It was no proof of grace that certain texts inspired such delight that he sang over the words: "it never came into my thought that there was anything spiritual, or of a saving nature in this."

He discussed his state with his father, and then walked in his father's pasture, exalted with a realization that in God are conjoined majesty and meekness; year after year he walked in forests, in New York "into a solitary place, on the banks of Hudson's River, at some distance from the city, for contemplation on divine things and secret converse with God," or near Northampton, alighting from his horse, where a view of the glory of Christ kept him in tears for an hour. He had owned his baptismal covenant in 1722 and been taken into the communion, and he would refer to this as "my first conversion," but in all honesty he could not find, even then, when his affections were most raised, such a conversion as conformed to "those particular steps, wherein the people of New England, and anciently the Dissenters of Old England, used to experience it."

Slowly he realized that he had gone about it by the book, trying to force himself through the stages marked out by seventeenth-century scholasticism, a method he now could see was "miserable," while Sarah Pierrepont, unlearned in technologia, simply possessed herself of a universal benevolence. Had he permanently disabled himself from encountering pure experience? By 1725 he faced the realization: whatever he now was, for better or worse, he would remain; "whether I am now converted or not, I am so settled in the state I am in, that I shall go on in it all my life." In his Northampton laboratory, he took his youthful ecstasies apart; experience, he found, had not then taught him, "as it has done since," the corruption of his own heart, and he concluded the *Personal Narrative* with a report on his findings: when his people came to him with their souls' concerns, and said that they were as bad as the devil himself, "I thought their expressions seemed exceeding faint and feeble, to represent my wickedness."

Allowance must be made for conventions, literary and social; an unshaken assurance was supposed among Puritans to be automatically suspect. But Edwards was reporting objectively on an insect; he was a secretive man, who looked unblinkingly upon all reality. He could not say that he was converted, but he could say that Sarah was. When he foresaw that he might be destined to the lowest place in hell, he was not attitudinizing: he was stating bare fact. Who then was the spider held over the pit? Who better could comprehend to what extremities nature will go in the attempt to simulate a reality it knows not? Who that hungered for love should more thoroughly know man's incapacity for it? Who else should pray God so desperately that his brain might be possessed of Sarah Pierrepont's happy distemper?

Solomon Stoddard long ago had decided that nobody could tell for certain who was elected. Multitudes, he said, have come to Christ all uncertain of their salvation; not out of Locke but by rule-of-thumb he concluded that the *a priori* scheme of the faculty psychology was not true, but since he had no philosophy to put in its place, he solved the crisis by extending, or trying to extend, the church to include all the town, and let God do the selecting. He never entirely succeeded, even with five revivals, in getting the whole community inside the church; the royal government would not let him force them in by law, and enough of the Congregational tradition persisted so that those who would not consent could not be compelled. Of course, as throughout Massachusetts, they were obliged to pay ecclesiastical rates, and, since taxes were community matters, these were voted in town meetings, where leading members of the church—generally leaders of the "court" party—ruled by what were supposed to be parliamentary procedures. The best Stoddard could do was to abolish the profession of faith, so that nothing stood between any citizen and the membership but his own shyness or recalcitrance. At Stoddard's death, 630 members had been admitted; in the surprising conversions of 1735, thirty admissions were received each week, and a total of over three hundred were enrolled before Joseph Hawley killed himself. They came when and if they wanted to come. Deacon Hunt kept count on everybody he heard to be hopefully affected, and of the 210 in his list, 185 appear on the records as new members. But Edwards held the policy of the church to Stoddard's line: no professions were asked for, and he did not officially certify that these recruits were true saints or necessarily had any real goodness. In 1740 and 1741 still more came in. In 1742 applicants fell off, and Edwards went on tour, leaving Buell in his pulpit and Sarah a prey to fears she dared not name. He came back in February, to find the town "running wild." Many were not merely leaping for joy, they were falling into twenty-four-hour trances, under a strong imagination that they were in heaven beholding glorious objects.

Edwards had learned in 1736 that this was the moment when Satan could be expected to rage, and he wanted no more throats cut. In the last glow of the Awakening he persuaded the people—if you will, he bullied them—into drawing up a covenant. Not, he specifically said, such a covenant of incorporation as Stoddard had disowned, but simply a public memorial which, since the people had gone through an immense experience and since true converts had the moral ability to make a commitment, testified the people's determination to abide by the results of the outpouring. In order to follow the

tragedy that was now preparing on the Northampton stage—
and to perceive its representative value for American history
—it is essential to note what Edwards asked in this covenant
of March 16, 1742. He committed the signers, of course, to re-
nouncing evil and seeking the Lord; he bound them to refrain
from backbiting and gossip, and enjoined them against revenge
or getting private ends or party ends by wounding religion;
he swore them to avoid bitterness in public affairs; but also, by
their own consent, he made them promise that they would not
overreach or defraud their neighbor, cheat him out of his debt,
or in any commercial transaction violate the slightest rule of
moral equity. This is a hard oath for an expanding economy
to observe to the letter; any aggressive interest would resent
being subjected to the moral surveillance that Edwards proposed to exercise over businessmen in Northampton. I am not
putting an "economic interpretation" upon the Northampton
story; the events are too obscure, the actors were too reticent,
to permit any oversimplified version, and this was, if I may insist, tragedy in the highest and most complex sense. Still, the
clash between Edwards and his people (egged on by his Williams cousins) was, among other things, a clash between America's greatest spokesman for absolute Christian morality and
representatives of the American business ethic.

The story is, as I say, complex, and there is another factor
that can hardly be put into words, but which is a reason why
this village fracas has tragic import. Edwards did not come to
it with clean hands, and he knew it. I mean not only that he
was proud and overbearing and rash; something more fundamental was at work in him—that trait inherent in his deepest
thought, a habit of mystification, a concealment practised until it became second nature. His arrogance was a symptom of
a more profound dislocation; he had reasoned as a youth, "If
I had more of an air of gentleness, I should be much mended,"
but his mature years were spent proving that virtues cannot
earn salvation, and that none can be acquired merely by taking
thought. When among friends, says Hopkins, who was as in-

timate with Edwards as any could be, he was affable, "tho' not talkative." Others found him "stiff & unsociable." Hopkins attributed this reserve to his early resolution to guard his tongue, but also (to our conception more pertinently) to his low stock of animal spirits, which "lays a Man under a natural inability" to be an affable, facetious gentleman, which compels him to reserve what he has for higher services. In the preface to *Some Thoughts*, Edwards declared New England engaged in a more important "war" than the skirmish with Spain, and "somebody should speak his mind, concerning the way in which it ought to be managed." As spokesman for Stoddard's empire, Edwards was under the greatest obligation to speak out; his revival oratory seemed to be ingenuous if any ever was. Yet he had resolved at twenty, "When I am unfit for other business, to perfect myself in writing *characters*," and all his works are a code, hiding some secret that would not come out. He was driven at last from Northampton because the people found him a man of deception.

There is something peculiar in the whole story, which no participant, not even the guilt-stricken Hawley, could ever say outright. Hence, I suspect, the spectacular vehemence it engendered. Nowhere else did a small band adhering to the protagonist worship him as did the followers of Edwards, the twenty heads of families, "besides others, women and young people," who stood by him; but nowhere else did the mass of a town hate a man as the citizenry of Northampton hated Edwards. Every student will read the Northampton story by his own lights—which is one reason why it belongs, along with Harpers Ferry or Homestead, to the symbolism of America. But to comprehend the fury of the people, we must understand that to them Edwards' long-delayed disclosure of his deviation from Stoddard was a criminal tergiversation, a masterpiece of treason to the community, "as if I was secretly doing the Part of an Enemy to 'em, so long as I had a being in the Town."

He had taken unto himself the prestige of his two years with

Stoddard; he was carried to the summit of distinction by Stoddard's polity and people, and he became an international figure because Northampton was the citadel of revivalism. The town paid him the largest salary of any inland minister, and it was voted in town meeting—or after the meeting was subdivided, by the "precinct"—by scores who were not members of the church. Then in 1744, he repudiated Stoddard. He demanded a profession of faith and experience before he would admit any to the communion. He showed, by the manner of the announcement, that he had long practised what he had not believed. And he dared to berate them for hypocrisy! A people who in 1735 and in 1741 reached the pinnacle of praying for the conversion of their enemies turned like a pack of animals upon him who had twice led them up the slopes of the delectable mountains, and Edwards was cursed from one end of the Valley to the other. When the battle was over, Edwards could say by whom he was actually defeated: the people looked upon Stoddard "almost as a sort of deity," so that "my teaching and insisting on the doctrine, which Mr. Stoddard opposed, appears to them a sort of horrid profaneness." The old Pope was never more alive, but he was alive, we should note, not only because of the veneration of the people but also because he was deliberately exploited as a shibboleth of propaganda by the Williamses and by young Hawley.

Edwards came to his conclusion slowly, reluctantly, out of empirical observation. In 1735 and again in 1741 numbers flocked to his church under the stress of revival and were admitted, without examination, with no commitment that he could hold over them afterwards, and many of them proved, measured by Sarah's happy distemper, to be ephemeral Christians. However, one is bound to suspect that his maturing decision to stand or fall on the issue of profession was formed, not so much from the external evidence, as within the recesses of self-analysis of which the *Personal Narrative* is the record. Signs of this growing determination can be traced in *Some Thoughts:* as he turned his fire from Chauncy on the right to the censorious enthusiasts on the left, he let fall a clear intimation that he would like to have a covenant in his church by which he could call his people to order. In places where the churches receive members by profession, he lectured the enthusiasts, they should bow to the judgment of the church, and not denounce pastors or brethren on the basis of private opinion—although, he added ominously, "I do not now pretend to meddle with that controversy whether such an account of experience be requisite to church fellowship."

His "covenant" of March 16 was an effort to acquire some such lever, but it was a makeshift as long as Stoddard's theory ruled. He knew all too well that Stoddard's doctrine had "been fully and quietly established, for a long time, in all the neighboring churches and congregations," so that in the provincial perspective, it would seem, were he to dissent, "that all the world, almost, was against me." As the event quickly showed, "my most crafty opposers improved this advantage, and abundantly represented me as all alone in my opinion." Stoddard had stripped Edwards of the only weapon that could avail him, but if he was weaponless, was not this the one challenge he must accept to show whether he was really as bad as the devil himself? Knowing what he must contend with, he knew even more the mounting compulsion of the *Personal Narrative:* "How happy are they which do that which is right in the sight of God!"

The published version of the *Religious Affections* may not be the same that he delivered in 1742-43, because by 1746 his decision was public; still, the structure of the argument shows the unfolding of his thought. After the first four and theoretical definitions of a true emotion, the remaining eight are specifically directed against revivalistic excess. The discussion revolves around the "imagination," which is the source of all abuses; there are two hundred pages of masterly and pitiless denunciation of those who, having images in their heads, "have very ignorantly supposed them to be of the nature of supernatural discoveries." The list of true signs—humility, meekness, tenderness, humiliation, and finally "a practice, which is universally conformed to, and directed by Christian rules"— is a prose elaboration of the love lyric to Sarah. He could now put succinctly the crucial distinction: it is between "lively imaginations arising from strong affections"—such as Sarah's— and "strong affections arising from lively imaginations"—such as those of the wild mob. A right judgment depends upon a right apprehension of things, just as, said Edwards (making one of his few excursions into literary criticism, which may, however, show his meaning more clearly to an era that has substituted literature for theology), "there is need of uncommon force of mind to discern the distinguishing excellencies of the works of authors of great genius"—notably Milton, where those things that appear tasteless to mean judges "are his inimitable excellencies in the eyes of those, who are of greater discerning and better taste." (Chauncy, we noted, could not understand Milton.) He that truly grasps the divinity of things "not only argues that they are divine, but he sees that they are divine," and such a sight is not obtained "by arguments fetched from ancient traditions, histories, and monuments," not even, the implication was obvious, from the traditions and monuments of Stoddard, who, ironically, had been outspoken in his day against the idolatry of ancestor-worship!

Northampton listened with incredulity and then with fury as Edwards drew out the conclusion that the best way of testing this insight, in the social context, is "a profession of Christianity," which, while it may not be the final evidence of conversion, "yet it is a thing requisite and necessary in it." He asked only for a few words, "briefly expressing the cardinal virtues, or acts, implied in a hearty compliance," but the people knew he wanted them in order to rebuke the spiritual pride of those who declared their experiences without discretion, without distinguishing, or wanting to distinguish, between impressions on the imagination and spiritual experience, just as critics publish judgments on Milton without understanding him. He asked only for a token, but the people were not to be trapped; they knew that to yield would be to put themselves in his power, so that he could discipline them out of their own mouths, and they knew that it would mean acceptance of his thesis that they had given way to impulses and imaginations, and so had thwarted the Awakening. He found the ways by which the affections can simulate grace without being gracious so numerous, the natural springs so secret, that "no philosophy or experience will ever be sufficient to guide us through this labyrinth and maze, without our closely following the clew which God has given us in his word."

Thus, out of the sensationally instigated passions of the Awakening, he who had started them and defended them with his mastery of the sensational method came, like the first Puritans, to believe that a public confession was not only the most reliable test for the brotherhood, but the only possible solution to enigmas that philosophy, even Locke and Newton, could not resolve. He still rejected the scholastic metaphysics out of which the founders had devised their argument for profession, and he did not propose to set up again the complex theology of the covenant; he simply wanted a submission of the will, if only a pro-forma one. The people were bound to oppose, because to accede would be to condemn themselves. A howl of rage went up, and, as Hopkins says, "before he was heard in his own defence, or it was known by many what his principles were, the general cry was to have him dismissed, as what alone would satisfy them." Men seldom fight successfully with society on the sole condition that society denounce itself; when a man deliberately undertakes a battle on such terms, he must be prepared for, even ask for, defeat. So, it appears, did Edwards.

In March 1744, as the issue was coming to a focus, Moses Lyman, head of one of the twenty families faithful to him, came with a story that certain children were gathering in barns or pastures to giggle over a "bad book," what proved to be a handbook for midwives, or, as the town called it, the "Granny Book." A man's blunders tell more than his successes, and Edwards blundered as monumentally as any statesman. As he later evaluated the drama, he could reproach himself for the diffidence that kept him from testifying against false appearances until too late, but also, "in some respects, doubtless, my confidence in myself was a great injury to me." He called the church to stay after the service, related the charge, and had them elect a committee of investigation, which included Col. Stoddard. Then, only then, he read the names of the children. The piece of paper he had on his desk survives; some of the names are marked with one sign, some with another, signifying that he discriminated between suspects and others whom he merely wished interrogated, but he read them all with no explanation, and so recited names from practically all the best families in town. Was he stupid? He was capable of a fantastic insensibility to the merely human. Was he arrogant? If he knew, then or later, he never told. But then and there, "the town was suddenly all in a Blaze." He could not, had he tried, have played more abjectly into the hands of Israel Williams.

How serious was the blaze can be gauged from the fact that for four years nobody in Northampton applied or dared apply for admission to Edwards' church. This, in the "enthusiastical town," the city on a hill, the stronghold of the Awakening, the throne of Stoddard! Relative to time and scale, no fall of princes was ever more steep than that of Edwards between 1741 and 1750.

This study does not require that the complicated and sordid maneuvers be retold by which Edwards was finally ousted from Northampton. The great works of his exile systematically disregard the episode, but nevertheless certain insights acquired, or rather confirmed, therein subtly pervade them. The story has been represented as a sort of anticipation of 1776, a rising of the democracy against the aristocracy, with Edwards cast in the rôle of Tory reactionary. This version gains plausibility because in the Granny Book investigation the ringleader of the juvenile obstetrical sessions was one

Timothy Root, otherwise unknown to history, who definitely did not belong to a best family but did belong to that limbo of society which even in the Great Awakening stubbornly remained outside the church. Timothy Root confronted Edwards with a declaration that stirs the hearts of Americans, "I won't worship a wig" (the clergy and gentry alone wore wigs), and pronounced upon the church's committee, including Col. Stoddard, a still more egalitarian judgment: "They are nothing but men moulded up of a little Dirt; I don't Care a Turd, or I don't Care a Fart for any of them." Certainly, the democracy of the 1740's was restive; at Suffield in 1746 a certain John Adams—no relation to *the* John Adams—said that Col. Stoddard was a lazy devil who sat in Northampton "on his cussed ass," for which exercise in free speech he was fined five shillings.

However, expletives from the lower strata at this time must be interpreted with reference to the situation. Throughout the Awakening, despite the inflation that worked hardship on the masses, merchants and land speculators consistently made money. When Edwards turned his eyes, even momentarily, from the glory of God, he could become an acute sociologist: "In latter times," he said of Northampton, "the people have had more to feed their pride. They have grown a much greater and more wealthy people than formerly."

Solomon Stoddard died in 1729 with what was considered a good estate, valued at £1,126; Col. John Stoddard's property was inventoried in 1748 at £35,432, which, even allowing for inflation, is an index of the prosperity of the upper classes during the years Edwards was defining the nature of gracious affections. The Colonel owned a gold watch worth £150, thirty-five shirts worth £90, the first china and the first teapot known in the Valley, and a Negro maid named Bess priced at £80. Madame Stoddard and her three daughters, who visited nobody lower in the scale than Hawleys and Dwights, wore the first hooped petticoats, and as they went to meeting down Moses Lyman's lane, "one lapped over the other so as not to spread too far." Social distinctions, in other words, growing out of increasing differences in wealth, were transforming the Valley from the pioneer simplicity of Stoddard's time, and Edwards, with only an intermittent appreciation of the process, was a victim of it.

Col. Stoddard's estate represents the process, but not the Colonel himself, who belonged to the older conception of aristocracy, the military squirearchy; he was almost the last of that line of which John Winthrop was the first, of which John Hancock was the empty shell. Having pledged support to his father's grandson, he remained faithful. From 1744, when Edwards' change of heart was first known, though the town might mutter, Edwards could not be touched until June 19, 1748, when Stoddard, nursed by Sarah, died in Boston of an apoplexy. Edwards preached the funeral sermon, one of the finest of his short pieces. "A man of honor," Edwards called him, "and not a man of mean artifice and clandestine management, for filthy lucre"; with an extraordinary ability to distinguish right and wrong in the midst of intricacies, he frequently surprised Edwards by his ability to foresee the consequences of things. Also, he was a wise casuist, "as I know by the great help I have found from time to time by his judgment and advice in cases of conscience"; and he understood experimental religion, not only doctrinally "but as one intimately and feelingly acquainted with these things." "Truly," Edwards cried, "the son of nobles."

His successor as commander of the militia and lord of the marches was Israel Williams, already possessed of so many land-grants that men called him "the monarch of the Berkshires." Only the remnant of the old gentry, Dr. Mather and Timothy Dwight, stood beside Edwards. It was not the democracy that unseated him; it was the oligarchy of business and real estate, of which Israel Williams was the manager and Hawley, the merchant's son, the instrument. The pattern of their operation is painfully clear: certain leading men of the town, esteemed for their knowledge and estates, who yet had "not been the most famed for piety," assisted "by some at a great distance, persons of note, and some great men in civil authority," stirred up "the more ignorant and less considerate people" by crying to heaven that Edwards was un-Stoddardean. They turned loose the mob "to prosecute the views of their bitterness and violence without a check of conscience," spreading rumors that Edwards aimed to overthrow religion and to ruin the present and future generations, and so built up such a pressure of public opinion that for a person to appear the friend of Edwards was to expose himself "to the immediate persecution of his neighbors, and perhaps of his nearest friends." These tactics tell a, by now, stale story in American history, and the point of it, as it concerns group behavior, is obvious: the river gods were out for Edwards' scalp, and the masses, played upon by the solid citizenry, did the screaming. When Israel Williams succeeded to Stoddard's command, though he was no son of nobility and incapable of conducting himself as a noble, Edwards' fate was sealed; it was only a question of time and a few formalities. In so far as there is an economic or class angle to the expulsion, Edwards was hustled out of Northampton, not by the populace, but by the entrepreneurs.

Tension was aggravated by an argument over Edwards' salary. In every town, as rising costs made difficulty for pastors on fixed salaries, they and town meetings were at loggerheads, and though the precinct of Northampton voted Edwards his increases, it smarted under his "haughty" manner, and whispered criticisms of Sarah's expensive dresses. When he ended his account of "a person"—her identity, of course, was an open secret—with the distinguishing mark of her scorning to manifest grace by cheap attire, he was rebuking village gossips; his anger against those who found fault "with our manner of spending, with the clothes that we wear," dictated the most trenchant denunciations of Main Street to appear in our literature until Ed Howe and Sinclair Lewis. Still, exacerbating though the salary dispute was, it was not the divisive issue, and up to the end, the precinct did its financial duty, although grudgingly, even while it was forcing him out.

The real issue could no longer be concealed by December 1748, when Edwards told the first applicant in four years that he must make a profession, and he, after consulting with his friends, refused. The campaign now began in earnest; in the spring of 1749 a young girl was ready to make a confession, but was scared out of it, and the church descended so far into the abyss that it voted to discontinue the Lord's Supper entirely! By the end of 1749 Edwards could report to Bellamy —with a calmness impersonalized to a degree that rejects sympathy—to what a pass the situation had come in Northampton, in that city God had formerly made such a place of wonders: "All that I do & say is watched by the multitude around me with the utmost strictness & with eyes of the greatest uncharitableness & severity and let me do or say what I will, my words & actions are represented in dark colours." The incredible factor in the story is Edwards' serene assurance of the outcome; he made no effort to hold his pulpit, but fought day and night, with a concentration that exhausted and infuriated his opponents, to compel the town to take its stand openly—to damn itself before the world. It was as much the way he drove them as their own rage that brought them to the point, which he could describe without passion, where "they seem to be sensible that now their Character can't stand unless it be on the Ruin of mine."

Israel Williams managed the town's strategy from the safety of Hatfield, and strove to make it appear that Edwards was blameworthy and scandalous. Hawley and his friends were outwitted fifty times by Edwards' ruthless diplomacy; but Israel, with "the countenance of other members of the family, of a character superior to his own," supplied the wits they lacked. Their most adroit move was to take the conduct of the debate out of the church and into the precinct meeting, where Edwards could not speak and where a mass of non-members, of the Timothy Root persuasion, could pack the votes. "I then gave them some reasons, why I thought it not a regular proceeding, for the Precinct to take the consideration and management of this Ecclesiastical affair into their hands, in the manner they had done." They had no reply except to assert that it was not irregular, and jammed through their votes, though Edwards warned them that they were setting New England a precedent by which the church would no longer count, by which ministers would become "a cypher." Both by implication and by direct effect, the opposition wrecked the order they claimed they were defending.

For a year and a half there was so much coming and going that nobody in Northampton had time for anything else. There have been, Edwards wrote to Bellamy in December of 1749, "abundance of meetings about our affairs since you was here, society meetings & church meetings, & meetings—of Committees, of Committees of the Parish & Committees of the Church, Conferences, Debates, Reports, & Proposals drawn up, & Replies & Remonstrances." Edwards remained a marvel of objectivity and a fiendish torturer of writhing spiders. If God was with him, he was certain, "I need not fear ten thousands of the People." By the evidence, the odds were in that proportion. So he met every move with the one challenge that the ten thousands could not face: that they either refute his arguments or confess that they were acting out of peevish and sinful rebellion. He put together a defense of his position, and Dwight made a trip to Boston to bring back copies of *An Humble Inquiry Into the Rules of the Word of God Concerning the Qualification Requisite to a Compleat Standing and Full Communion*. Edwards made the church a dismaying proposition: let the people read his book and then vote, none to be allowed to cast a ballot who had not read it; if then they wanted him to leave, he would resign with no further fuss. By now the town was plunged headlong into hysteria, and Edwards strove only to score such points as would demonstrate, if not now, then eventually, its recklessness—a program in which he was inadvertently assisted by Hawley's blunt and blundering lieutenant, the village blacksmith, Major Seth Pomeroy.

Hawley and Pomeroy took care that few read Edwards' book, but they were afraid of it, and wanted it answered. The Williamses came to the rescue; Elisha, Edwards' tutor at Wethersfield, the former rector of Yale, started the job; he had been assisting half brother Israel from the beginning, but just now being diverted by an offer to go to London, he turned over the task to his other half brother, Solomon of Lebanon, who laboriously produced a reply in 1751. He thought he was evening the reckoning against the funeral sermon for William Williams in 1741. By the time he got his book out, Edwards was no longer in Northampton, but Edwards had no pity on Williamses. He published in 1752 *Misinterpretations Corrected and Truth Vindicated*. The legend is that nobody in Northampton dared let on that he had read it.

Today, the two books are the least rewarding of Edwards' works since the issue is utterly forgotten. For sheer destructive argumentation, they are a joy to those who like that sort of thing, and if ever a man was cut into small pieces, and each piece run through a meat-grinder, it was Solomon Williams. But more illuminating is the treatment of the real opponent, Solomon Stoddard. Edwards' struggle, at this crisis in his life, with the ghost who would not down is, as I read the books, a confession that he was haunted and obsessed. He freely admitted that now he differed with Stoddard, and sheltered himself under Stoddard's scorn of ancestor-worship. "If I should believe his principles, because he advanced them, I should be guilty of making him an idol." Yet the body of the books, after admitting the departure, is an elaborate, a strained effort to prove that the departure is not opposition. Partly, no doubt, Edwards was countering his opponent's use of Stoddard as a rabble-rousing slogan, but partly, and all too patently, Edwards was wrestling with himself, and not too successfully, to prove himself no great traitor "against what my honored grandfather strenuously maintained." I have no wish to psychologize, but I think it striking that Edwards spoke constantly of Timothy Edwards as though of an elder brother, and if ever he showed signs of struggling with what is today called a father-image, Solomon Stoddard was the target. "I can truly say," he wrote in considered words, "on account of this and some other considerations, it is what I engage in with the greatest reluctance, that ever I undertook any public service in my life." Read against this background, these volumes are fascinating, for Edwards wrote them knowing that his reputation and his usefulness—"even my very subsistence"—were at stake, in the certainty that his enemies would not listen, yet determined to put the facts before his people, his country, and posterity.

For students of American institutions, the books are useful for their astute tracing of the effects of the Half-Way Covenant, of the multiplication of covenants and the degeneration of the ceremonial owning of the covenant into formality, and of the historical logic of Stoddard's abandonment of all covenants, showing these to be a single process which produced, by imperceptible stages, the indigenous form of Arminianism that Edwards first attacked in 1734. For the social historian these are invaluable though neglected works, but they produced as little effect on Israel Williams as they have on historians; as he fought Edwards in 1734, so he now replied, not only through the weak pamphlet of his brother, but through the more effective method of rigging the Council of Churches in order that the dismissal of Edwards might at long last be realized.

By the original theory of Congregationalism, a church was autonomous and could settle its own quarrels, but when a dispute grew violent, it should ask the "advice and counsel" of the neighboring churches. The clergy and lay delegates of the adjoining bodies would listen, as impartial arbiters, and give an opinion, which was not legally binding, but which the church could disregard only by defying public opinion. Disgusted with the impotence of councils, Stoddard organized his

Hampshire Association as a standing corporation with compulsory powers; lacking legal warrant, it went its way throughout his regime and up to 1735, but then the church in Springfield broke loose and chose Robert Breck for its pastor. The Association, urged on by Edwards, thought Breck too much an Arminian, whereupon it tried to act as though it were a synod in Connecticut, and the Massachusetts government stepped in to break up the power that Stoddard had usurped. During the Awakening, the Hampshire Association had worked together harmoniously, though, for reasons still obscure, Edwards attended infrequently after 1740. Now, working through the Association, Williams and Hawley maneuvered the calling of a Council to give definitive "advice" to Northampton. Knowing that all Hampshire churches were Stoddardean in practice, Edwards strove, as was his right according to custom, to secure one or two delegates from outside the county, hoping that Foxcroft, still the most respected of Boston revivalists and still, though shattered in health, carrying the prestige of the First Church, could be appointed. He wanted to make a last stand for the revivalist party.

After lengthy and tedious stratagems, a Council of nine churches convened on June 19, 1750, its results a foregone conclusion because, of the nine ministers, one was a Williams (the minister from Hadley to whom Sarah had talked indiscreetly); one was Israel Williams' own pastor, who would vote as Israel told him; another, Ashley of Sunderland, was the brother of Williams' brother-in-law; while the fourth was Robert Breck, out to get revenge for 1735; and the fifth, the moderator, Jonathan Hubbard of Sheffield, hated Edwards as violently as any of them. By a vote of five to four, the Council recommended that the relationship be dissolved. A minority of the Council protested, but when the question was put to the church of Northampton, on June 22, and the moderator expected that the people would vote with reluctance, "to his Surprise, their Arms flew as if they went with Springs;

which plainly shew their former Love to be waxen cold, for they did their Part with a good Will." Thus Northampton and the Valley repudiated Edwards, and Chauncy won. With his large and chargeable family, fit only for study, aged forty-six and physically exhausted, Edwards was thrown onto the world, a major artist and America's foremost philosopher.

All through the ordeal Edwards showed not "the lest Symptoms of displeasure in his Countenance," which only exasperated those who could not rest until he was expelled. But what the effort cost him, deep in his secretive soul, can be estimated. His Scottish correspondents, whom he kept informed and to whom he predicted the result, were shocked, and one of them asked if he could subscribe to the Presbyterian government, and if so, would he consider emigrating to Scotland? Edwards replied that as for Presbyterianism, though it might have defects, it was no problem: "I have long been perfectly out of conceit of our unsettled, independent, confused way of church government in this land." As for removing to Europe, there were practical problems of family and of finances, but otherwise, "my own country is not so dear to me, but that, if there were an evident prospect of being more serviceable to Zion's interests elsewhere, I could forsake it." In this mood, on July 2, 1750, within a week of nineteen years after the defiance of the Boston lecture, Edwards delivered his greatest oration in Northampton, his acknowledgment of failure, the *Farewell Sermon.*

It is the ultimate in his peculiarly cool, scientific objectivity. The "doctrine" is a straightforward assertion that ministers and people will meet before Christ's tribunal on the day of judgment; then—and not in packed councils—will merit be determined. Edwards deployed the "reasons," following the venerable Puritan form, in abstract and logical terms; but they amount to a review of his pastorate, leading to the declaration (Newton and Locke in the background) that there comes a time in the world of cause and effect when no further debate can avail. The people will not be convinced, the minister has no infallible signs for determining the will of God. In this world, such contentions are usually settled by the prevailing interest of a party, but eventually they will be adjudicated by the word of God and by the reason of things. From out the gulf of defeat, Edwards asserted his prerogatives as a messenger of God, and in his "applications" let Northampton have it full in the face: for twenty-three years he had worked among them, "perplexed, but not in despair; cast down, but not destroyed"; now "you have publicly rejected me, and my opportunities cease." But when all stand together before the chief shepherd, to whom Edwards must give an account of his stewardship, they will have to account for their conduct toward him, and then every argument will be stripped of its veil. Every specious pretense shall vanish, hearts shall be turned inside out, the ends they aimed at and the truly governing principles shall appear.

No summary can do justice to Edwards' rolling chant, which is not so much a reproof or an indictment as a somber keening, in which the confidence he had not found within the *Personal Narrative* is now placed where it cannot fail, in the assurance of a final and absolute justice which swallows up all rancor and resentment:

> And then it will appear whether my people have done their duty to their pastor with respect to this matter; whether they have shown a right temper and spirit on this occasion; whether they have done me justice in hearing, attending to and considering what I had to say in evidence of what I believed and taught as part of the counsel of God; whether I have been treated with that impartiality, candor, and regard which the just Judge esteemed due; and whether, in the many steps which have been taken, and the many things that have been said and done in the course of this controversy, righteousness and charity, and Christian decorum have been maintained; or, if otherwise, to how great a degree these things have been violated. Then every step of the conduct of each of us in this affair, from first to last, and the spirit we have exercised in all shall be examined, and manifested, and our own consciences shall speak plain and loud, and each of us shall be convinced,

and the world shall know; and never shall there be any more mistake, misrepresentation, or misapprehension of the affair to eternity.

How his opponents, who flocked to the church on their day of triumph, endured what they heard, passes comprehension. How the Williamses, who professed the *Dies Irae*, compounded with their consciences, remains their secret. At the end of the discourse, Edwards reminded the people that sixteen years ago he preached against Arminianism; the danger then was small compared with the present. "I know the danger." Now there are many young gentlemen of corrupt principles, concealing themselves in fair, specious disguises. Possibly this barb struck young Hawley; perhaps—Edwards would be the first to agree that these matters are bound up with circumstances of a different order—it was that when he chose to marry, Rebekah his mother, who had turned the cheeses while his father died, did not approve his choice and sulked in a separate apartment. At any rate, by August of 1754, Joseph Hawley, whom Edwards described to his Scottish friends in 1750 as "my mother's sister's son, a man of lax principles in religion, . . . very bold in declaiming and disputing his opinions," could no longer live with his conscience, and wrote Edwards a letter, begging, if not for forgiveness, at least for a frank judgment upon his part in the persecution.

I have called Edwards' style, in Broch's phrase, the style of old age. Your letter, he replied to Hawley, obliges me to revolve "that most disagreeable and dreadful scene, the Particulars of which I have long since very much dismiss'd from my mind." He dragged up, as from the bottom of the sea, his certainty that he had come to his own position honestly, that the town had refused to listen to him, that his every move had been represented as policy, and that the insensate people had simply determined that "nothing would quiet 'em till they could see the Town clear of Root & Branch, Name and Remnant." Hawley asked Edwards' judgment on himself, and Edwards gave it to him, remorselessly but remotely, working it all out again as in a dream, forcing himself to it; he could see it no other way but that "That Town & Church lies under great Guilt in the sight of God," but now he had said it, and he begged Hawley not to argue with him. "I have had enough of this Controversy, and desire to have done with it. I have spent enough of the precious Time of my Life in it heretofore."

He could, he said, mention more things, "but I am weary." Edwards is a power in literature and philosophy mainly for the works he produced in the eight years remaining. His dissertations on the will, original sin, true virtue, and on the end of the creation are great works; for a hundred years a school of Yankee theologians lived off them as from their intellectual capital, and only with the collapse of the school which tried to monopolize them are they being restored to their proper place in the main line of American thought. Yet they are tired books, as the *Religious Affections* is not. He did not grow weary of thought; on the contrary, ideas were as vivid at the end as at Wethersfield, but tired in the sense that in human and mortal outcomes he knew the answers. Henry Thoreau said that he traveled much in Concord, but he was an observer from the side-lines; Mark Twain said that after he left the steamboats, he encountered no character he had not already met on the river, yet he contented himself with description. Edwards had seen humanity, and he could define it. Stoddard and Abigail Hutchinson, Chauncy, Whitefield, Col. John Stoddard, Israel Williams, Seth Pomeroy and Timothy Root, Joseph Hawley and then his son Joseph, who pressed upon him the disagreeable task, and "I must leave you to judge for yourself concerning what I say." Boston and the Valley, the animosity of cousins, the studied indifference of Harvard and repudiation by Yale, Jerusha dying for Brainerd, and Sarah rapt in Elysium. Experience, said Locke, is grounded in sensation. Was there any limit to the amount of sensation a man could absorb?

As he was leaving Northampton, letters came telling of revivals in Holland, and he wished, out of a disillusionment that still was not disillusioned, that "they had all the benefit of the late experience of this part of the Church of God, here in America." Momentarily he could imagine retreating to Scotland, into the security of an established (though imperfect) church, out of this unsettled, independent, and confused country; instead, he went in 1751 to Stockbridge—as deep into America as though in 1851 a man had gone, let us say, from Albany to the Dakotas—and he went rich with American experience. "For the temptation to religious people, in such a state of things, to countenance the glaring shining counterparts of religion, without distinguishing them from the reality, what is true and genuine, is so strong, that they are very hardily indeed restrained from it." For a culture that had been transported *en bloc*, that was not yet aware, in terms of cause and effect, of the inviolable connection between environment and inclination, there was every temptation to take the glaring, shining counterpart for the reality.

The beauty and excellency of the world, he reasoned in his notebooks, should not be hidden or kept secret; God has given man a nature "which, if it be under the influence of true virtue, and be not depraved, desires above all things to behold this kind of order and beauty." An exile in the wilderness, realizing that God had been pleased to manifest His power at Northampton through the weakness of Stoddard's successor, Edwards faced the task yet to be done: the expounding of the meaning of desire, true virtue, depravity, and this kind of order and beauty, and how it is beheld. Now full of experience and ripeness of judgment, he must explain to himself, and through himself to America, the final difference between counterfeits and reality. "There are many things," he wrote in 1742, "that make it probable that this work will begin in America." There are some convictions that withstand the analysis of a *Personal Narrative*, that survive the onslaught of an Israel Williams, that sustain a man through both his own and his country's failure.

THE EXTERNAL BIOGRAPHY IV

The tension between Edwards and his church became open controversy in December 1748, when he refused to admit an applicant without a public profession of faith. In February 1749, he communicated his views and arguments to the standing committee of the church. Mary Hulbert then applied for admission, and Edwards drew up for her a form of profession; she became alarmed at the now inflamed public outcry, and would follow Edwards' prescription only if the church would consent. The committee objected; in April Edwards made his offer to resign if the church could honestly say that it was still unconvinced after it had read his forthcoming *An Humble Inquiry;* in August Col. Dwight brought back the copies from the printers in Boston.

The precinct committee then usurped the conduct of the dispute, and in October appointed a standing committee of nineteen (overwhelmingly opponents of Edwards) "to oversee and manage the affair affectually." Edwards took the ground that the church should read the book and allow him the chance to expound it from the pulpit. The precinct replied on November 6 by calling upon the church to summon a Council of the neighboring churches. Edwards countered that the precinct had no constitutional right to initiate such action. On November 27 the committee of the church called for a Council; the church thereupon voted to suspend the administration of the Lord's Supper.

After several stormy meetings, the church voted on December 16, at the end of a session of "long debating and much earnest talk," lasting from two o'clock until after sundown, to call a "Preparatory Council" of the neighboring churches to decide whether a formal Council was in order. Edwards now advanced his demand that if a Council were called, he should be allowed to nominate as delegates two ministers from outside Hampshire Country. The four neighboring ministers met on December 26, and considered a lengthy letter from Edwards justifying his demand. They recommended that the Sacrament be resumed, that Edwards and his people discuss the issue further, but that there be no public proceedings— such as his preaching on the topic. Obviously this body was afraid to face the question and tried to evade responsibility.

Through the first months of 1750 there were carried on negotiations and intrigues of a complexity that defies exposition. The Preparatory Council reconvened in February, and Edwards again addressed the ministers with a masterly demonstration of his right to call in foreign delegates. They again hedged. Edwards thereupon forced the issue: he announced his intention to devote the Thursday lectures to stating his views. The church was packed on these Thursdays, but with persons from other towns; his own people stayed away.

The Northampton church then appealed to the church of Hadley, where a Williams held the pulpit, to provide a minister to refute Edwards. On March 26 the church at last took the fatal plunge by voting to call a Council, but the dispute about Edwards' right to nominate outside members raged unabated. The Council finally convened at Northampton on June 19, consisting of ministers and delegates from nine churches, five of whom were opponents of Edwards. By vote of five to four it recommended on June 22 that an immediate separation between Edwards and the church of Northampton was necessary. Despite the strong protest of the minority, the church acted on this recommendation, and on July 2, 1750, Edwards preached his *Farewell Sermon*.

He remained in Northampton for almost a year, actually preaching several times in his now vacated pulpit. A group of his friends entertained a project of setting up a separate church for him, which threw the town into a new turmoil. A certain John Miller is recorded speaking of Edwards thus: "it would be well if his head was seven feet underground but he thot Six would do his turn and Mr Edwards was Just like his old Cow Lowing after a good mess." When Edwards claimed the rights in the meadow lands formerly used by him, the town refused. He received offers from Canaan, Connecticut, and Lunenburg, Virginia; possibly he received help from his Scottish friends, who were eager that he migrate. In December 1750 he received the invitation from Stockbridge, but felt he should not accept without observing the proper forms, and so requested the advice of a Council. The embittered church, led by Joseph Hawley, drew up scandalous charges against Edwards and those who had proposed the separate church, but abjectly refused to maintain them before the Council. On May 19, 1751, the Council advised Edwards that his duty was clearly to accept the Stockbridge call.

Edwards' eleventh and last child, Pierrepont, was born in April 1750. In June his daughter Sarah was married to Elihu Parsons, and in November his daughter Mary to Timothy Dwight of Northampton. In this year appeared Joseph Bellamy's able exposition of the Edwardsean theology, *True Religion Delineated*, with a preface by Edwards.

He began his work in Stockbridge in the summer of 1751, being installed in August; he returned to gather his family in October, and on the 16th they all definitely left Northampton. In September of 1752 he traveled to New Jersey and preached before the Synod of New York assembled in Newark.

His life at Stockbridge was so deeply involved with his writings—although not in the sense that he made any mention of his circumstances in print—that I have summarized it along with my discussion of the later works. The struggle with Ephraim Williams and Joseph Dwight engrossed most of his time and energy until 1754; the practical demands of the mission and the Hollis boarding school were incessant. The evidence is conclusive that he was a good administrator. He wrote voluminous letters to officials and friends, so that this period is the most completely documented portion of his career. He preached to both the Indian and white congregations, but relied mainly on old notes. His sermons to the

Indians are simplified to the utmost. With the outbreak of the war in 1754 the situation became dangerous, and in addition there was the distraction of having troops quartered upon him. His health was precarious. The letters of his daughter Esther, who married Aaron Burr of Newark in 1752, and who visited her parents in 1756, give a lively picture of a frontier post. The *Freedom of the Will* was published in 1754. The "Miscellanies" for the last years are filled with verbatim extracts from books he was reading, and show a diminishing vitality. The treatise on *Original Sin* was published in 1758.

Aaron Burr, chosen President of the College of New Jersey in 1748, died on September 27, 1757. On the 29th the Board chose Edwards to be the successor. Edwards requested the advice of his neighboring ministers, and they in Council on January 4, 1758, decided that the call was from God. When Edwards heard their decision, he wept; but of course he undertook the duty. He reached Princeton on February 16, was inoculated for the smallpox on the 23rd, and died on March 22. He is buried at Princeton.

But what, quite as much as the inconceivability of absolutely independent variables, persuades modern men of science that their efforts must be predetermined, is the continuity of the latter with other phenomena whose predetermination no one doubts. Decisions with effort merge so gradually into those without it that it is not easy to say where the limit lies. Decisions without effort merge again into ideo-motor, and these into reflex acts; so that the temptation is almost irresistible to throw the formula which covers so many cases over absolutely all. . . . Nor do I see why *for scientific purposes* one need give it up even if indeterminate amounts of effort really do occur. Before their indeterminism, science simply *stops*. She can abstract from it altogether, then; for in the impulses and inhibitions with which the effort has to cope there is already a larger field of uniformity than she can ever practically cultivate. Her prevision will never foretell, even if the effort be completely predestinate, the actual way in which each individual emergency is resolved. Psychology will be Psychology and Science Science, as much as ever (as much and no more) in this world, whether free-will be true in it or not. Science, however, must be constantly reminded that her purposes are not the only purposes, and that the order of uniform causation which she has use for, and is therefore right in postulating, may be enveloped in a wider order, on which she has no claims at all.

William James

The Will

EXPERIENCE in a town already launched upon the American career taught Edwards one memorable fact: in temporal affairs men figure long-term risks. The farmer plows in the spring to reap in the autumn, and lays up in summer for the winter; also, there is that marvel of continuity: "How careful and eagle eyed is the merchant to observe and improve his opportunity to enrich himself!" Men need no sermons to teach this wisdom, only "the experience of their neighbors and forefathers." All this is, of course, agreeable "to what has been cited from Mr. Locke." Sensation is a cause, but it registers on a man, not as collision upon a stone, but as a power that forms his inclination, and once he accumulates a disposition, he reacts to sensations in the manner to which he is predisposed. It was equally explicable according to Locke that farmers and merchants should heap up provision for their children, "though it be quite uncertain, who shall use and enjoy what they lay up, after they have left the world." In all such transactions, a Yankee trader will weigh pleasures against pains, and estimate the difference between a long run and a short, the incidence of opportunity, and the worth of securities.

Now, the eternal things, Edwards contended, are no more obscure or abstruse than the lore of field and shop. Perhaps this eminently Puritan declaration is also a revelation of how much Edwards was the product of an American society; however, what fascinated him was the ambiguity at the heart of the sensational version of humanity. Men work day and night for estates which their children will dissipate, but they are cold, lifeless, and dilatory about their eternal welfare. "How many arguments, and often renewed, and variously and elaborately enforced, do men stand in need of, to convince them of things that are self-evident!" Up to a point, the Lockean psychology readily accounted for their conduct: the farm, the shop, the son are immediate and powerful sensations each day of the year. Pleasure, Edwards said, is a good, coequal with excellency, and arises from what is seen or foreseen. But Locke also insisted, as must every environmentalist, that in the process of seeking its objective good among extrinsic objects, the organism discovers how to discriminate among sensations. If it did not, it would acquire nothing but piecemeal impressions, and would never achieve ideas of space and duration, which contain the units of perception and arrange them in connections and dependencies. The senses in themselves do not err, but intelligence learns that the moon is not really resting on top of the house on the next hill where the eye sees it.

Here then was the problem: there appears to be a limit in time and space beyond which the calculation of pleasures and pains falters. Men will make provision for the security of a loan that rests on so uncertain a foundation "as the life of a neighbor or friend," but when it comes to the self, which is the center of their calculus: "How are they like the horse, that boldly rushes into the battle! How hardly are men convinced by their own frequent and abundant experience, of the unsatisfactory nature of earthly things, and the instability of their own hearts in their good frames and intentions!" In the light of such common experiences, the basic principles of religion are "self-evident"; yet when man is closely studied, he does not behave as the sensational psychology predicts. When the wind blows from the field or counting house, he is sane;

when it blows from eternity, he loses the power of computing. If the natural man were only a register of pleasures and pains, then according to the utilitarian arithmetic, he would proportionately subordinate temporal considerations to the eternal, just as, in daily fact, he subordinates his efforts to plans for his children. What prevents him from an equally distinct perception of this end? "It must be from a dreadful stupidity of mind, occasioning a sottish insensibility of their truth and importance, when manifested by the clearest evidence." The lesson of Northampton (and of the *Personal Narrative*) was that in the center of every sensory being there is a factor which deflects stimuli into action, not according to the determination of the thing, but according to a previously settled disposition of the will. The hinge of the human problem is not the unhuman universe, which is a perfection of automatic balance, centrifugal and centripetal, but the human will.

It would be inaccurate to say that Edwards dissented from the Enlightenment simply by asserting, against the confidence that whatever is, is right, the sinfulness of man. Such a description would characterize Whitefield and Tennent, or what is called in general Pietism. But the Enlightenment was, and remains, a challenge to Christian culture that cannot be summarily disposed of, nor can its successes in physics and analysis be ignored, as the "romantics" attempted. A categorical proclamation of original sin cannot restore either the scholastic universe, which the laws of motion destroyed, or the scholastic faculties, which Locke once and for all identified with organic functions. To retreat into orthodoxy or the authority of a church, or to hold to faith apart from, in despite of, science and psychology, is to reject not rationalism but intelligence. With all his defects and the limitations of his techniques, Edwards is a great modern in his refusal to confess that the eternal world is an utter mystery, by his summoning Christians to realize that "to understand and know which, it chiefly was, that they had understanding given them." The apologist for emotion is no fundamentalist or anti-intellectual, and he could criticize the Enlightenment because he was enlightened. He would not speak of the will except out of full cognizance of psychology and physiology, and he would not merely shout that men are depraved.

Therefore he had to orient his discussion toward a philosophical tendency which had grown, with every show of logic, out of the Lockean doctrine, of which in English thought the two major spokesmen were the third Earl of Shaftesbury and the Scottish moralist, Francis Hutcheson. He had particularly to take stock of them because he himself had anticipated their position in his "Notes on the Mind," deducing it, as did they, from Locke. He may have read Shaftesbury's *Characteristics* before he wrote the "Notes," but he had certainly worked out the thought before he encountered Hutcheson's *An Inquiry into the Original of Our Ideas of Beauty and Virtue*, published in 1725, and *An Essay on the Nature and Conduct of the Passions and Affections* of 1728. These works had an immense vogue among rationalizing Dissenters, and their influence was pervasive throughout the century. They are the form in which Edwards confronted most directly the fundamental tenet of the Age of Reason, so that in his effort to utilize and correct Hutcheson, Edwards struggled not only with Hutcheson, but with that of which Hutcheson was the spokesman. This argument called for the closest examination because, being nearest to the truth, it most subtly perverted the truth, and the duty lay with peculiar weight upon Edwards since in his notes on "Excellency" he had worked out an almost identical system, and had been preaching it for years. When the *Religious Affections* offered as the second sign of a genuine emotion that it be grounded upon the nature of divine things as they are in themselves, with no conceived relation to self-interest, he was putting into simple language the result of both his own thinking and his rethinking of the most formidable tendency in contemporaneous moral speculation.

Things, said Locke, are in themselves morally neuter. They are good or evil only in relation to our pleasure or pain. That which hurts a man, a stone or a bullet, is innocent. All values are inward. Edwards found in Hutcheson a clear statement of the starting point they shared, which to Edwards was the point from which all modern thought, after the destruction of scholasticism, must perforce begin: beauty cannot be understood as a "Quality suppos'd to be in the Object, which should of itself be beautiful, without relation to any Mind which perceives it: For Beauty, like other Names of sensible Ideas, properly denotes the Perception of some Mind." Edwards, again in the solitude of the "Notes," had already seized upon the identical clue: to define the good and the beautiful he must analyze the contents of the perception, discover its structure, its anatomy. There is no difficulty, within the calculation of pleasure, in defining the good of a dinner or a piece of property. But scatter a few dots or lines on a paper: there is no "good" to be found in them; then group them into symmetrical patterns or designs, and immediately the mind recognizes a pleasure which is not gain, but a disinterested joy in the "equality" of the arrangement. The dots or lines, like stones in an arch or sounds in a melody, remain what they were, but the mind is so constructed that along with perceiving what is useful for nutrition or shelter, it perceives things in systems of order, in time and space, in proportion and law. The mind beholds and is pleased with beauty no less because it has itself bestowed that beauty upon things which in themselves are neither beautiful nor ugly.

Above all, in the perception of beauty no new "faculty" is added to the physiological mechanism. Nothing more is required than what materialism must grant: "the organs are so contrived that, upon the touch of such and such particles, there shall be a regular and harmonious motion of the animal spirits." But this perception has come, not as the idea of heat from the flame or of redness from the sun, but as an idea which is not any one of the things, not the stones or the sounds, but their organization into rhythm. The self-seeking animal, hunting for pleasure, fleeing from pain, beholds beauty as a by-product of the process, and in the contemplation of this utterly nonutilitarian glory, discovers a greater pleasure than in any "use." "Of these consist the beautiful shape of flowers, the beauty of the body of man, and of the bodies of other animals." By the same token, the mind is unhappy in the presence of disproportion, although objects may or may not lie scattered about the universe in haphazard arrangements.

Edwards' break with the past was here complete, with the technologia that placed intelligible arguments in the things God had wrought; he was also prepared to dissent in advance from the Emersonian form of transcendentalism that would maintain a correspondence between nature and the mind, that would seek the good and the beautiful in sunsets and woodchucks. Again, I believe, his thought is peculiarly interesting today, but his problem was how to explain the insight to colonial New England. Beauty gives the highest pleasure the mind can know, but it is not a photographic reproduction of the external order. As Locke had taught him, Edwards set himself to sift out the contents of the concept—to understand and to know what constitutes the beauty of the beautiful. The answer, he reasoned, is that in a beautiful pattern there is a "consent" of one thing to another, of stone to arch, of note to melody. And the locus of the consent is in the mind of the artist; he contributes it by perceiving *as though* objects and sounds and colors were willing to enter into harmony with others, *as though* each were willing to be where it is. Therefore, what gives the pleasure is a "sense" that the proportioned work comes from a conscious intention, from a self-conscious volition. In the final analysis, beauty is the recognition of a will. There is no need to ask if stones have an inherent disposition to fall into arches or notes into songs, so long as, out of experience with them, the architect, the musician, the beholder can come through sensation to the idea of created harmony. By such mutual respect, the notes "carry

with them, into the mind of him that sees or hears, the conception of an understanding and will exerting itself in these
appearances." Were we not led by reflection to the extrinsic
intelligence of the composer, "it would seem to be in the
notes and strokes themselves"; they would "appear like a society of so many perceiving beings, sweetly agreeing together." Through all the years, after the first public hint of
1731, Edwards expounded little by little his conception of excellency, but he had from the first formulated the universal
definition toward which he strove to lead New England:
"*The Consent of Being to Being, or Being's Consent to Entity.*" A firm rule of aesthetics and of morality followed:
"The more the Consent is, and the more extensive, the greater
is the Excellency."

The fascinations of this discovery for Edwards were numerous, in some of which we may share. It gave him, as the
crown of his thought, a conception of beauty that was not
a priori or transcendental, but which arose out of concrete
experience, without being dependent on the chance beauties
of nature. It particularized a moment of insight which includes and justifies the system of pleasures and pains. It showed
that since the idea of the beautiful arises not from any one
thing alone—because a single thing, one note, one stone, one
person, obviously cannot become excellent by itself—but from
a society, then the beautiful is something that the universe as-
pires toward, but which, being finite, cannot achieve beauty
out of itself. Particles can consent to being this or that individual particle, and call upon God as the ultimate beholder to
give them significance by perceiving them. Nature itself, analyzed as the content of perception, discloses an anatomy of
beauty which requires for completion something beyond nature, without which there is no method, no science, no society.
Natural things and natural events (which would thus include
history) are "images" or "shadows" of a divine thing, a divine
event, and their meaning resides in that of which they are the
image or the shadow. Nature requires grace, not as a super-

natural invasion or correction, but as an aesthetic fulfillment. The mind does not come to perception of beauty by enlarging the canvas, by extending the range from one structure to another, hearing more and more music; it comes to the point, within itself, where no more additions make for beauty, but only the leap from finite instances, single or several, to the one idea.

"Only," Kierkegaard was to say, "only when reflection comes to a halt can a beginning be made, and reflection can be halted only by something else, and this something else is quite different from the logical, being a resolution of the will." The logic, leading to the resolution of the will, can thereafter be discarded. Edwards, much more than Kierkegaard, was restricted by the language of his century, the language of scientific rationalism, but nevertheless he broke through this restraint to a psychological perception that anticipates Kierkegaard, to that of "the beginning without presuppositions." The logic of the *Freedom of the Will*, interpreted from within and not from without, is a demonstration of the emptiness of presuppositions; Arminianism was a conceited presupposition to facilitate a comfortable and facile beginning. Just as in the search for the atom, Edwards found that by dividing and subdividing a particle, the mind gets no closer to a termination, and so is obliged to jump to the concept of an indivisibility regardless of size, so he came triumphantly to the sight of a single system of mutually consenting entities as the adequate idea of a universe, and found that upon the beholding, it is lovely.

To say that bodies or sounds consent, Edwards agreed, is to borrow a term from consciousness. But the ordering of bodies into intelligible sequences bespeaks a consent somewhere, either in the artist or in the beholder, or in both; therefore, to move into the realm of conscious beings, the concept of consent becomes the mold of both society and theology. "There is no other proper consent but that of *Minds*, even of their Will; which, when it is of Minds towards Minds, it is

Love, and when of Minds towards other things, it is *Choice.*"
Wherefore it could be worked out, step by step, that from
rudimentary sensations, from the first dawning of a disinterested pleasure which overtakes the self in the midst of his pursuit of the objective good among extrinsic objects, he approaches a vision of what must be, of what is, excellency. He
finds all virtue "resolved into *Love to Being.*" Virtue is an
act of will, but an act of will follows and is determined by a
perception, and the perception of virtue is love, love to the
totality of being. The love of self can be extended indefinitely
(just as the particle can be indefinitely subdivided), from the
self to family, to town, to nation, and still not become the perception of love, not until the mind leaps from all specific loves
to a love of all being. Out of selfishness arises a disinterested
benevolence that adores the order in which the self is one
without reference to that self's particular pleasures—or pains.

Thus, by faithfully restricting himself to the limits Locke
imposed, and seeking the principle of the good not in the
ocean of being but in the mind, Edwards found a rule of
beauty that is at the same time the rule of virtue, and that both
for loveliness and for righteousness is resolved into a single interior motion, a consent to serve in the total scheme of things
where and how, in the system of objective causes, the self
would be obliged to serve in any event, whether or not he
gave consent. But the moment of beauty and virtue depends,
not on what he is called to do or predestined to do, but upon
the consent, upon an act of will, which follows upon the
depth of the perception.

When Edwards turned to Hutcheson, he found a logic that
followed his own, almost to the end. Denying that the idea of
beauty or of the moral good is anything *a priori* or innate,
Hutcheson also found it in a sensational analysis of the mind,
defined it as an all-inclusive love of proportion and harmony
for their own sake, and made it simultaneously the law of
aesthetics and of ethics. But the difference between his con-

clusion and Edwards' was immense. From the argument that we perceive a beauty in the actions of others even though they are unrelated to our own advantage, and that we always apply this principle in judging whether actions are good or bad, Hutcheson posited the existence within each man of a "moral sense" guided solely by "disinterested benevolence." He established the existence of this sense by arguing, out of Locke, that the mind is obliged to receive the impressions given it, and since it receives moral impressions within the frame of a concept of benevolence, the moral sense must exist. Therefore he gained what he and the Enlightenment most wanted, a method of refuting Hobbes and Mandeville and the Christian tradition, of denying that self-love is the only motive for natural human action. But the method had even greater charms: the conception of the moral sense as an inherent power rendered unnecessary (Hutcheson offered the conventional gestures toward Christianity, but Edwards could see how perfunctory they were) any supernatural interposition, because the natural principle operates automatically. All evil thus becomes a derangement of the mechanism, produced by faulty education, bad diet, a particularly strong temptation, or accident. Since virtue appeals to men by an inherent loveliness, all men will be virtuous—unless something prevents them. And even these breakdowns of the machinery can be accounted for as partial evils incidental to the universal good. No further ground of accounting is needed than that "our Reason may be very deficient in its office, by giving us partial Representations of the Tendency of Actions." The remedy would be obvious: education in benevolence.

The system of Shaftesbury and Hutcheson has been called smug. It certainly contains in essence the eighteenth-century confidence that the laws of nature demonstrate this to be the best of all possible worlds, and that lapses from perfection can be righted by natural correctives. If, as Hutcheson contends, variety of judgment, including error, is not irregularity in the moral sense, but only the result of wrong opinions, the ills of the world and of society can be cured by the rectification of opinion. When obliged to define the standard of correct opinion, Hutcheson answered, not with a vision of entity's consenting to being, but with a formula that was destined to lead an active life in the next two hundred years: "that Action is best, which procures the greatest Happiness for the greatest Numbers; and that, the worst, which in like manner, occasions Misery." As Leslie Stephen put it, God enters this theology not as a judge but as a skilful contriver of an harmonious system. Yet, if Hutcheson's argument appears a little too pat for modern taste, it is worth noting that the criticism is frequently leveled by those who no less than he expect to cure evil by such natural implements as education and sanitation.

The interest of Edwards' interpretation, on the other hand, is that he, while taking stock of everything in Hutcheson, and affirming no less that whatever is, is right, also could further discover in the workings of a perfect universe a principle of absolute, ineradicable evil. It was, he could say as early as the "Notes," self-love, or what today would more readily be called egotism. It is evil not because it mars in the slightest the perfection of the best of all possible worlds, but evil in the inward sense, where it is a want of beauty. It is, in fact, not love at all, it is "merely an inclination to pleasure, and averseness to pain." It is life as lived solely for the objective good, on only the one level instead of on both levels, without the perception of both the objective and the inherent. Devils and damned creatures love themselves, not for any good they see in themselves, but because they have an aversion to the disagreeable. But in nature, what is agreeable to the self is simply agreeable, and what is disagreeable is just the disagreeable, and this is exactly what "mere Entity supposes." Self-love, in short, is evil, yet it is no affection, "but only the Entity of the thing, or his being what he is." As Edwards declared in the *Religious Affections*, take away this insight, and God Himself, with all the created universe, is an infinite evil. Which is to say that the will of man must do what nature calls for;

there can be no evil in the scientific order, but evil exists, and its hiding place is the will of man.

When he found time, in the thick of the Northampton crisis, to edit the papers of Jerusha's lover, and to bring out in 1749 *An Account of the Life Of the late Reverend Mr. David Brainerd*, he treated Brainerd as another case history, giving a minimum of biographical detail and interpreting him as a rebuke both to enthusiasts and to Arminians. He made Brainerd a text for the definition of true piety, emphasizing the key word: his love of God "was primarily and principally for the supreme excellency of his own nature, and not built on a preconceived notion that God loved him"; Brainerd's joy was in views "he had of divine things without himself," not within himself. Arminians, who place all their religion in morality, cannot bring one instance of Arminianism's working such a moral transformation as was wrought in Brainerd. Edwards edited the journals with skill and affection, and the volume is a minor masterpiece of psychological confession; at the end, Edwards thanked Providence that Brainerd "should be cast hither, to my house, in his last sickness, and should die here," but deeply though he was involved with his friend and protégé, he presented him analytically, as representative rather than as an individual, as a vindication of "this one grand principle, on which depends the whole difference between Calvinists and Arminians," which is simply the discovery of the beauty of God "as supremely excellent in itself."

Edwards never knew a man who came closer to excellency than Col. John Stoddard: "Perhaps never was there a man that appeared in New England to whom the denomination of *a great man* did more properly belong." In pursuit of the objective good, "he was probably one of the ablest politicians that ever New England bred," but also he manifested his consent to a society of perceiving beings by caring for the country "as a father of a family of children, not neglecting men's lives and making light of their blood; but with great diligence, vigilance and prudence, applying himself continually to the proper means of our safety and welfare." In the literary tradition of New England, the funeral oration or the biographical memoir was a sort of Puritan equivalent of the Plutarchian character-study, the portrait of a generalized type, suitably improved into an abstract moral, rather than the presentation of a particular individual; when the Puritan tradition broke apart into contending armies, the faction that followed Chauncy and Mayhew wrote eulogies with an increasing emphasis upon what novelists call characterization. But Edwards, always the artist within an established form, remained on the heights of Homeric generalization, and his creations, whether Phebe Bartlet or Col. Stoddard, are not so much representations of the subject as expressions of an ethos.

So when he said of Stoddard, "he had a far greater knowledge than any other person in the land, of the several nations of Indians in these northern parts of America, their tempers, manners, and the proper way of treating them," he was formulating a principle for his frontier society. And when he spoke of "nations," no one missed that he meant the Six Nations, the Iroquois, upon whose choice of allegiance hung the outcome in the struggle between Britain and France. Yet in his threnody Edwards did not descend, as might a less archaic bard, to the particular project that had been closest to Stoddard's heart, the mission to the Indians at Stockbridge. As chief architect of this enterprise, Stoddard neatly combined consent to being in general with a shrewd calculation of policy. On the one hand, the aim was to bring Christianity and civilization to the remnant of the Houssatunnuck Indians, but on the other it was to educate them in the ways of peace, which might be worth as much to the border as a whole regiment of militia. And furthermore, there was a chance to set before the Iroquois such an example of the white men's benevolence to the red as would persuade them to trust the good will of the English, which would be worth twenty regiments.

The mission was organized at Stoddard's house in 1734,

with Edwards present. The undertakers had the good fortune to find in a Yale tutor, John Sergeant, who had studied with Edwards, a devotee of disinterested benevolence, who accepted the dual call as missionary to the Indians and pastor to the tiny congregation of whites. Money was contributed from both Boston and London by the Society for the Propagation of the Gospel, and Benjamin Colman worked upon Thomas Hollis to obtain funds for a school for boys. Formal and solemn covenants were entered into—Edwards' rebellion against the covenant theology did not lessen the Puritan awe of a covenantal commitment—by which the English bound themselves to respect Indian land-titles. Edwards was always a party to these negotiations. The whole colony deemed the project of such strategic importance that Sergeant's consecration was turned into an elaborate ceremony when the Governor and Council came to Deerfield for a consultation with the Iroquois—who looked on suspiciously—and Nathaniel Appleton traveled all the way from Cambridge to preach the ordination sermon.

In 1737, the Williamses, so it seems, persuaded Col. Stoddard that a few whites were needed to strengthen the settlement; that judicious patrician let Israel select one of his uncles, Ephraim, who with his son Ephraim and his daughter Abigail settled on the Stockbridge hill overlooking the Indian town. In 1739 Abigail married Sergeant, and bore him two children; in 1749 Sergeant died. Of all the Williamses, Ephraim is much the most unsavory, and of him it is perhaps enough to say, in Edwardsean terms, that he was moved exclusively by self-love, if we understand Edwards' point that love of family is an extension by calculation of love for the self.

For some months after the *Farewell Sermon*, Edwards meditated his future. The move to Scotland was not practically or emotionally feasible, and no settled town would dare invite him. Northampton, finding to its surprise that it now had no minister, hired him Sabbath by Sabbath, at £10 the day, so that the *Farewell Sermon* was not technically his last. The small band of his friends held a consultation, and the rumor got about that they intended to set up a separate church, whereupon there was again "great violence of feeling," and apparently (though the town records on this point are defective, possibly on purpose) the precinct voted that Edwards was never again to be heard in Northampton. He delivered his last sermon on October 13, 1751; three days later he moved, with his family, to Stockbridge, to take up Sergeant's mission to the Indians and the pastorate of the little church that Ephraim Williams had dominated for fourteen years.

Ephraim did not want Edwards. A clear light is thrown upon what was at stake, on both sides, by a letter that Ephraim, Jr., wrote to Ashley of Deerfield (who, married to a sister of Israel and Solomon, was one of Edwards' dedicated opponents). Edwards, wrote this youth, is not "sociable"; he is a "very great Bigot" who will admit none to heaven except in his own way, "a Doctrine deeply tingd with that of the Romish church"; young Ephraim tried to read Edwards' book on the Northampton controversy, but could not understand it, as neither could "almost every gentleman in the country," and he doubted that Edwards understood it himself. However, he concluded, the decision has been made, so let Edwards come: "Not that I think he will ever do so much more good than an other, but on account of raising the price of my land."

For five years Edwards fought his last battle, which was the ultimate, but the bitterest, in his long struggle with the Williamses. He nominated one Joseph Dwight to be deputy for the Boston Commissioners; the widow Abigail (she was reputed an attractive woman) married him, and he went over wholesale to the enemy. Elisha Williams in London got himself appointed to the governing board of the Society for the Propagation of the Gospel. The simplest way to describe what the Williamses were attempting in Stockbridge is to resort to non-Edwardsean language: they were grafters and land-grab-bers. Edwards fought with no weapon but his pen and his courage, and he fought them to a standstill. Had he been merely a misguided idealist crying for justice to a collection of mangy Indians, he might be pitiable, but he expended him-self, as ought to have been obvious to any but an infatuated lot of speculators, in order to hold the Mohawks in line, some of whom had been lured into the settlement, and thus to spare the frontier a repetition of such massacres as that of fifty years ago at Deerfield, where now Israel's brother-in-law received the intelligence that Edwards was a bigot. The calamities of his family, he patiently wrote, were as nothing compared with "the much greater Calamities to the important affair of the In-struction of the Six Nations," though indeed "we suffer not a little by them."

Edwards finally won the Stockbridge fight by default, be-cause the French and Indian War distracted the Williamses. The younger Ephraim was killed in battle (leaving the legacy that named a college), and Abigail, who was no heroine, fled the frontier. Edwards stayed, although Israel wrote to him that if the Stockbridge Indians took up arms, "Farewell peace & prosperity to New England, yea to North America"—an ironic note, indeed, considering how much his clan had done to exacerbate the savages. Edwards' daughter, Esther Burr, on a visit to her family, wanted to run as had Abigail, but her father would hear no word of it; so, Esther concluded, "if the Indians get me, they get me, that is all I can say," and though he taught her to be willing to die in any way God pleases, she had to confess, such is the hold of love for self among even the daughters of a saint, "I am not willing to be butchered by a barbarous enemy nor can't make myself willing." In 1754 troops were quartered on the town, and Edwards submitted a bill for the 800 meals and seven gallons of rum that Sarah pro-vided them. Under such conditions, Edwards put the finishing touches to, and published in Boston, *A careful and strict En-*

quiry *Into The modern prevailing Notions of that Freedom of Will, Which is supposed to be essential to Moral Agency, Virtue and Vice, Reward and Punishment, Praise and Blame.* The germ of the treatise lay in the "Notes on the Mind," and was stated again and again in the various works; the journals show that he worked over the argument for thirty years. Beyond all peradventure, the *Freedom of the Will* is the cornerstone of Edwards' fame; it is his most sustained intellectual achievement, the most powerful piece of sheer forensic argumentation in American literature. It became the Bible of the New England theology, and is considered by logicians one of the few proofs in which the conclusion follows inescapably and infallibly from the premises. But it is not so rich or human a book as the *Religious Affections*, nor is it the great writing that are parts of the three tracts yet to come. Actually, most of it is sterile to our reading, because it is devoted to pulverizing a few hapless Arminians like Whitby, Turnbull, and Chubb. The problem of determinism is, I take it, not yet solved, but today few hold indeterminism in so crude a fashion as did Edwards' opponents, and his book seems like a battleship wasting broadsides on a flimsy target. It is a debater's triumph, and taken by itself—apart from his entire system—it is the least valuable of his major productions, or at any rate the least valuable for American literature. It was not written, as were the others, to be an integral part of the "Rational Account," but for a prologue, to clear the ground for the construction of his monument. Its principal interest for the student either of Edwards or of modern thought is not the lengthy demolition of feeble arguments, but the opening sections, wherein, forced to clarify his terms, Edwards made explicit the meanings of many words he had used as oracular symbols ever since the Boston lecture. It would burden this study to retrace the extensive dialectic, but the book has a deeper significance: its confirmation of motifs we have watched taking shape under the pressure of history. In relation to the works of the revival period, the *Freedom of the Will* is a coda, while the later books are the opening of a new and magnificent, though abruptly truncated, slow movement.

"It is the man that does the action; it is the agent that has power, or is able to do," said Locke. The eighteenth century, if I may generalize dangerously, started with this unitary conception of man, but aside from a few notables, it ignobly surrendered to a new scheme of the faculties, and once more departmentalized the psyche. Edwards stood rigorously faithful to Locke's original discovery that faculties are modes of motion. Perhaps Edwards was obliged to make his break with scholasticism the cleaner because, his society having so complacently accepted it, he had to reject it either entirely or not at all. When Edwards wanted to make fun of Chubb—too easy an enterprise for his powers—he said that there is nothing more unintelligible than Chubb's notion of the will choosing its motive "in all the writings of Duns Scotus, or Thomas Aquinas." He knew little of Scotus or Aquinas at first hand, but he could make out enough to know whereof he spoke. When he contended with Chauncy, he was fighting not only the rationalism of the Enlightenment, but that rationalism grafted onto the Aristotelian and Thomistic strain which had been transplanted to New England in the form of the first settlers' technologia. Calvin himself was the source of the difficulty: though he warned Protestantism against linking theology to psychological theories, since these "will involve us in their obscurity rather than assist us," still, because he had no other terminology, he riveted Calvinism to the medieval doctrine of the faculties. His entire theory of the enslavement of the sinful will was erected upon his notion of the will as that "whose place it is to choose those things which the understanding and reason propose to it," and Puritan New England was his pupil. There is no better epitome of the scholastic position than Calvin's: the office of the will is "to choose and follow what the understanding shall have pronounced to be good; to abhor and avoid what it shall have condemned." The essential point of the distinction is the temporal sequence: the will must wait until the reason "shall have pronounced."

Edwards said that it does nothing of the sort, as all experience shows. Those who argue thus have an ulterior motive, which two centuries of Protestant rationalization had now made clear. Calvin had no choice but to describe the fall of Adam as the rebellion of Adam's will against his reason; by 1700 or 1750 Protestants had worked it out that therefore the image of God can be restored, or at least rehabilitated, by training the will to heed the reason. They would still say that grace was necessary, or at least helpful, but words, as the sensational analysis shows, may be used long after the idea has become "dim and transient, and exceedingly confused, and indistinct." Thus Protestantism was rushing headlong into ethical meliorism.

Behind this development lay a still more fatal error. Calvin declared that when the will is without grace it is "necessarily" sinful. He might, in his day, have understood that it sins because it is sinful, but by conceiving of the will as a faculty, Calvin left Calvinists of the eighteenth century to deduce that it is sinful only because the machinery of the soul is out of joint, because the reason misinforms it or the senses seduce it. In his pristine state, Adam had the faculties all in order—and so, according to this doctrine, he was originally independent of nature; no matter what impressions he received from objects, his will stood at attention until his reason came to a conclusion. At the root of Calvin's conception there is—carried down from the Middle Ages—a belief that man acts outside the field of cause and effect, that he is a self-originating power. Though by sin he has become enmeshed in nature, by grace he can escape from it. The regenerate will comes back into obedience to reason, and man can act, at least ideally, upon his sovereign decisions, let the laws of motion and the dance of atoms be what they may. But Edwards placed the illumination which makes all things glorious—the perception of excellency—inside the frame of nature, and denied to any man, regenerate or sinful, "a self-determining power in the will." Thus he strove to emancipate Protestantism from the winding-sheet of the Middle Ages, although many who call themselves Protestants, in his day and in ours, cling to the shreds of that garment.

In the Arminianism of his day Edwards saw what follows upon the separation of reason and will: as the sense of sin grew indistinct, and as the scientific reason grew more distinct, Protestants began to insist that if the reason be properly informed, and if adequate persuasions be offered the will, sin can be overcome by argument. Arminianism always took its stand upon the common-sense proposition that if men are predestined, they cannot be persuaded. Whitby spoke for the lot:

> To say God seriously requires them who are not elected to make their Calling and Election sure, is what we call a Bull. To say God seriously invites, exhorts, and requires all Men to work out their Salvation, and yet by his Decree of Reprobation hath rendered that Even to the most of them impossible . . . is to make the Gospel of Christ a Mockery.

Edwards could see, if Chauncy could not, that Whitby's argument was entirely sound as long as the reason and the will are conceived as separate agents, as long as the will waits outside the council-chamber of speculation. But neither Chauncy nor Whitby could detect the arrogance concealed in their humanitarianism: they said by implication that the sin of man actually upsets or throws out of line the order God established in creation (wherefore whatever is, is demonstrably *not* right!), and they said by an even clearer implication, which in our day has swelled to a chorus, that a man of trained intelligence can command his own will, and that while he is making up his mind, God stands helplessly by, hoping that the decision will be good.

The core of the *Freedom of the Will* is the assertion of the unitary and functional nature of the organism. If the will is that by which the mind chooses, it is not a faculty or a talent or a knack, but it is the man choosing: "the very willing is the doing; when once he has willed, the thing is performed." It is not some power of volition that breaks a covenant with the Indians, it is Ephraim Williams. Edwards added that he would say little on this head, "Mr. Locke having set the same forth, with so great clearness, in his *Essay on the Human Understanding*," but even Locke was not too clear: he could imagine that the willing man might choose against his desire, but Edwards said that the unity is complete. Desire is the will, and the will is the emotions. The connection of stimulus to reaction is not arrested while the reason takes stock, but "such an alteration instantaneously follows." This does not mean that logical proofs are to be despised—far from it; but it does mean that rational arguments prevail only as do objects or as does the spectacle of the universe, by being perceived. They have weight when they appear to be what is most agreeable. The mistake of all rationalists, of whatever variety, is their defective view of the total human situation. The dictate of reason is, indubitably, "one thing that is put into the scales"; when it concurs with "other things," its weight is added to them, but if—as at Northampton or Stockbridge—it is a weight in the opposite scale, then "the act of the Will is determined in opposition to it." What constitutes perception—Edwards' whole system revolves constantly around this pivot—is not the import of the object, for the object is without significance, but the object as seen, the manner of the view, and the state of the mind that views.

His opponents said, as would many today, that by merging together "an appearing most agreeable or pleasing to the mind, and the mind's preferring and choosing," he conceived man as a puppet pulled by the wires of sensation, with the internal manner of perceiving become a mechanism to which the wires are attached. In one sense, the criticism is just, because on the plane of the objective good Edwards presents man as just such a contrivance. Yet the criticism is blind, because Edwards contends that man lives also for the inherent good. Hence man makes a true and revealing choice; the instantaneous motion of love or hate is according to "something that is extant in the view or apprehension of the understanding, or perceiving faculty." Again Edwards used the word "faculty" because he had no other, but he meant it in "a large sense"—not as reason or judgment, but "as including the whole faculty of perception or apprehension," as the entire man perceiving. Responsibility for conduct belongs to the intelligence, because "nothing is in the mind, or reaches it, or takes any hold of it, any otherwise than as it is perceived or thought of." And how a thing is perceived, while it depends somewhat on the health of the organs, is for each man not a day-to-day affair, but a long accumulation of experience, out of which is formed his inclination to perceive in such and such a manner. A person disposed to perceive the melody running through the tones will perceive it; to another they are noises, and without the illumination they remain noises. By such a disposition, Edwards' first thesis runs, every man is determined and predestined, let him pretend what he may.

A nineteenth-century biographer, a Unitarian, pronounced sentence upon Edwards: "The illusion under which Edwards labors is in looking at man as part of nature, instead of as a personal being, who rising above Nature, has in himself the power of new beginnings." Most criticism of Edwards, from his day to ours, comes down, in one form or another, to this objection; it is unperceptive because it assumes to be illusion exactly what Edwards reports as fact. Even his followers in the nineteenth century, even Lyman Beecher to whom Unitarianism was as fire in his bones, were so filled with the optimism of the age that they never appreciated Edwards' radical naturalism. In 1752 Edwards remarked concerning the "liberals" of his day, the forerunners of those who for two centuries have told our civilization that man rises outside of nature, that their opinions "are commonly attended, not only with a haughty contempt, but an inward malignant bitterness of heart, towards all the zealous professors and defenders of the contrary spiritual principles." These gentlemen, he noted, are advocates of freedom of thought, but they easily become persecutors "under some good cloak."

In the American tradition, Edwards is the most formidable defiance yet leveled against the liberal spirit, against the cult of progress that starts with a denial of man's kinship with nature and claims to elevate him above the workings of cause and effect. Therefore, the second thesis of the *Freedom of the Will* is that just as the will follows perception's view of things rather than things themselves, so the will lies within the tissue of nature, and is "caused" by something outside itself. Choice "arises from nature, as truly as other events." Man transmits stimulus into effect, in accordance with "that established law and order of things." He is in the chain of events, and he cannot interrupt it; his motion is not, and can never be, "entirely distinct from nature," nor ever be set in opposition to it. He is guilty of spiritual pride (and an ignorance of physics) when he pretends anything else.

Edwards, we must remember, did not take "cause" in the positivistic sense of that which determines the effect, but rather as that which is necessarily and aesthetically antecedent. So he said that the will is caused by the motive which, at the moment of action, lies strongest in the view of the mind, that the view is caused by the prevailing inclination. A man does what he does, not by becoming every moment a new beginning, but "necessarily," by an inevitable sequence of connections, in which the will is a link. Here he had to explain his distinction, already expounded in the sermons, between natural and moral necessity, a distinction which he took from Locke but developed along with his deepening insight into the difference between, and the coincidence of, the objective and the inherent. Natural necessity is physical, as it is necessary that one walk around and not through a wall; moral necessity is the "habits and dispositions of the heart." It is an inclination or want of one (Ephraim had no inclination to treat the Indians fairly). It is as absolute a necessity as the physical, at least to those skilled in the knowledge of causes: "That is, the effect may be as perfectly connected with its moral cause, as a natural necessary effect is with its natural cause." I think it not quite a vulgarization of Edwards to summarize his position thus: you are free to do what you can do, but you are not free to do what you won't do. You are prevented by walls or by congenital idiocy, but you are free to be righteous: "There are faculties of mind, and capacity of nature, and every thing else sufficient, but a disposition: nothing is wanting but a will." He had the authority of Locke behind him, that no man can be any freer than to be able to do what he wills; what higher notion can Arminians and rationalists conceive?

They insist, of course, that they have a higher, the notion of a power that chooses differently in given cases, some kind of self-motion. They can buy and sell, become politicians, and drive Edwards out of his pulpit. As Edwards saw them, these men "aim at they know not what, fighting for something they have no conception of," and they substitute confused words for things and thoughts. "They may be challenged to explain what they would have: they never can answer the challenge." Edwards most infuriated the liberal by placing upon him a responsibility, entirely within the order of causes, not for overcoming obstacles nor for constructing churches and factories, but for being the kind of person he is. A person is one who looks upon the heavens and earth in his kind of way. "An evil thing's being from a man, or from something antecedent in him, is not essential to the original notion we have of blameworthiness; but it is its being the choice of the heart." As Edwards says, this is a hard challenge.

Edwards further exasperated his opponents, as well as modern critics, by pushing to the limit a technique of disputation he also borrowed from Locke. Since concepts are mental, Locke contended, the test of knowledge is not factual verification, but the inner consistency within a pattern of ideas; refutation of a proposition then becomes a demonstration that it does not hang together. Edwards mastered the method in the "Notes on the Mind"; the only foundation of error "is inadequateness and imperfection of ideas," for if the ideas are perfect, their relations will be perfectly perceived. The greater part of the *Freedom of the Will* is a remorseless dissection of imperfection in the notions of a breed of spiders called Arminians. He scored most heavily with a reduction of the Arminian proposition of the free, self-determining power of the will into intrinsic nonsense: if the will determines its own acts, there must always be a will before the act; each act must be preceded by an act of will, and that by another, and so on, *ad infinitum*, until we come to the theoretical first act; if this is determined by a still previous decision of will, we take up the march again, but if we call a halt, and say *this* act is first, we have an act that flows from no volition, which is just simply an initial fact, an arbitrarily given, which cannot be the selection of a free will. In the life of the universe or in the lives of particular men, Arminians must reach back into time until they get to an imposition, to an uncaused fiat with which their freedom, if it exists, must commence. "If the first act in the train, determining and fixing the rest, be not free, none of them all can be free."

No believer in free-will ever was disabused by logic. Dr. Johnson said that all theory is against it, all experience for it. Edwards conspicuously appealed to experience in his apologies for the revival, yet now he appeared especially irritating because he seemed satisfied with dialectics. When, for instance, he came to the stock Arminian charge that Calvinism makes God the author of sin, he contented himself by proving that free-will gets no further from this disturbing reflection than does predestination: it is "a difficulty wherein the Arminians share with us." Edwards seems through most of this book to be altogether happy with Dr. Holmes's characterization of it: that logic is logic is all he says.

However, the strength of the book is not the logic it says, but the inner principle that sustains it. The surface play of dialectic is supported by a deeper and hidden flow of energy. Explicit as Edwards now became in defining his terms, the open tactic of debate was only a more subtle mask, except to those in the secret, for the spiritual strategy. Yet he scattered clues in abundance; he was never more courageous than in declaring, after his demonstration that the Arminians no more than the Calvinists could exonerate God from the charge of creating evil, that if by God be meant "a disposer of the state of events, in such a manner, . . . that sin, if it be permitted or not hindered, will most certainly and infallibly follow: . . . I do not deny that God is the author of sin." He had already said, in the *Religious Affections*, that unless that is seen without which nothing is seen, God is an infinite evil. The Arminians, by robbing man of an inner principle of continuity, by telling him he can do as he pleases, that he can pick and choose for himself among objects and ideas and motives, were in fact so enslaving him to the domination of objects that they destroyed the very freedom they vaunted. "It is not to leave the Will to its own self-determination, but to bring it into subjection to the power of something extrinsic, which operates upon it, sways and determines it, previous to its own determination." To impose upon man the unswerving rule of an automatic principle of freedom is, as with Hutcheson's moral sense, to subject him to a worse tyranny than the Calvinistic God. Sustained by his inward vision of the inviolable sequence of things, by his assurance that throughout the universe, and into the utmost fastnesses of the Godhead, cause perpetually reigns, Edwards turned the tables on the liberals, and declared that they and not he reduced men to automata, under the fatal illusion of becoming self-willing individuals.

I have said, perhaps too often, that our age is better prepared to comprehend Edwards than was his own. Thus Eric Fromm, for instance, wrote in 1941:

> The illusion helps the individual to remain unaware of his insecurity, but this is all the help such an illusion can give. Basically the self of the individual is weakened so that he feels powerless and extremely insecure. He lives in a world to which he has lost genuine relatedness and in which everybody and

everything has become instrumentalized, where he has become a part of the machine that his hands have built. He thinks, feels, and wills what he believes he is supposed to think, feel, and will; in this very process he loses his self upon which all genuine security of a free individual must be built.

What seems in the *Freedom of the Will* to be a methodological legerdemain, the demonstration of the logical inconsistencies of the Arminian position, is an oblique assertion of the inherent dignity both of God and of man. The secret was stored up in the "Notes on the Mind," but the substance of his first as of his last utterance was that truth is a consistent supposition of relations among ideas, not because truth is separable from the empirical test, but because only by a consistency of ideas can the mind participate in order and law. Jumbled and muddled systems, with their *ad hominem* arguments that without uncaused freedom no man will listen to reason, are false because they violate the order of nature. Edwards prophesied, in the language of his day, that they are bound to lead eventually to what Fromm has called "escape from freedom."

Arminianism was an insult to God because it set Him "to mend and patch up, as well as he could, his system, which originally was all very good, and perfectly beautiful; but was marred, broken and confounded by the free Will of angels and men." It secured the freedom of man only by supposing that the divine will is carried hither and thither at random. In order to remove the compulsion of moral necessity from the will of man, to leave merchants free to charge what the traffic will bear, it told of a supreme glory, dear to the hearts of river gods, that consists in being "left to senseless, unmeaning contingence." But when an age becomes insensible of the honor of the universal principle, it will sacrifice that honor to the enhancement of man, or of some men, by showering upon them the illusion that they know what they want and that their wills determine themselves; it will end by debasing them lower than any theory of original sin ever called for. Mankind have conceived of liberty as of some dignity or privilege worth claiming; the man who held his course through both the Awakening and the expulsion from North-ampton knew what is worth claiming. On whatever stage, at the head of a nation or of a town, a man learns this much, or he learns nothing. Edwards found what it meant:

> But what dignity or privilege is there, in being given up to such a wild contingence as this, to be perfectly and constantly liable to act unintelligently and unreasonably, and as much without the guidance of understanding, as if we had none, or were as destitute of perception, as the smoke that is driven by wind!

There are arresting parallels between the minds of Edwards and of Pascal, not only because Pascal too was a better physi-cist than his contemporaries, but that he, precisely because of that fact, could write: "A cipher has a double meaning, one clear, and one in which it is said that the meaning is hidden." The *Freedom of the Will* is an immense cipher. Intellectually, the hidden meaning is "Excellency." The necessity Edwards pled for is not the certainty that a stone or a bomb will fall at high noon tomorrow, but the necessity of "the full and fixed connection between the things signified by the subject and predicate of a proposition, which affirms something to be true." If, as Edwards contended, the laws of motion and gravitation, "laid down by Sir Isaac Newton," hold univer-sally (the case is not altered when further laws are laid down by Albert Einstein), then not an atom exists in the material universe but causes every part to be otherwise than would be "if it were not for that particular corporeal existence." The effect may be for the moment, or for a long time, insensible, "yet it may, in length of time, become great and important." Edwards lived at the moment when the new world, that which is now grown, shall we say, to years of discretion, was deliv-ered into the arms of the old. Because he denounced the lib-erals who were destined to preside over the formative years of the new society, because he wore a wig which the democratic virtue of Timothy Root refused to worship, he is rated a conservative and a reactionary. Had he attempted to arrest the course of history, as did Cooper, Sewall, Foxcroft, and the metropolitan revivalists, only by thundering old dogmas in the path of change, the estimate would be correct. But Edwards took into his mind and into his heart the fundamental insight of the new world. The hidden meaning of the *Freedom of the Will* is not only the great vision of Excellency which the youth confided to his "Notes"; it is also a consequence of his testing of that vision in the field of an emerging, competitive America. He was not cut off from society, as conventional history declares. He did not need graphs, charts, and statistics to be a sociologist; he did not accumulate a mass of detail in order to describe, but he seized upon details so close to the heart of the matter that they do not have to be checked against documents. From that vantage point he could gauge the difference between the short-term and the long-term, and work his way out of terms to the definition of a society of full consent as the only possible goal of a modern universe. But consent, to be worth anything, must be universal and disinterested; it must be, in the full meaning of the word, gracious.

The *Freedom of the Will* is an arraignment of all partial and half-hearted forms of consent, of cheap substitutes, of false shows of benevolence. Read as a cipher, as all Edwards writings must be, it is a penetrating analysis of modern culture, and specifically of the American variant. Which is to say that the writing of it posed for Edwards still more urgently the problem that the Awakening first thrust upon him, the problem of history, and most importunately, the problem of America's rôle in the sequence of things throughout time, which is what men call history.

Though the question of realism and nominalism has its roots in the technicalities of logic, its branches reach about our life. The question whether the *genus homo* has any existence except as individuals, is the question whether there is anything of any more dignity, worth, and importance than individual happiness, individual aspirations, and individual life. Whether men really have anything in common, so that the community is to be considered as an end in itself, and if so, what the relative value of the two factors is, is the most fundamental practical question in regard to every public institution the constitution of which we have it in our power to influence.

CHARLES SANDERS PEIRCE

Sin

IN AUGUST of 1752, Edwards charged, in one of his periodic reports to the Speaker of the General Court, that events were forming into such a shape "as tends to establish a dominion of the Williams family over the affairs of Stockbridge"—a tribe, he added (unaware that in this opinion he and Chauncy were agreed), who "by their natural disposition, . . . are sufficiently apt to engross all power, profit, and honour to themselves." His old tutor, now known as "Col. Williams," just back from London, paid a visit, and was "abundantly resorted to by his friends to Stockbridge," but not, one gathers, by Jonathan Edwards. When Edwards presented a petition for the purchase of a parsonage, Ephraim went to work on the committee "with his Lime-juice Punch & Wine"; Edwards could give them only facts, and so lost the petition. Ultimately, however, facts proved more powerful than punch, but they prevailed more slowly. By the time he finally discredited the Williamses, the Mohawks had decamped, alienated by the familiar English perfidy, and Col. Stoddard's diplomatic project was ruined. Edwards kept up the mission to the Houssatunnucks as long as possible, delivering them little lectures against "getting too much Drink," and when the mission dwindled he continued pastor at what was left of the church. Suffering "Feaver and Ague, having a severe fit almost every day," he filled up pages of notebooks, though the entries now begin to show a tired man, with whole sections literally copied from books he was reading. Amid constant fears of Indian raids, he put together segments of the journals, desperately constructing, if not the whole "Rational Account," at least coherent sketches. By May of 1757 he had one portion ready, and in 1758 published in Boston *The Great Christian Doctrine of Original Sin defended; Evidences of it's Truth produced, And Arguments to the Contrary answered.*

The tactics of the free and catholic faction in coping with the *Freedom of the Will* soon became standardized. They condemned the book on two accounts: it was too "metaphysical," and by establishing a theoretical necessity of sin, it destroyed the sinfulness of sin. Therefore it was "unfavorable to the cause of truth and piety." Chauncy Whittelsey (who endures for posterity because Edwards transfixed him with Brainerd's *mot* that he had as much piety as a chair) protested in 1768 to Stiles against teaching the book in the Yale curriculum, lest Deism, if not atheism, ensue: by Edwards' reckoning "Dr. Watts is the Arminian, and Mr. Lock the Calvinist." By this late date, the liberal spirit had appropriated Locke, and proclaimed at every opportunity that Edwards' use of him was abuse. Ultimately, in 1841, William Ellery Channing would sum up the development by fixing upon Edwards responsibility for compelling the inward revolt against Calvinism to become the open one of Unitarianism; happily, however, his argument never proved his pernicious case: "It is a demonstration which no man believes, which the whole consciousness contradicts." The liberals answered Edwards mainly by asserting that while logic may be logic, men do not live by logic alone, or even at all.

Though Edwards did not live to confront the matured Unitarian argument, he was preternaturally gifted in detecting trends. A few hints sufficed, and consequently, by an artistry that was wholly conscious, the *Original Sin* is a complete methodological contrast to the *Freedom of the Will*. Instead of a dialectical demonstration out of given premises, or a destruction of opponents with a logical and semantic *reductio ad absurdum*, it is a strictly empirical investigation, an induction, in the manner of Boyle and Newton, of a law for phenomena. This time the Arminian position is refuted as an inadequate hypothesis to account, scientifically or historically, for the facts, either because it does not take cognizance of all of them, or because it does not explain those it recognizes. "As I study brevity," he advertised, "and lest any should cry out, *Metaphysics*, as the manner of some is, when any argument is handled against any tenet they are fond of," he proposed to argue, not from the "nature of things," but from what "is plainly demonstrated by what has been shown to be *fact*." If the liberals took the line that consciousness instinctively abhors the metaphysics of the *Freedom of the Will*, Edwards would now demonstrate that their precious consciousness was a timorous evasion of reality. The two books are complementary, but for a variety of reasons—because the intellectual pyrotechnics of the *Freedom of the Will* fascinate even those they repel, because the subject has a wider appeal, but mainly because the liberals concentrated their fire on it and deliberately ignored the sequel—Edwards' philosophy is generally represented as comprised entirely in the one work which was merely prolegomenon to a majestic drama, of which *Original Sin* provided the plot.

By either book, by both logic and induction, we come to Edwards' basic prerequisite to all experience: the course of nature, as infallibly shown "by late improvements in philosophy," is an inviolable sequence of events. All Christians profess an "immediate agency" of God, but they may no longer vulgarly invoke it as a miracle, as a break in the coherence. Even when bringing the soul of a child to birth, God works "as much according to an *established* order, as his immediate agency in any of the works of nature whatsoever." If any should object to the word "nature"—liberals were certain to charge that he degraded the spiritual into the natural—let them, unless they wished to reveal how little they understood Newton, call it "a *constitution* or *established order* of successive events"; the result would be the same. Whether we discuss the will or the sin of man, we have no choice, let the liberals wail as they may, but to commence with "an established method and order of events, settled and limited by divine wisdom."

Now then, to discover a law within the established method, we must go about it as Newton studied the law of such hit-or-miss phenomena as tides or comets: we must resolve surface eccentricities into a regularity that accounts for them all. We get nowhere by generalizing from a single event or a random collection. We must seek "some stated prevalence or preponderation in the nature or state of causes or occasions, that is followed *by* and so proves to be effectual *to*, a stated prevalence or commonness of any particular kind of effect" —some matter of record, like the laws of motion and gravitation. A law of nature is "something in the permanent state of things, concerned in bringing a certain sort of event to pass, which is a foundation for the constancy, or strongly prevailing probability of such an event."

In a word, an empirically verified law is a "tendency." An effect argues a cause, and a steady effect argues a steady cause. It proves, not by logic but by evidence, that there is "a prevailing exposedness or liableness in the state of things, to what comes steadily to pass." We obtain our idea of such a tendency "no other way than by observation." And the subject of our investigation must be the events—all the events. "How ridiculous would he make himself, who would earnestly dispute against any tendency in the state of things to cold in the winter, or heat in the summer; or should stand to it, that although it often happened that water quenched fire, yet there was no tendency in it to such an effect." Edwards was so far ahead of his contemporaries in comprehending scientific method—ahead even, as I compare them, of Professor Winthrop of Harvard College, who observed certain reticences

—that he was handicapped in debating against minds of lesser compass, with the ironic result that he comes down to the generations as one opposed to scientific progress.

These principles established, Edwards sprang his scientific trap. Study the expanse of human nature, in society and in history; examine it objectively, and plot its tendency, as Newton plotted the orbit of a comet. Take the over-all result, not the occasional variant. Not even common sense will induce a fixed inclination from a single action: "We see that it is in fact agreeable to the reason of all mankind, to argue fixed principles, tempers, and prevailing inclinations, from repeated and continued actions, though the actions are voluntary, and performed of choice; and thus to judge of the tempers and inclinations of persons, ages, sexes, tribes and nations." Or take, if you will, the principle so celebrated by Hutcheson and all rationalists, "evidently agreeable to the nature of things, and the voice of human sense and reason," that the actions of men are dictated, not by sagacious calculation of advantage, but by a disposition to pursue "from instinct" the happiness of the agent. Then, having amassed all the evidence, ask what tendency is manifested. Go to the past, to the recorded facts of experience, and enquire what must be the prevailing cause, what alone will account for the totality of the phenomena?

In the liberals of New England's Enlightenment, in Chauncy, Gay, and Johnny Barnard, Edwards recognized the prophets of what Howells finally called the smiling aspects of American life. He invited them to a reading of history, a realistic report of village gossip, and a frank inspection of the police blotter. He left each to judge for himself—he was always the Protestant!—"from his own opportunities and information concerning mankind," as to how far disinterested love to God, "this pure divine affection," rules the world. He was confident out of his own opportunity and information of the inescapable conclusion that mankind are naturally in such a state as leads to their destruction. Applying to moral as well as to natural philosophy what his enemies vaunted as "the experimental method of reasoning," he could extract only one inference, "that the natural state of the mind of man, is attended with a propensity of nature, which is prevalent and effectual, to such an issue; and that therefore their nature is corrupt and depraved with a moral depravity, that amounts to and implies their utter undoing." Edwards invited an America just become aware of vast resources awaiting exploitation, already commencing to utilize the scientific order of things not as a lesson in humility but for the happiness of the agents, to a consideration of certain facts and laws of nature demonstrable not only in science but more especially in history.

On the whole, for almost two hundred years, Americans exercised their right of judging from their own information, and even more from their opportunities, by deciding against Edwards. Until relatively recently, and even today in most quarters, the American creed is optimistic, centered upon Channing's high estimate of human nature, and vindicated by a geometrical increase of wealth and comfort. Dr. Holmes spoke for more than Boston Unitarianism when he called Edwards' teaching an old-world barbarism that would have been unthinkable had he "breathed the air of freedom" a hundred years later. Artists who shared the historic Christian insight into what hitherto was called sin had a hard time in America. Hawthorne won an audience for his romances, but none for his theology; Melville's cry that an inscrutable malice sinews the White Whale was not heeded; and Mark Twain's recognitions were concealed by indirections.

Edwards, it is true, did have followers in the dynasty of New England theologians, who continued his war with liberal theology, but petrified his philosophy into dogma, reduced his revivalism to a technique for mass manipulation, and then destroyed the architecture of his thought by splintering it into factions and schools. By this process, Edwards was lost to the American tradition; the belief that he was an anachronism, a retrograde leader of a rear-guard action against science, became a premise of America's opinion about its past. Even in the twentieth century, when the smiling aspects largely ceased to smile, and Hawthorne, Melville, and Mark Twain were re-evaluated, Edwards remained identified with what Dr. Holmes called "the nebulous realm of Asiatic legend," and therefore could not be supposed of value for critical realism. Edwards was thus relegated, through failure of comprehension, even further into an unusable past.

Yet a distinctive mark of the contemporary crisis has been a rediscovery of history—not only of the reality of the crimes and terrors of the past, made convincing by those of the present, but still more of the applicability of the world's experience to America. Conflicts, anxieties, and cruelties, which in the air of freedom were supposed the lot of other men and nations but never of the United States, now appear as much the heritage of Americans as of Europeans. Faith in democracy can no longer be maintained by ignorance of the recurrent lessons of history. The remarkable device of Edwards' *Original Sin* is precisely its appeal, "according to such rules and methods of reasoning, as are universally made use of, and never denied, or doubted to be good and sure, in experimental philosophy," to the facts and experience of all the ages. Brutes are destructive to each other, but have not mankind, he asked, been a thousand times as hurtful as any of them, "yea, as all the noxious beasts, birds, fishes, and reptiles in the earth, air, and water, put together, at least of all kinds of animals that are visible?" Edwards called upon America not to submit to time-worn dogma, but to surrender its pretensions to exceptionalism, to acknowledge its share in the propensity of the race, and to confess from the evidence "that wickedness is agreeable to the nature of mankind in its present state."

The evidence, then, was clear. If for a thousand years men cultivate a piece of ground that produces only a thicket of briars and thorns, they must conclude that the product is agreeable to the nature of the soil. But a study of history shows that circumstances have been so infinitely various—good, evil, and indifferent—that had they been the only determinants, effects would have been equally various; yet an unvarying result has always followed. Again, the answer must be that when things work through the human perception, the effect is determined not by the things but by the manner of the perception. Events thus demonstrate "that the fixed cause is internal," and their uniform tendency bespeaks "the greatness of the internal cause, or the powerfulness of the propensity." Empirical or statistical tabulation confirms the lesson of logical or psychological analysis: the persistence of evil is an effect, of which the prevailing disposition of the human will is the adequate cause.

Edwards' conception of history, at least in this work, suffers from the limitation which, in post-Darwinian eyes, vitiates most eighteenth-century history, a static interpretation. Even thus limited, he made certain vigorous comments upon the rationalism of 1750 that are no less pertinent to later forms of evolutionary progressivism. The Arminians, for example, explained evil as that which must exist in order that virtue may have something to strive against, to which Edwards replied that history is "a prevailing, continual and generally effectual tendency, not to men's victory, . . . but to the victory of evil appetites and lusts over men." Even supposing a trial is ordained, the question to be put to history (and to historians) is, wherefore so unfailing a "failure"?

Edwards achieved even more trenchant asperities when he came to the Arminians' treatment of death: they could not deny that it came into the world as a punishment, but in their effort to prove all things right and God benevolent, they maintained that in the cosmic economy even death is a good, because it emphasizes the vanity of earthly things and excites sober meditations. Edwards replied to this palliation with some of his finest pages, calling it a cheapening of death. How really depraved men must be, he wrote in the satirical vein he could frequently employ, if even after God has given them life and prosperity, they must remain under this terrible rod, or else run wild! Even though God has expelled the race from

Eden to labor and sorrow in the world, and then imposed the utmost penalty, they still cannot conquer their passions! No wonder Adam and Eve, having a nature like ours, but without the fear of death to wean them from the world, succumbed to the first temptation! And the authors of this muddled thinking dared accuse Edwards of making God the author of sin! Edwards' scorn is charged with the old and abiding Puritan conviction that whatever the theoretical justice, death itself is terrible. Arminians debase it into "only a medicine; it is preventing physic, and one of the greatest benefits." Yet they say Christ redeemed us from death, which is to say, by their reasoning, from a thing agreeable to divine goodness! The upshot of the Arminians' inability to distinguish between the objective and the inherent is that they seek for the good in an objective evil, and so are left without pity or dignity in the presence of the most agonizing of New England's trials, the mortality of infants. Edwards' realism is firmly planted upon an indomitable knowledge that pain is pain, and he would not degrade mankind by pretending that for the living death is not evil.

John Taylor's *The Scripture Doctrine of Original Sin* reached America in the midst of the Awakening, and made, as Edwards put it, a noise, because it published the glad tidings, as though they had long been suppressed, that "what is natural to us, as the Passions of Hunger and Thirst, or the Frailty of our Bodies, we can by no means help or hinder," and that therefore nothing done under such compulsion can be sin. So (Edwards' opponents drew interminably upon this passage) what divines call a moral inability is only a natural deficiency, and therefore not blamable. As for what unassisted nature can do—here Taylor spoke for his century—though God provides the wool and the trees, "human Wisdom and Sedulity work *this* into Garments, and *those* into Ships and Houses." This left one clear deduction: if children grow up undisciplined, it is "the Fault of careless, ungodly Parents, not of that Nature which God in much Goodness hath given."

One may understand why Edwards, who devoted pages of the *Original Sin* to Taylor, was growing weary. He had insisted upon nothing more clearly, in his emphatic preaching of the objective good, than that the order of nature cannot be corrupted: the stomach must be filled, the child begotten, the bullet fired. The last thing he ever meant was that the sinful disposition is implanted in the foetus in the womb. The leader of pioneers in the Connecticut Valley knew infinitely more about what sedulity can do with wool and trees than a gentle Nonconformist in Norwich. But, he repeated, bring the intellect to bear upon the machinations of sedulity, and trace them into infinity, as merely the workings of "the common natural principles of self-love, natural appetite, &c.," without any government of higher principles—without the leap into excellency—and they will fully account for the historical performance of mankind. They will also show that no matter what the inventions and improvements, these "will certainly be followed with the corruption, yea, the total corruption of the heart." Taylor and the liberals saw nothing in human activity but a calculus of pain and pleasure, and so the future like the past was to them a continuum of appetites and passions, an interminable projection of man's "love to his own liberty, honor, and pleasure." They destroyed all inwardness of life, and condemned the race to a destiny that would be like its past, a tedious chronicle of wickedness.

At this point Edwards amplified his distinction between the objective and the inherent into a definition of Adam's original righteousness which, though he may privately have formulated it earlier, he had hitherto kept under cover—a theory which strangely reproduces, out of the forests of Stockbridge, a teaching that Thomas Aquinas centuries before had systematized. The holy image of God, according to the Angelic Doctor, was a gift over and above nature, which was withdrawn at the fall, leaving man possessed of simple "natura." Or, as Edwards phrased it, when man sinned, the superior principles were removed from his heart, as light ceases in a room when the candle is withdrawn; and so the regulations of self-love and natural appetite ("which were in man in innocence"), being left to themselves, "*of course* became reigning principles; having no superior principles to regulate or control them, they became absolute masters of the heart." Taylor attempted to construct a coherent policy out of this mere remnant of nature, and took it for an adequate description of a divine order. Hence he said that bereft nature is inherently good, and he accounted for all its defects and tribulations as mismanaged policy, whether by faulty information, accidents, or careless parents. Understanding nothing of the inward life, the liberals drew up a diagram of the perfect universe, and saw no reason why man should not respond in diagrammatic perfection to every stimulus if only he were properly educated, had careful parents, and were trained to think in terms of the greatest good of the greatest number.

It would be an ironic comment on Edwards should it turn out that his distinction between the objective good and the inherent was merely a private restatement of the scholastic distinction between the natural and the supernatural. It may be that a persistence of this doctrine from the schoolmen through Puritan technologia gave him the idea. Yet in an enigmatic footnote Edwards endeavored to explain his use of terms, saying that by "natural" he did not mean what was created first as opposed to what was introduced afterwards, but rather what belongs to "that nature which man has, merely as man," as against those things "above this" by which man is truly virtuous, holy, and spiritual, things not essential to the natural man on the level of pain and pleasure. If, he said, I use these words "in an uncommon sense, it is not from any affectation of singularity, but for want of other terms more aptly to express my meaning." He was, indeed, using "natural" and "supernatural" in a sense wholly new to the federal theology; still, the footnote must be read in the light of his then unrevealed meditation on excellency: the superior principle, without which man remains man but is predestined to the treadmill of history, in Edwards' thinking is not a "principle" at all, but an insight, a perception of harmony and consent, a subjective vision of full disinterestedness, the new simple idea that forms the vision. That it is a "supernatural" gift distinguishing saints from natural men, Edwards said again and again, but always he insisted that it is composed of nothing but what nature supplies. For the want of this internal conception, history is a chronicle of selfishness and violence, yet the objective goods—the bread, the house, the child, the property—remain unalterably good. Human nature is human nature still, as Taylor blandly announced, but order, peace, and beautiful harmony are gone, because there is lacking that sense of the heart of which Arminians proved themselves totally ignorant by their effort to locate virtue in the weaving of woolens and the construction of ships. One may follow Edwards with perfect sympathy in his contempt for Taylor, and note his assertion that superior principles are supernatural, but also note that he calls them supernatural only "in some sense." The student is never wholly convinced that Edwards' conception of a supernatural arising out of sensation is what traditional Christianity conceived as the divine. His *Original Sin* is a powerful indictment of utilitarian liberalism and of the profit-motive, but it is delivered in the name of what seems rather a glorified naturalism than an eternal transcendence. Thus, I more than suspect, the book leads us to the very secret of Jonathan Edwards.

However, no matter how the misfortune that fell upon mankind in the wake of Adam's transgression be defined— whether as a corruption of nature (which Taylor said it must be if it is anything) or as healthy and natural self-love (as Edwards strove in vain to make liberals comprehend it)— there remained an objection which, from the time of Pelagius, the rational mind of Europe, in its manifold incarnations, persistently offers against the central mystery of Christianity: "it is not being just to charge Adam's sin to his posterity." Why should I suffer for another's misdoing? Taylor's book achieved its vogue in New England mainly because it posed anew the perennial question: "How Mankind, who were perfectly innocent of Adam's Sin, could for that Sin, and upon no other Account, be *justly* brought under God's Displeasure and Curse, we cannot understand." Nor can we judge it anything but monstrously "unjust."

In Edwards' tradition there existed two methods of defending what theologians called the "imputation" of Adam's guilt to his posterity; the one went back to Augustine and was taught by Calvin, the other was the peculiar invention and delight of New England Congregationalism. Augustine's reply was that Adam's sin is somehow transmitted in the bloodstream, a sort of inherited virus of concupiscence. But the founders, just men and students of the English common law, were uncomfortable with that solution, and so propounded, out of the federal theology, what seemed to them a thoroughly just arrangement: Adam stood as the legally appointed representative for the race, and God entered into a contract with him, agreeing that as he should merit, so his constituents would be treated. When he fell, his guilt was imputed to his heirs as a liability on the human estate. For the seventeenth century this forensic conception was entirely satisfying, and on it the social order of New England was erected.

Now, with the importation of Taylor's book, New England found both the traditional and the federal doctrines riddled. Taylor neatly disposed of the older theory: "If we are wicked, it must be our own Fault, and cannot proceed from any Constraint, or Necessity in our Constitution." No man can justly be damned for "a Taint, Tincture, or Infection" that alters his faculties independently of himself. Though throughout the centuries this argument was advanced times without number, in the enlightened climate of the eighteenth century it struck with a fresh cogency that Edwards would have been the last to deny. In a *Supplement* Taylor turned his attention to the federal version, and exploded it. "A Representative, the Guilt of whose Conduct shall be imputed to us, and whose Sins shall corrupt and debauch our Nature, is one of the greatest Absurdities in all the System of *Corrupt Religion*." Taylor precipitated a crisis in the Puritan mind because he frankly announced what cultivated Puritans had long suspected, none being more convinced than Edwards, that in a Newtonian universe the federal notion of imputation was absurd. Taylor, by invoking formulae out of Locke's treatise on government, revealed the real impetus for the Arminian theology: it is utterly unreasonable for any man, "without my Knowledge or Consent," so to represent me that I become guilty of his transgression. Such sentences made an irresistible appeal to stalwart citizens of the commonwealth, and I believe historians have not sufficiently appreciated the extent to which Arminian doctrine was a seed-bed for 1776. Any talk, Taylor concluded, of a corrupt tendency in human nature is a slight upon God's handiwork, and "neither can any corrupt my Nature, or make me wicked, *but I myself.*"

Edwards' *Original Sin* declares on the contrary that an observable propensity extending over the ages cannot adequately be explained as a discontinuous series of private decisions. Here exactly is the issue between his mind and the liberal. If all the decisions go in one direction—that is, "without the interposition of divine grace"—if the machinery of pain and pleasure invariably, left to itself, augments the misery and vice of humanity, there must be some deeper law at work than each individual's resolution to make himself wicked. To define the adequate scientific axiom, Edwards again reached back to Locke (and to his own "Notes on the Mind") to propose his most original and brilliant conception: in the realm of the mind, all humanity, like the atom, is a single concept. Thus God, working as always according to established laws, "has in a constant succession communicated to it many of the same qualities and most important properties, as if it were *one.*" The only hypothesis capable of matching the array of historical evidence, Edwards wrote in the most profound moment of his philosophy, is the unity of the race. The investigator of depravity, the dissector of spiders, found in the depths of sin the basis for a new definition of the brotherhood of man that merged all men into one conception, that discomfited the prosperous and the proud, the merchants and the river gods, by telling them that in the nature of things God treats them all as one, along with Negroes and Houssatunnucks.

John Locke is one of those dangerous men who set in motion forces beyond their reckoning. In order to clear the mind of scholastic rubbish, he classified one type of our complex ideas as ideas of relation, aiming only to show that whatever the mind conceives as a pattern of relations is a sufficient description of how things stand toward each other. At Molyneux's suggestion, he added to the second edition a chapter on identity, to employ the same technique for proving that identity is an idea, not an essence, a substantial form, or a unity of substance. If all the atoms in a man's body were changed overnight, and he still thought of himself as the same person, his identity would endure. "In this consists *identity*, when the ideas it is attributed to vary not at all from what they were that moment wherein we consider their former existence, and to which we compare the present." A plant that has "one common life" is one coherent body, no matter what branches are lopped off.

The young Edwards pounced upon this concept as one of the most liberating in the *Essay*, and immediately deduced from it the further consideration—which Locke would have distasted—that if identity is an idea, it is a natural necessity, "arising from a Law of nature which God hath fixed." If identity is a perception, through which countless atoms may flow without altering the focus, then identity is an act of God, sustained from moment to moment at His pleasure, for as long as God thinks of that unit as one. Even this early, Edwards grasped that there must be a connection between the theory of identity and the continuity of sin: "What is the positive cause of corruption?" he asked himself. For thirty years he matured the reflection, constantly reworking it in the journals, and at last brought it forth as a definitive answer to history. Even if, he guardedly put it, we do not quite allow that personal identity consists wholly "in that which Mr. Locke places it in, i.e., *same consciousness*," still this is an essential. Clearly the communication or continuance of an identical consciousness through successive durations "depends wholly on a divine establishment," is an "arbitrary constitution of the Creator." Hence, because on the evidence of "plain fact" men are sinful, Taylor's notion that each particular entity makes himself sinful by a disparate act of choice is patently "a false hypothesis." "For it appears, that a *divine constitution* is the thing which *makes truth*, in affairs of this nature." By being one in idea, mankind are one in being. The plant has one common life, no matter how many branches are cut away, because in any sector of the created system it is an establishment that makes for the unity. Sin is the apostasy of all mankind by virtue of the full consent of all their hearts; it is theirs, not because God assigns it to them, "but is *truly* and properly *theirs*, and on that *ground*, God imputes it to them."

Edwards realized that he was again employing what his enemies would sneer at as "metaphysics," but he felt that the undeniable "fact" of the dependence of things upon a sovereign constitution would convince persons "of common modesty and sobriety" of the justice of God in deriving the guilt of Adam to posterity. To our reading, the conclusion at which he aimed, the "justice" of God, may be of less moment than the great thesis he propounded along the way, the conception of a divine constitution as the cause of a sustained identity. The body of the moon cannot be the effect of its existence in the previous moment; the settled course of nature must be, as Newton divined but was afraid to say, a continual and immediate efficiency of God, according to the constitution established. Things would drop into nothingness upon the ceasing of the present moment were there no new exertion of power to cause the next pulsation. God's maintenance of continuity "is altogether equivalent to an *immediate production out of nothing,* at each moment." The structure of the race, like the organization of the atom and of the void itself, depends upon a predetermined resolution that one thing shall remain one, even though, as with the tree a century old, not a single particle of its original substance abides. By this "metaphysic" an individual is responsible for a crime he committed forty years ago, and on the same account, on this sufficient account, the race is responsible for a crime forty centuries past.

Nowhere is Edwards' confinement by a "want of other terms more aptly to express my meaning" more tragically exemplified than in these compacted pages. He had no equipment for generalizing his insight beyond Locke's rudimentary notion of identity; yet somehow he managed to say it, compelling language to serve his turn. We must remember that as he wrote these words, he was isolated in Stockbridge, he was a discredited leader of American society. He could remark only in passing that the divine constitution concerning the method of men's coming into being naturally unites them, "naturally leading them to a close union in society, and manifold intercourse, and mutual dependence." He had no better way of saying, seventy years before Hegel, that society is organic, and so fell back upon the language of the Bible, "all made of one blood," though he could add that therefore all are "to be united and blended in society, and to partake together in the natural and common goods and evils of this lower world."

The social problem was always for Edwards a lesser problem, a concern of the lower world, but as for what should follow in the lower as a result of determinations in the higher, he was altogether clear; the rising of the river gods against his rule in Northampton did not seem to him an exercise of democracy. Chauncy and Mayhew, not to mention Franklin, who outlived him, finally devoted the new nation to the principle that society is a contract for given and specified purposes, designated by the contracting parties. This was their reading of Locke. But Locke, recklessly exploring all things out of the liberal insouciance, hit upon more truths concerning mankind than he put into his treatise on government. Edwards was a reminder, although in 1776 a disregarded one, that if Locke's analysis of the mind was as valid as his theory of society, there exists a singleness of conception in which men must find themselves involved, a coherence more fundamental than the formal terms of a Declaration of Independence, more pervasive than the legalistic guarantees of the Constitution. To enlightened individualists, rejection of the concept of original sin was a way of asserting, along with Taylor, "a Spur to our Diligence," but to Edwards, retention of belief in the historic Christian doctrine, bulwarked by the testimony of history, was a profession that we must bear the shame for things done, not only by ourselves, but by others with whom we are nearly concerned.

These are none of them roughly sketched drafts, but fair copies of unfinished scores, the completion of which was prevented by outward circumstances. Again we meet with confirmation of the fact that Mozart never began to write until his composition was in all essential points completed in his own mind. When only a few bars are written they offer a perfected melody, a motif only requiring its further development. When the sketches are longer, they form a well-rounded, continuous whole, that is evidently interrupted, not because the continuation is not ready to hand, but because some chance has prevented its further transcription. It may be plainly discerned also that not only are detached ideas put into shape, but the different characteristic traits of execution are indicated in the usual way, so that the chief effects and capabilities of these motifs may be clearly inferred.

OTTO JAHN

The Uncompleted Summa

IN THE SPRING of 1755, after a winter of fever, Edwards commenced work upon two manuscripts which, his journals reveal, were culminations of private meditations. Presumably he worked on them for the remaining three years of his life, but still considered them unfinished. His editor, probably Hopkins, published them in 1765 as *Two Dissertations*. *The Nature of True Virtue* and *Concerning the End for which God created the World* were intended to be digested into the "Rational Account," but each is, as the editor remarked, "concisely sketch'd out"; they are, he further noted, designed for the learned and inquisitive, and "something above the level of common readers." These fragments are Edwards at his very greatest. The man for whom such studies as weary ordinary minds were "a natural play of genius" here let his mind play freely and spontaneously. He was prevented from completing the monumental system, but the heart of it is in these two extracts, albeit in miniature.

The Nature of True Virtue is Edwards' only purely non-polemical work; its perfection of form shows what he could have done with pure thought had he not for all his life been obliged to sacrifice himself to controversy. It takes Shaftesbury's and Hutcheson's definition of that by which, in the optimistic mechanism, the moral sense is supposed to judge:

the rule of disinterested benevolence; and analyzes the internal structure of the idea. It is Edwards' supreme application of the method he learned at the beginning: "Truth consists in having perfect and adequate ideas of things." If we had perfect ideas, the "Notes on the Mind" predicted, we would need no ratiocination, because we should have all things in one view; we reason only "in consequence of the paucity of our ideas." To no other reflection do the journals come back more frequently: "Seeing the perfect idea of a thing, is, to all intents and purposes, the same as seeing the thing. . . . Now, by seeing a perfect idea, so far as we see it, we have it." The distinction which he declared the most important of all distinctions, between the speculative and the sensible, is here vindicated, for the book is not a reasoning about virtue but a beholding it. "All was easy to him," said his editor, adding significantly that ideas were as clear to him as "many things in the works of Newton and Locke," which appear difficult, were clear and bright to those illustrious authors. He looks hard upon a conception until it yields up meaning beyond meaning, and the simulacra fall away. The book approaches, as nearly as any creation in our literature, a naked idea.

Edwards' conclusion is that what Hutcheson and the rationalists conceive as a natural possession of all mankind, the criterion of disinterested benevolence, is actually only a compounding of pleasure as against pain, nothing more than an extension of the principle of uniformity through wider and wider variety, a long-term instead of a short-term calculus, which nature can achieve unassisted by adding more and more to a column of figures. But true virtue, Edwards insists, is not a compound. It is, like the atom, a single insight; though it arises out of measurement, and recognizes the beauty "which consists in the visible fitness of a thing to its use and unity of design," it is not attained by a quantitative extension of the design. It is different in kind rather than in degree; it is an elevation of consciousness above the web of relations to the idea of relationship itself. Dr. Holmes, again voicing the attitude that for almost two centuries has prevented an understanding of Edwards, said that Edwards prescribed a rule of virtue more suited to angels than to flesh and blood—a statement with which, aside from the flippancy of tone, Edwards would agree. He was fully aware of how in fact humanity behave, but in his last years, freed from the oppression of the Williamses, he expanded to the full his mastery of the old Puritan disposition to expect the worst from mankind even while demanding the best, and composed a hymn to virtue which, upon the ultimate beholding, is pure intellectual beauty.

Behind the *True Virtue*, the reader must make out the long and enforced indoctrination of the *Religious Affections*, of that terrible trial which compelled the champion of the revival, in the very moment of triumph, to divert his onslaught upon the rational enemies of piety into an effort to stamp out counterfeits and pretentious travesties. These, and not the avowed opponents, defeated the Awakening and involved him in their ruin. In November of 1754 he was left, as he wrote to Hawley, "with a trembling Hand, as you may easily perceive," convinced that "palliating & extenuating matters, and dawbing themselves over with untempered mortar, & sowing Figleaves will be in vain before him whose pure & omniscient Eye is as a Flame of Fire." But also he was left with more than a suspicion that what had happened in Northampton was a frown of heaven upon himself as well as upon the people. *True Virtue* is the weary voice of a man at the end of tragedy, all passion spent, who, sparing himself no more than others, prays only that God shall "make me to know how that I deserve to be cast away, as an abominable branch and as a vessel wherein is no pleasure." Not only had he for too many years concealed his true opinion when open confession might have rallied the people to his side, but when the crisis arrived, though his congregation showed themselves intemperate, he proved himself, even in the cause of righteousness, proud and intransigent. *True Virtue* is all the greater a study because its composer knew that, by the absolute standard therein declared, he himself was as culpable as any.

Hence the greater part of this concentrated essay is a tracing out, with no rancor, as from an incalculable height of observation, of the manifold masquerades that self-love can resort to in the endless effort to simulate benevolence. By policy, by the craft of interest, the self will take into himself family, country, justice, conscientious righteousness, even admiration for noble deeds from which he receives no benefit, but which he can conceive as tending to his advantage "if there were opportunity and due application." Edwards called all such virtues, wherein a man loves others in "some way or other as appendages and appurtenances to himself," secondary virtue. Even in its most extended or intricate form, the secondary betrays its derivation by operating exclusively within the scheme of the objective good. It arises from a principle that unites the self to another being, "whereby the good of that other being does in a sort become his own," and must always be, in the necessary nature of a perceiving and willing being, an operative principle, even in his love to God. It is a gross misunderstanding of Edwards to conceive of him as condemning the natural goods, even the love of the self for itself, as in any sense intrinsically evil. On the contrary, when there is an agreement of desire with object, of an instinct with satisfaction, just as when the parts of a regular building agree with each other, there is a "natural beauty." But Hutcheson took this beauty for the only beauty, for the supreme test, whereas it is simply an "image" of the "cordial agreement, that consists in concord and union of mind and heart." What rationalism claims for the moral sense is true, "which is no more than to say, the more there are of different mutually agreeing things, the greater is the beauty." The pleasure men acquire from the contemplation of such beauty, especially when the tabulation makes it appear that the personal increment is slight, rests upon the nature of perceiving organisms, upon "their sensation of pleasure."

Within the frame of secondary virtue, therefore, the self-congratulatory apprehension of beauty is equated with animal delight, "immediately owing to the law God has established, or the instinct he has given." What the natural man calls virtuous and beautiful—social justice, the mother's love for her child, the happiness of those he happens to love, a regard for the public good which includes himself even when it calls upon him to sacrifice himself, ultimately even the approbation of an inward conscience that gives him invincible pleasure despite the censure of his fellows (despite the malevolence of Williamses)—all these, analyzed into elementary terms, are no more than "the order and proportion generally observed in the laws of nature." They are reactions, like the cry of the anvil hit by the hammer, like the perpetual fall of the moon toward the earth. Though they seem virtuous, especially when most complicated, they have nothing virtuous in them beyond the seeming, and in truth are as decipherable by the laws of physics as are the motions in one arm of a lever with relation to the length and velocity of the other.

Everything that Hutcheson and the liberals ascribe to normal human nature, armed with its sensitive moral discrimination, can be resolved into the mechanics of instinct, as an insect feels out its course with its antennae, or into a scheme in the furtherance of instinct, "and may be without any principle of true virtue in the heart." In the twentieth century, to readers of Marcel Proust, it should come as no surprise that "such limited private benevolence, not arising from, not being subordinate to benevolence to Being in general, cannot have the nature of true virtue." There are men, said Edwards before Laurence Sterne was published, who will weep upon seeing a brute creature in torment, but who suffer no uneasiness whatever in knowing that thousands are slaughtered every day "at butchers' shambles in great cities." Pity, when gratifying to the ego, may not only be without benevolence, "but may consist with true malevolence, or with such ill will as shall cause men not only not to desire the positive happiness of another, but even to desire his calamity." The instincts serve for men's preservation and comfortable subsistence, which are objective and legitimate goods, for the regular satisfactions of appetite by extrinsic objects, which God by a divine constitution joined in sequences within the order of causation; but though these instincts perpetually manufacture attitudes of aversion and approbation, within the field of instinctual behavior they can be plotted by arithmetical equations only a trifle more complicated than those of the *Principia.* They can be formulated into rules as objectively beautiful, but as utterly irrelevant to moral worth, as incommensurate with the dignity of suffering and the agony of decision, as the insensate laws of motion.

So Hutcheson was correct when he identified morality with aesthetics. For Edwards, the Puritan in pioneer America, the definition of the ethical is beauty. But Hutcheson, and all utilitarians and humanitarians after him, failed to proceed from beauties to the beautiful, and so set up for perceiving beings a criterion applicable only to stones and planets. True virtue, therefore, is no law of inanimate things, but "is *that*, belonging to the *heart* of an intelligent Being, that is beautiful by a *general* beauty, or beautiful in a comprehensive view as it is in itself, and as related to every thing that it stands in connection with." The familiar process of perception still furnishes the distinction that a Hutcheson blurs: what sensation receives as the instigator of a reflex act is also received as a perception predetermined by the disposition of the agent, and according to the conception, not according to the thing, the motive compels the will. If the conception is of things as they are in themselves, without relation to the desires of the self—though all this while the self must eat and dress and marry—then in that identification of the objective and the inherent consists true virtue. No poet was more sensitive to the beauty of nature than Edwards, but he concluded that the disinterested benevolence which is the inescapable rule of virtue among sentient beings "doth not necessarily presuppose beauty in its object." The Lockean clue, followed through the years, tested in a community that offered prototypes of almost every kind of American who was yet to figure in American history, led in the serenity of exile into realms Locke never dreamed of, into the affirmation that the beauty of holiness is one with the nature of the objective universe.

It is obvious, Edwards remarked, that none can "relish" pure beauty who has no temper for it. The coherence of his system shows that he identified the relish with the new simple idea, which is supernatural grace, and the possession of which makes certain men other (or more) than "natural" men. Yet it is remarkable that *True Virtue* contents itself with setting forth the inward beauty wholly in terms of the psychological pattern. The road out of the maze of secondary beauties up to the ideal beauty which no longer gloats upon its possessions or evaluates them in proportion to their amount of beauty, to that sight which bestows beauty on objects by regarding them, is so plain that in the simplicity of Edwards' presentation it appears open to all mankind. That it is traveled by only a few becomes a matter of biography; the determination is not from an intervention of the spirit, but from the nature of things. Man lives on the plane both of the objective good and of the inherent, not because he is both body and soul, but because he is one being, and the law of his life is that he must perceive things, yet as he perceives them, so they are and so he is. *True Virtue* can be called, if I may use the word in its primitive rather than in any of its sectarian connotations, a magnificent *humanism*. The rule of pure benevolence is implicated in every human act, so that every satisfaction of appetite, even of the lust which, within its own system, perceives the object as beautiful, has "in it some image of the true, spiritual, original beauty." By the uniformity of the cosmos, "diverse things become as it were one," and in the system of things even the fundamental distinction between the speculative and the sensible is merged into the pure beauty which is the final goal both of the reason and of the heart.

Yet this beauty is not a Platonic idea, no flame which the moth desires, no devotion to something afar from the sphere of our sorrow. It arises by discoverable processes out of motion and perception. Critics like Chauncy Whittelsey never understood Edwards, but their instinct was not far wrong when they accused him of atheism—except that they could not conceive an atheism more profoundly conscious of God than they could experience. Channing came closer to the truth when he said that by making God the only active power of the universe, Edwards annihilated the creature, became in effect a "pantheist," and obliged men at last to question whether any such thing as matter exists. Rational liberals do not want the creature annihilated, and they want matter to remain matter. I believe no one aware of recent physics and logic can be so confident as was Channing, or certainly so confident as were his colleagues and followers in liberal Protestantism, that matter is as solid as he would have it. As for annihilation of the creature, sociology and anthropology as well as history do not exactly enhance his independence of circumstance. Edwards ended the *True Virtue* with a startling recognition: "that sentiment, at least as to many particulars, by some means or other, is different in different persons, in different nations," and therefore the specific content of virtue and vice is arbitrary, being determined not by the nature of things, "but by the sentiments of men with relation to the nature of things." Edwards' scholarship, especially his anthropology, was narrow (although he could make first-hand comparative studies of English and Indian cultures); yet his experience was deep if not broad, and though he never saw a cathedral or an art gallery, never heard a symphony or an opera, out of the beauty of the world and the beauty of virtue he came to a vision of beauty for which the existence or nonexistence of matter is but a verbal quibble, a beauty which, being seen, puts the creature beyond all anxiety concerning his own annihilation.

In day-by-day existence, all men profess disinterested generosity, though it may be only the tribute vice pays to virtue. Political history, especially in parliamentary or democratic traditions, is a record of leaders successively broken as their attachments to self or to party become more evident than their devotion to the general welfare. Turn the rascals out, is ever the slogan, and is practically always in order; an ethical standard which few or none observe in private is repeatedly the undoing of those who fall publicly short of it. Edwards was cast out of Northampton upon the charge of subverting the community to private ends. Once self-love is exposed to view, nobody mistakes it for virtue. There is, it is true, occasionally a man "who, through the greatness of his pride, may imagine himself as it were *all*"; and as long as his mind is large enough to encompass a great range of selfishness, a vast knowledge of extrinsic goods and of the fitness of things to their use, his self-love "is exceeding necessary to society, besides its directly and greatly seeking the good of one." Edwards' ethical system comprehends perfectly why the great peculator wins social esteem while the petty thief is promptly jailed: the large-scale enterprise has more resemblance to the primary operation of virtue. Yet presiding over the career of every public man, ecclesiastical or political, as it presided over and terminated the career of Edwards at Northampton, is a rule of judgment that is the premise of every act of human perception, and finally comes, out of the multitude's observation of the leader, to bear upon him. Once it is articulated, the rule measures the man, and the people reject him. There comes a time when the law of the general, to which by the very mechanism of cognition a democracy is committed, declares that the self-love of the dictator, of the prime minister, or of the town parson, "if it be not subordinate to, and regulated by, another more extensive principle, it may make a man a common enemy to the system he is related to." History

would cease to be a tale of sinfulness, there would be true redemption in it, could it show even one society wherein the
limits of a particular system, communal or national, were
fixed, and were kept so fixed that a single leader, some Col.
John Stoddard, could organize it within his personal ambition, and never thereafter have to face the challenge of a still
greater possible organization of goods. In politics, secondary
virtue constantly appears to be attaining, but never quite suc-
ceeds in becoming, the primary.

The extent to which the politician or the cleric identifies
self with the community—"its extent may be to a system that
contains thousands of individuals"—determines the duration
of his power; for he holds office, or the authority of office,
only so long as his gratifications appear, to the view and comprehension of men's minds, one with the whole system of virtue, or at least bear "some resemblance of the universal
system." We might be inclined to discount Edwards' calling
himself an abominable branch as so much pious cant had he
not, though in this highly indirect fashion, in the guise of an
abstract reading of the universal failure of power, offered a
full confession of his own fall. By this law he measured and
condemned himself, and while the rule particularly applies to
dictators, he also invited social reformers and political ideal-
ists to come to a similar reckoning with themselves.

What insures the defeat of politicians is simply the fact that
any calculus can be extended indefinitely, beyond their ability
to cope, beyond any limits that private virtue can keep pace
with. Within a limited sphere, the system of the father, of the
priest, of the statesman, is beautiful as long as it shuts out of
consideration all other systems—other families, churches, or
nations—with which it actually stands in a vital relation. "If
that private system contained the sum of universal existence,
then their benevolence would have true beauty; or, in other
words, would be beautiful, all things considered." The rationalists were right in sensing that in the moral and political universe as in the natural, a self-operating law is at work which

eliminates aberrations, but they made it merely mechanical, the mutual cancellation of self-love and social; in Edwards' philosophy, it is the law of beauty, which ultimately is the consent of all beings to being in general, and it operates in the social community as a judgment. So all private systems, even the system of a major political power, are doomed to defeat, because there is bound to be a competition among systems, economic or moral.

For a time, men mistake such social mobilizations of private affections—especially when participated in by their town, party, or nation—for demonstrations of true virtue, because of "the narrowness of their views." When experience forces an enlarging of the view, they discard the now inadequate or incompletely virtuous leader, whose views of policy have proven too straitened in relation to the enlarged corporate aims; yet men constantly strive to set a limit to the social aspiration, and while they demand of the statesman that he go to the limit of their standard, they resent his passing beyond it as furiously as they despise his falling short. All societies parade their devotion to virtue by denying that anything virtuous exists outside their own formulae. They even attempt to enlist God in the service of their delimited objective, praying that He prosper their town against others, or their nation over rivals. A few men perceive that this logic is endless, and they alone are able to free their affections from a specific segment of the created system. Only they perceive that the self-contained and illimitable unit of virtue, which is the beauty that cannot be defined, is the entire universe. For this system, there is indeed an adequate statesman, who so defines His love of self that it perfectly comprehends and furthers the welfare of all. God's private ambition is the universal system of benevolence. Among men, only those who perceive and take to heart this paradox achieve the moral ability to will in conformity with Him who is all in all, "in comparison of whom all the rest is nothing, and with regard to whom all other things are to be viewed, and their minds be accordingly impressed and affected."

Here Edwards was brought, after years of unceasing cogitation, face to face with the doubt which all the while lay in wait for him. He could pronounce judgment on himself without flinching; as one in authority, he had failed to cast the net of his pride sufficiently wide to gather in all his townsmen, although in 1735 and 1741 he almost succeeded. But to condemn himself—did that vindicate the principle by which he accounted for the fall of both parsons and Caesars? Suppose the politician or the priest should learn from Edwards' example that an indefinite extension of calculation will bring him no closer to true virtue, and that he should give over the effort to organize numbers, parties, or churches, spurn the quantitative for pure perception, and suppose at last he should behold the simple idea of disinterested benevolence: what guarantee would he have, after all the expenditure, that his notion of benevolence is not a fantasy? How can he know for sure that it is not just another particular disguised as the universal? What proof exists that the sense of the heart, even after liberated from utilitarianism and humanitarianism, even after it accepts the totality of all systems and the absolute unity of the race, is not simply dreaming? Men of worldly experience, schooled in the dismal science of pleasures, will call the simple idea of pure virtue a merely subjective consolation. Imagine Sir Robert Walpole reading *The Nature of True Virtue*!

"For," wrote Edwards in what, considering all that he had undergone and all he had wrought for good or bad, may be regarded as one of his basic sentences, "if there were no correspondence or agreement in such a sense with the nature of things any more than there would have been in a diverse or contrary sense, the idea we obtain by this spiritual sense could in no respect be said to be a knowledge or perception of any thing besides what was in our own minds." Edwards held that the problem which has tormented modern philosophy—the technical issue of epistemology: whether our ideas of objects correspond to the objects themselves—has no real urgency, as it never has to men in action or in suffering. Edwards could dismiss it, and would have saved the modern intellect an untold expenditure of time and paper had it heeded him, by the reflection arrived at in the "Notes," that since things exist to the mind as they are perceived, it is all one whether the so-called objects be mental or material.

But the real problem of our culture, he insisted, is the other kind of correspondence, not of ideas and things, but of virtue and reality. If there is no meeting place of ethics and science, "this idea would be no representation of any thing without." By the nature of the organism, sensationally and environmentally conditioned man, having no innate or *a priori* standards, is forced by the battering of experience and by his constant failure to measure up to the sheer physical immensity of the universe, to fall back on what he divines to be the pattern of the world. There he takes his stand, his last stand, upon the conviction that persons who have a true knowledge of God have their minds greatly enlightened "in the knowledge of divine things in general." Is this illusion? Must the only remaining stronghold of sanity be surrendered, and shall an utter chaos of partial and conflicting systems of secondary virtue engulf us? In only one direction could Edwards find the answer upon which all other answers hang, only by putting this question, and only by answering it explicitly: for what actual end did God, in the first place, ever create such a world as this?

The second half of *Concerning the End for which God created the World* is a study of what may be learned from Scripture. Fixing upon texts which the Arminians were constantly citing, Edwards argued them in a literalistic—and to us unrewarding—vein, elaborating still one more polemic against his foes. Like much of the argumentation in the *Freedom of the Will*, he proves merely that the Arminians can make out no better case than the Calvinists. But the first half of the dissertation, entitled "What reason dictates concerning this affair," is Edwards' explanation of explanations. We should, I trust, be prepared to find that it is a projection of the Lockean psychology into the Godhead itself, of the pattern of a disposition of the heart that predetermines perception. But there is a crucial difference between God and man: God is by definition a Being who perceives not separate entities in succession, but the totality of being in a single, eternal glance. His will is therefore always and invariably determined toward the order of things as they are in themselves, in accordance with the method of true perception; yet for Him, for Him alone, perception of objects is perception of the naked ideas, because He, by willing to perceive them, creates them. True virtue is the rule of God's sight, it is God's ever new simple idea, as the grace of God is man's. The determinant of God's moral ability is pure virtue, but because with Him to see is to know, so for Him to perceive is to enact, and what He is disposed toward is what exists. The guarantee that the moral insight of man, the anatomy of the idea of excellency, is one with external reality lies in the continuity of the pattern of perception throughout all mind, from God down to man, the ultimate "fact" that there is a necessary connection of volitions with motives. By grace man is lifted into the perception of a coincidence of the objective order of pleasure with the inherent order of virtue, and discovers from afar that both converge in beauty. But God Himself is eternally both orders in one, for He alone can choose the motive with which His volition shall be connected. In Him are reconciled necessity and freedom, because He selects the necessity to which He submits Himself. In order that this beauty may be manifested, and not for the particular good of any creature or the incorporated good of any society of creatures, for that end alone is God "disposed" to create a world in time and space.

Perhaps a simpler way of putting it would be to say that the internal contradictions of the sensational psychology become harmonies in the psychology of God. The objective and the inherent are demonstrably one in Him, because He, and no other intelligence, can be portrayed as perceiving and so being motivated, yet as perceiving nothing but Himself. Therefore what He sees as pleasurable and excellent is exactly so, and thus provides Him with an extrinsic object in the possession and enjoyment of which He is happy. Egotism and benevolence become one in God, and not in the self-regulating mechanics of Pope's *Essay on Man*. "If God himself be in any respect properly capable of being his own end in the creation of the world, then it is reasonable to suppose that he had respect to *himself* as his last and highest end in this work; because he is worthy in himself to be so, being infinitely the greatest and best of beings." Edwards dares to say that "we must suppose" that God had a perception of this fact "before" He created the world, in order that God Himself should have a "motive" for so doing.

Undoubtedly Edwards betrays much by this "we must suppose," for he knows that with God there is no "before" and "after." Still, he ventures to read the pattern of perception and motive into the celestial understanding, and the divine act must be "supposed" an eternal consequent of an eternal vision. In man, a perception of true virtue, once really beheld, is followed by a disposition enabling the will to practise it; or else, a perception of secondary virtue, among those incapable of perceiving the difference, becomes a moral necessity inclining them toward a counterfeit instead of a reality. Does necessity, the necessity of the motivated perception, then rule all intelligence, even that of God, so that even He must submit to the postulates of John Locke?

Edwards lent color to the charge that he enthroned fate above Jehovah by a hypothetical supposition of how the case would have been decided if before the world were created it had been submitted for arbitration "to some third being of perfect wisdom and rectitude, neither the Creator nor one of the creatures, that should be perfectly indifferent and disinterested." On the invincible logic of the situation, this arbiter would decide that God should fall short of the end He had in view, that His will should not correspond to His idea, if He created a world for the benefit of any number of particular persons. These, being concrete, must be in competition for the goods of creation, and are bound to deprive each other of some degree of full pleasure; the whole system of created being would thus be found, in comparison of the Creator, "as the light dust of the balance (which is taken no notice of by him that weighs), and as nothing and vanity." Hence the arbiter, deciding how matters should proceed "most fitly, properly, and according to the nature of things," would determine that the whole universe, including all creatures both animate and inanimate, planets and minds, "should proceed from a regard and with a view, to God, as the supreme and last end of all." Of course, Edwards added, the supposition of such an arbiter (who does oddly resemble Jonathan Edwards!) is an impossibility; it serves only to help us conceive a rule of "what is most fit and suitable in itself." Actually the rule exists not in any umpire between God and man, but in the intention of God, and to say that God is bound by it is absurd, because the will of God is itself the rule. What the supposition proves is that "there must be some supreme judge of fitness and propriety in the universality of things, as otherwise there could be no order nor regularity"—that is, no sequence of causes— and obviously it belongs to God to state all these things "as much as if perfect rectitude were a distinct person."

Edwards' real point was that no partial system of rectitude, no man's or no nation's definition of the good, can be taken for perfect rectitude because, no matter how inclusive it may appear, there are areas beyond it. Whereas an atom is one complete unit, whether it be the point of a pin or a universe. God's aim in creating a universe according to perfect goodness could be only to express the good that is in Him, not to make charming creatures. There is in God a "fulness"—Edwards again was at the frontier of language, and used this word because he could find no better, to signify all the good which is in God, both "natural and moral"—which cries for emanation *ad extra*, and this was His "motive"; the determining idea was not a prevision of the good of the creature, but of the pure beauty of expression.

But the diffusive disposition that excited God to give creatures existence, was rather a communicative disposition in general, or a disposition in the fulness of divinity to flow out and diffuse itself. Thus the disposition there is in the root and stock of a tree to diffuse and send forth its sap and life, is doubtless the reason of the communication of its sap and life to its buds, leaves and fruits, after these exist. But a disposition to communicate of its life and sap to its fruits, is not so properly the cause of its producing those fruits, as its disposition to communicate itself, or diffuse its sap and life in general. Therefore, to speak more strictly according to truth, we may suppose, that a disposition in God, as an original property of his nature, to an emanation of his own infinite fulness, was what excited him to create the world; and so that the emanation itself was aimed at by him as a last end of the creation.

The lesson for the creature, once he comprehends this secret of the universe, is not to enlist God in the service of his private pleasures, or to pray that he be given house and land and estate, but to reflect the diffused light of God, whether he be in heaven or hell, as a jewel that gets all its radiance from the sun reflects back the light of the sun. For man this conception is a real solution to the problem of his existence, for it gathers up and unites the distinctions so abruptly enunciated in the Boston lecture of 1731. If it be valuable that the understanding have an idea of God's perfection, which is the idea of the physical universe, then the love of the heart, which is the man willing in accordance with his idea, is still more valuable, "as moral beauty especially consists in the disposition and affection of the heart."

Puritanism is the essence of Protestantism, and Edwards is the quintessence of Puritanism. This thesis of an emanation of God for the pure joy of creation, in which the creatures find their justification by yielding consent to the beauty of the whole even though it slay them, will be recognized as his approximation to a spiritual vision that the saints, Augustine or Pascal, have variously expressed. What is peculiarly Puritan about it is the courageous—or, some may say, presumptuous—invasion of the Godhead by that pattern of reality Edwards had learned on earth. As far as language could go, he would say how and why God actually operates. He would not be content with worship and ignorance, and because scientific law and the method of perception were the great discoveries of his age, he applied them to God, and emerged with a description of the indescribable. One may charge (as have his critics) that Edwards simply projected into heaven the problem given by his age—the conflict of science and value, of reason and faith, of head and heart—and achieved only a theoretical solution by constructing an image of God after the necessities of his own mind, in which he could logically resolve the tension of his own thought, in which he could combine verbally what would not be merged in fact, the objective and the inherent. He could unite them in the mind of God by identifying God's creation with God's perception.

To the extent that this criticism is justified—as up to a point it is—it is a comment upon Puritanism, especially the pure Puritanism of New England. In this tradition, all intermediaries between God and man are resolutely taken away; there is no relaxing of the quest, no indulgence and no confessional. Those who try to evade the ordeal by seeking contentment in ships and banks, or in the persuasion that man is not really very bad and that reason and decency make adequate rules of life, are bound to be left with uneasy consciences. But there is a deeper comment to be made upon this Puritan habit of subjecting the Godhead to analysis: even after the Puritan has said what God is, even after Edwards has explained just how and why God created a world, and after he has expounded the system of it, the secret has not been told. Neither the secret of God nor that of Edwards!

There is constant progress toward the telling. The more

the divine communications increase, the more the creature becomes one with God: "The image is more and more perfect,
and so the good that is in the creature comes forever nearer
and nearer to an identity with that which is in God." The
elect, who are eternally with God, must be, in a system disposed according to an idea, the end of creation—yet if that
reflection makes them proud, they may suspect that possibly
they are not really among the elected! As all things are from
God, and in their "progress" come nearer and nearer to Him,
He who is their first cause must be their last. But—and here
Edwards put, on the final page of this dissertation, the heart of
the Puritan conception—"the particular time will never come
when it can be said, the union is now infinitely perfect." By a
constant motion the world eternally strives after God as its
center, "though the time will never come when it can be said
it has already arrived at this infinite height." Even after the
mystery has been analyzed into the forms of the new psychology, and the will of the inscrutable has been specified into the
laws of motion and refraction, into atoms and gravity, the
mystery abides, and the Puritan God is still hidden. For the
mystery is not in time, but the Puritan is.

So, if to God be ascribed a motive which is called a consequence of perception, a disposition by which it is said that His
will is determined, the Puritan is not thus reducing the divinity to a logarithm. He is pointing out anew where God
and man may converse, for in mankind the instantaneous act
of God is broken down into temporal sequences. For man, the
object is not brought into existence by his perception, but it
exists, whether as thing or as concept, before he perceives it;
since he does not create it, he can know it only as idea, and
his life must consist in a never-ending effort to merge his idea
with the object. God's disposition to diffuse Himself *ad extra*
is for Him a sufficient motive; by seeing and loving, man
shares in the motive, but instead of one comprehensive intention, man must have a succession of motives aroused through
perceiving successive things. The universal method is the

same, but this does not mean that man becomes God. God's inclination determines existence, but man's inclination is an existence; yet because he is the child of God, it is determined not by existence itself, but by existence as he comprehends it. And for him to form an idea in the brain about which a motive can cohere takes time.

As man reaches toward God, even in the act of sin, by his use of perception he exhibits his likeness to God; by knowing anything and affixing a name to it, he endeavors to triumph over time. Could man attain absolute excellency, the final aesthetic vision would be eternal and unchanging. Yet in time, "there never will come that particular moment, when it can be said, that now justice is satisfied." Were that possible, man would indeed be divine, beauty would become concrete justice. "There never will come the moment, when it can be said, that now this infinitely valuable good has been actually bestowed." Because the human predicament is given in time, it calls for the supposition of a beginning and an end, of a birth not only of particular men but of mankind, and of a consummation not only of lives but of the cosmos. Yet God Himself is without beginning and without end. Definition of the purpose for which God created the universe, even if it can be reduced to a psychological design agreeable to the terms of John Locke, is not definition of the mystery. Because the real mystery is in time, the field of investigation is not only the perpetual laws of physics and of the mind, not only the logical structure of virtue and of emanation, but the extension of these operations through temporal changes.

When planning the great "Rational Account," Edwards seems mainly to have intended, according to the evidence of his journals, another of those "vindications" of Christianity against free-thinkers and Deists with which the literature of the eighteenth century abounds, a work similar in design to Addison's or Butler's. But to repulse the foe at this or that bastion, by erecting fortresses of logic, was still not the same thing as fully justifying, in Milton's phrase, God's ways to man. The last dissertation shows that even had Edwards' *summa* been completed, there would have been at the core of his treatment an element of incompletion which for him would not have been entirely the mystery of God but the psychological limitation of man. The creature must perceive the complete work of God moment by moment, which is to say in time. Therefore a logical or structural system, even if irrefutable, would not be enough; in order that finite perception may meet with the eternal, there would be needed a chart of its successive insights, of the law of consciousness not only as formulated by Locke, but as extended over the centuries. By the end of his life, the logic of his investigation and of his experience brought Edwards, step by step, through an inexorable development hardly to be paralleled in the eighteenth century, to a realization that makes him intellectually the most modern man of his age: the heart of the human problem is history.

He that made man a reasonable creature of soul and body, and He that did neither let him pass unpunished for his sin, or yet excluded him from mercy: He that gave both unto good and bad essence with the stones, power of production with the trees, senses with the beasts of the field, and understanding with the angels; He, from whom is all being, beauty, form and order, number, weight and measure; He from whom all nature, mean and excellent, all seeds of form, all forms of seed, all motion, both of forms and seeds derive and have being: He that gave flesh the original, beauty, strength, propagation, form and shape, health and symmetry: He that gave the unreasonable soul, sense, memory and appetite, the reasonable besides these, phantasy, understanding and will: He (I say) having left neither heaven, nor earth, nor angel, nor man, no nor the most base and contemptible creature, neither the bird's feather, nor the herb's flower, nor the tree's leaf, without the true harmony of their parts, and peaceful concord of composition; it is no way credible, that He would leave the kingdoms of men, and their bondages and freedoms loose and uncomprised in the laws of His eternal providence.

AUGUSTINE

History

TO THE INVITATION from the trustees of the College at Princeton, Edwards replied on October 19, 1757, by listing his disqualifications, personal and scholarly, and offered one which we may translate roughly as a preference for research over administration. He had long been occupied with writing down his thoughts, "pursuing the clue to my utmost," filling the folio journals wherein his best thought is still concealed; by now, he felt, he had stored up "many things against most of the prevailing errors of the present day." But besides materials for the great rational and systematic account, he had another project, which he strove to explain to the trustees: "Beside these, I have had on my mind and heart, (which I long ago began, not with any view to publication,) a great work, which I call a *History of the Work of Redemption*, a body of divinity in an entire new method, being thrown into the form of a history." The trustees chose him because he was the foremost theologian in America, were prepared to take him on his own terms, and expected him to be original. It may be doubted, however, that they understood how entirely novel Edwards' projected method really was.

By saying he began the work long ago, he meant that in 1739 he gave a series of sermons on the idea. Thereafter, the journals show, he read with avidity every historical work he could lay his hands on, and made long lists of others he hoped to read. His thinking undoubtedly progressed far beyond the rough draft of 1739. He told the trustees that he would deploy the narrative "from eternity," through the Creation, to the end of the Creation which shall "last to eternity," along the way "particularly considering all parts of the grand scheme, in their historical order." He would carry on the story, he said in language that must have meant to the trustees either something entirely obvious or else something the like of which had not yet been imagined in theology (or at least in Protestant theology), with regard to the three worlds of heaven, earth, and hell; he would introduce doctrines as they emerged out of the course of change and alteration, in a manner entirely scriptural but also "most natural." The new method, he predicted, would be "most beautiful and entertaining"—adjectives not generally applied to theology, even by theologians—and would gather together the totality of divine doctrine by "shewing the admirable contexture and harmony of the whole."

When trustees pick a president, they do not mind if he has crotchets, and invariably assure him that a college presidency can be combined with private study. So Edwards came to Princeton in February 1758 to find a smallpox epidemic under way. He believed in science, and he never asked others to suffer what he himself would not endure. He was inoculated on February 13; his wasted and exhausted body could stand no more, and the experiment killed him on March 22.

Speculation on "what might have happened" if certain critical historical events had gone the other way—as, for instance, if Lee had won at Gettysburg—is unprofitable but irresistible. If Jonathan Edwards could have been both what he actually was by 1758 and yet also robust enough for another ten or twenty years of activity, the intellectual history of America would assuredly have become a different story. Against the Stamp Act and the Intolerable Acts he would have been a Whig: in the mundane political sphere he accepted the social compact and the bill of rights. His influence might thus have spread through the Presbyterian Church into the synods and the new colleges of the West (as Witherspoon's eventually did); but he would not have disseminated the Scottish realism which, emanating from the later Princeton, became for vast numbers of Americans a *rigor mortis* of the mind. He would have had difficulties with the Scotch-Irish elements in the Calvinistic entente, but his intellectual prestige would have sustained him. He might have equipped those bodies, whose influence on American life for the next century was decisive, with a comprehensive theology; he might so have fastened it on the American mind that all liberals would have had to make common cause to meet it. But it would have been an orthodoxy aware that metaphysical problems cannot be reduced to the blunt assertions of common sense. It would have been oriented toward science, infused with a love of beauty, and articulately critical of the ethic of business; it would have given to emotion the dignity of a mode of spiritual apprehension; it would have invited rather than forbidden the interpenetration of theology and philosophy, religion and aesthetics. If orthodoxy would have profited, liberalism would have profited even more. All this assumes, of course, that Edwards could have completed his work and could have taught it to Protestant intellectuals, the latter being the more dubious supposition. But had he done this much, he would then also have furnished America with the first glimmerings of historical method which, even though lacking the scholarship to support it, would still have been, in the reckoning of today, an immense enrichment of the intellectual heritage of the nation.

In 1774, Jonathan Edwards, Jr., sent the manuscript of the 1739 lectures—only a few pages of which had been retouched by Edwards—to a Scottish admirer, who published it in Edinburgh. The first American printing was in 1786; it was thereafter frequently reprinted, and was translated into Dutch and

Welsh. Jonathan, Jr.'s preface borrows a phrase from the letter to the Princeton trustees, calling the book a body of divinity in a new method, but it apologizes for a want of "elegance of composition"; despite this lack, the work may excite pious conversation. Erskine, the Scottish editor, remarks that in most of his works Edwards was too acute a philosopher to be understood by the vulgar, but here he addresses "ordinary Christians." The book had a vogue among simple people, who also read Foxe and Bunyan, but by the middle of the nineteenth century became too primitive for even such an audience. At first sight it is an uncritical retelling of the "Christian epic"—the Creation, the Fall, Saul, David, and the prophets, the life of Christ, the Reformation; it ends with a prophecy which is simply old-fashioned chiliasm—the thousand-year reign of Christ, to be followed by the last apostasy, and then the Day of Judgment and the end of the world in flames. Biographers avert their gaze from this tract, as though to treat it seriously would be to insult their own intelligence.

However, mankind have recently been taking the philosophy of history with increasing seriousness. I agree that if one stops with the surface narrative, *A History of the Work of Redemption* sounds like a story book for fundamentalists, and is hardly to be mentioned with Gibbon, Marx, Spengler, or Toynbee. Measured against modern scholarship, textual criticism, archeology, and comparative religions, it is an absurd book, where it is not pathetic. But the problem that compels the modern intellect to grapple with the philosophy of history is not the increase in historical data, it is the demand for an interpretation of data. As Justice Holmes remarked—to him were vouchsafed insights inaccessible to his father—"History has to be rewritten because history is the selection of those threads of causes or antecedents that we are interested in." For many, the rediscovery of this truism means only that the problem of history lies in the data, in arranging the facts so as to interest the modern mind; yet there is reason to suspect that such "new history," written in terms of economic factors, or of class warfare, or of sectionalism and the frontier, has a way of becoming as quickly dated as has Edwards' history in terms of the Old Testament.

There are others who find in Justice Holmes' remark an implication, not that the mind can make its own capricious selection, but that history is what the mind must perceive in a fashion dictated by the mind itself rather than by data and documents. If Edwards' book be read as a study of this problem, and the superficial narrative be stripped from the philosophical thesis, it becomes a pioneer work in American historiography. His tentative effort, arrived at in solitude, when none among his contemporaries, or for that matter among his disciples, neither Erskine nor his own son, could grasp what he was after, is an achievement truly staggering. For a mind imbued with Newtonianism to break away from the reigning conception of space toward an appreciation of time, to subordinate the idea of an eternal and immutable, or at best a cyclical, pattern of the past to a vision of a dynamic process of realization within temporal existence this was such a metaphysical excursion as his contemporaries could not begin to comprehend. In its divination of the methodology to which our culture has been more and more committed, the *History of Redemption* is a prophetic book.

Of course, Edwards came to his reading of history through the method which, from the moment he discovered Locke, was always the secret of his solutions, the method he used for his conclusions about the atom or the unity of the race. The "Notes" declared that because man knows only his ideas of things and not things themselves, then *"Pastness*, if I may make such a word, is nothing but a Mode of Ideas." Ideas fade in our minds, and this process is our very "sense" of duration; perception of historical fact, therefore, is not of something that occurred at such a moment in such a year, but a consciousness of how far the perception has receded. To the modern analyst this will seem too easy an approach to an intellectual law of history, since there now appear many subtle ways in which the past is prolonged into the present, both in the mind and in society. Still, for Edwards the essential conception was clear, that what men call history is the idea they have of the past, not the actual events which they never witnessed. But then, Edwards did not stop with merely this epistemological analysis; the *History of Redemption* is a more extensive philosophical enterprise, whose guiding principle is his doctrine of cause. The idea which determines the coherence of history is not just a whimsical notion of the historian; it would indeed be just that were it a supine induction from evidences (if one surrenders his mind to his footnotes, he can write untold monographs, and call them history!): "In order to see how a design is carried on, we must first know what the design is." Edwards first set forth the design of history as at Enfield he set forth the pattern of torment, in order to convey the naked idea, stripped of rhetoric, to the understanding of listeners, so that they, having their minds possessed of the concept, would necessarily see the truth and no longer lose themselves amid syllogisms and proofs. He expounded the "grand design" of history so that "this great affair of redemption may not appear like confusion to you" —just as he taught them the doctrine of cause in order that they should not suppose each phenomenon to be the determinant of the next. He taught a philosophy of history so that mankind could be "made capable of actively falling in with that design, and promoting it." Here, as in other realms, Edwards came through the Lockean mechanism to answers that, in our reading, transcend Locke. When he approached history as a collocation of atomic occurrences that must have their cause outside themselves, and demanded that by perceiving their coherence man should approach the principle in which they are organized, he also attained to the revolutionary insight (which James and Bergson were to discover by a more intricate approach) that what man sees as the truth of history is what he wills to prevail. The disposition of man not only makes true virtue—it makes the truth of history.

Edwards takes delight in showing how at every juncture of history, learned men, philosophers and academic historians, missed the significance of their epoch, and did nothing but collect facts without meanings. God suffered the wisdom and philosophy of the ancient world to come to their greatest height immediately before Christ appeared in order to demonstrate "that all they could do was in vain." He who goes across country, sedulously noting every stream, reports a jumble and confusion of watercourses; he who knows the whole topography can trace the course of all brooks as they converge in the great river and empty into the sea, and he perceives that no stream fails of its destination. Rationalists and Arminians, free-thinkers and Deists, did not perceive the design in time, even after Newton had compelled them, though against their wills, to confess a design in space.

Thus the *History of Redemption*—it is, remember, only a rough sketch, and the journals show that the finished version would have been more circumstantial—is an assertion that has value quite apart from the specific terms of its narrative. History, Edwards says, is a grand conception, a design, a chain of events within a scheme of causation. He slowly came to realize that by casting theology into the form of a history, he had indeed hit upon something entirely "new"—at least in America. It was so radical in its grasp of the problem, though not in its erudition, that by contrast the histories of Robertson and Gibbon are superficial organizations of the past in terms that become, to more critical scholars, private and subjective. Only that history which satisfies the mind by accounting for all things is worthy the name. "Shall we prize a history which gives us a clear account of some great earthly prince, or mighty warrior, as of Alexander the Great, or Julius Caesar, or the Duke of Marlborough," and not more prize the history which God has wrought for the redemption of His chosen?

Thus, in whatever terms (for Edwards they were those of the Christian epic), the real thesis of the *History of Redemption* is the unity of history. All phases "are but the several parts of one scheme." "It is one design that is formed." Successive events in different ages are parts of a continuous whole; the chain is never broken. The historical span, like the volitional, is "not disunited and jumbled, without connection or dependence, but are all united, just as the several parts of one building." There is, in short, "an orderly history." Which is to say that Edwards found the determination of this order, as in his 1734 treatise on justification, outside the sequence and yet presiding over it, not accruing step by step as though each event chose its own effect. The order is an instantaneous concept; translated into time, it becomes the historical record, and in this temporalized fragmentation of the eternal men may read through their senses, for they can learn by no other means, the idea of the perfect beginning and end. By that perception, their wills may be determined, so that they can play a constructive rôle in the historical process. This is their happiness, this their consent to what must be, this is excellency. There is never redemption *in* history, as the *True Virtue* made clear, but there is a history *of* redemption.

Arminians, like the modern sociologists, clinging to the fallacy of a causal sequence with no inner coherence, to a God who must mend and patch, write history as an assemblage of accidental conjunctions, and can tell nothing of tendency or of development. But the work of redemption is not a cycle of meaningless repetitions: "not merely by repeating or renewing the same effect in different subjects" does it move, but by evolution (although Edwards did not have the word, and called it "carrying on"): "all together making up one great work." Paul Tillich makes a distinction between "nonhistorical" and "historical" interpretations of history: that the former interpret the past through nature while the latter interpret history through history itself. In that sense Edwards, as opposed to all naturalistic and materialistic versions, to Marx no less than to Gibbon, wrote the first truly historical interpretation in American literature; and, until the contemporary crisis, wherein the nonhistorical has at last been challenged,

Edwards' was our only such example. Hence the book was long deplored as a childish venture, what Dr. Holmes called one of the "disorganizing conceptions" with which his powerful mind was regrettably filled, "like that which makes all mankind sinners thousands of years before they were born." Again, although we discount the peculiar mythology in which Edwards embodies his narrative, in a day when Dr. Holmes' mythology is also ripe for discounting, we may recognize that Edwards levied against naturalistic histories and historians the basic criticism that they are only today commencing to face.

This does not mean, however, that the *History of Redemption* pretends to recite history exactly as it lies in the mind of omniscient God. On the contrary, the book definitely embodies Edwards' time and place; it is the history of Northampton writ large. It is a cosmic rationalization of the communal revival, and the unrevised portions contain assertions, delivered out of sheer conceit, for which Edwards later did penance. It obliges the history of the world to conform to the experience of Abigail and Phebe and Sarah, and, as frequently happens with a work of art—with *War and Peace*, for example—the artist survives his creation to recognize that even at its finest it is rash and arrogant.

He saw the over-all design of history as a steady progress from the fall of Adam to Christ, then a reversal of direction with the coming of the Saviour, and thereafter "a finishing state," where all is spent "in finishing things off which before had been preparing, . . . in summing things up, and bringing them to their issues." But in each of the two phases, though the work is steadily carried on, there is a constant rising and falling; not deviations or repetitions, but the zigzag course of a ship making head against the wind, every tack putting it farther on its voyage. The systole and diastole of time is like that within the person: it "has its ups and downs," but all the while, "in general, grace is growing." A declension, thus, should be interpreted as a preparation for the next and greater exertion: "the event is accomplished in a further degree than in the foregoing." As there are ebbs, so there are floods, each mounting higher toward the goal of history.

Though the large design is constant progress, from Adam to Christ, from Christ to the Judgment, within these segments of time the morphology is retreat and advance, and the work "has mainly been carried on by remarkable pourings out of the Spirit of God." History moves through a pulsation of "special seasons," interspaced with exhaustion and backsliding. The prophets were revivalists, early Christianity was a revival, and so was the Reformation. The intervals are necessary in the design as times for the gathering of forces; in each resurgence more men are changed (or men are more changed) than in the preceding. And—here lay the martyrdom and the temptation—every revival must have a leader: a Paul, a Luther, or a Calvin. "Time after time, when religion seemed to be almost gone, and it was come to the last extremity, then God granted a revival, and set some angel or prophet, or raised up some eminent person, to be an instrument of their reformation." Edwards could not claim to be an angel, and modesty forbade that he think himself a prophet; but in the unchastened pride of 1739 he had no doubts as to what eminent person was to be the instrument of New England's reformation. With the experience of 1735 behind him, he prepared himself for the next and mightier surge which could be so great—who in 1739 dared deny?—as to sweep the race into the millennium itself.

Edwards, in art and in doctrine a conservative, preached in the very face of rationalism and Deism the fulfillment of prophecies. He preached chiliasm in its starkest form. According to this ancient doctrine, there will come "a very dark time," which will be followed by a thousand years of the reign of Christ on earth; then one more dip into apostasy, brief but violent; and at last the immense rush of "Christ's immediate appearance to judgment." And in 1739, as he looked upon the eighteenth century, did not the signs seem to be shaping toward an inauguration of the millennium? There had certainly been a long—longer than average—time of darkness (New England had listened for so many generations to its denunciation of itself that it could comprehend the age on no other premise). The state of religion was low indeed, riddled with heresies: Anabaptism, enthusiasm and Quakerism, Socinianism, and particularly Arminianism and Arianism, which spread among even Dissenters—among the saving remnant of the chosen—and now actual Deism, "which of late exceedingly prevailed among Protestants, and especially in England." And then, as all prophecies said would be the situation on the eve of the millennium, knowledge and science were grown great, surpassing even the zenith of the ancient world. "So now learning is at a great height at this day in the world, far beyond what it was in the age when Christ appeared; and now the world, by their learning and wisdom, do not know God; and they seem to wander in darkness, are miserably deluded, stumble and fall in matters of religion, as in midnight darkness." Since the last dilatation of the Reformation, which was the Puritan revolution, "the Papists have gained ground: so that the Protestants now have not so great a proportion."

All this, interpreted in the light of history, had meaning: it meant that piety had sunk so far only because it was about to rebound more gloriously than ever. "God in his providence now seems to be acting over again the same part which he did a little time before Christ came." And finally, there were signs that the upswing was commencing, exactly as the true light began to dawn in the darkest night of antiquity, in the Rome of Augustus and Virgil. There was already a revival of religion in Germany, "through the endeavors of an eminent divine there, whose name was *August Herman Frank*"; and there was also, of course, Northampton in 1735. It would be, said Edwards, ungrateful not to notice the pouring out that had lately come upon this part of New England, "of which we, in this town, have had such a share." He did not, however, need to describe it to those that had been eye-witnesses.

In preaching this chiliastic vision, and in centering it upon himself, Edwards appears perhaps at his worst, or at least at his most pitiable. He committed the mistake for which he paid in full: he insinuated that history could and might culminate in Northampton. True, he did not openly claim it, but he let slip some injudicious sentences that sounded as though he did, and rumors spread through New England "that I have often said, that the millennium was already begun, and that it began at Northampton." Charles Chauncy, to whom the chiliastic myth was stuff and nonsense, seized upon these stories, and Edwards was obliged to write in 1744 to Scotland that because "a doctor of divinity in New England, has ventured to publish this report to the world," he must explain that he had never considered the late revivals as more than forerunners of the ultimate glorious light. He always taught, he insisted, no matter how wonderful might be New England's reformation, that there were still conflicts, convulsions, and intermissions to come. Yet from the original sections of the *History of Redemption*, the historian has little difficulty in comprehending how ordinary Yankees, whose knowledge of history was highly impressionistic, gathered from Mr. Edwards that the revival which flared up again in 1740 was the commencement of Christ's reign, and that Northampton was its capital, and thereupon surrendered themselves to ecstasies that left them writhing on the floor of the meeting-house, or found them clasped in the arms of their neighbors' wives or daughters.

So it is hardly possible to exonerate Edwards entirely, or to term what he wrote to Scotland in 1744, after the reaction had set in, an accurate version of what he preached in 1739. The *History of Redemption* all too clearly brought the people to the very threshold of the millennium, and he was obviously intoxicated with the prospect. Here was the particular fault from which in the general censure his heroic virtue took corruption, and the *Farewell Sermon* declares that there shall be a judgment upon ministers as well as upon the people. But modern students will probably agree with Chauncy that it is not so much his appropriation of the chiliastic hope to himself that renders Edwards culpable as his believing such a manifest absurdity at all. It seems difficult indeed to take Edwards seriously as philosopher or scientist when he used his wisdom for declaring, "And now the time is come; now the seventh trumpet sounds, and the seventh vial is poured out."

Yet, before we dismiss the millennial lore as so much foolishness, let us note that Sir Isaac Newton, after his crisis of 1692, devoted the rest of his life to studying the fulfillment of prophecies, and spent more years than he devoted to devising orbits for planets and comets to fixing the precise date for the pouring out of the seventh vial. He used experimental methods to link the major events of history with the prophecies, and reached the conclusion that the millennium could not be far off. Fragments of these speculations were published, claiming the respect of the learned world, and were cited by Edwards in the *History of Redemption*. Neither may we comfort ourselves by calling these speculations the amusement of Newton's dotage, for that would be to miss the significance which chiliasm long had for Western culture, the hidden intellectual purport which justified minds as vast as Newton and Pascal and Edwards in occupying themselves with it. The scientific movement of which Pascal was the prophet, Newton the culmination, and Edwards the student, was not a laboratory for devising labor-saving appliances; it was an effort to capture in mathematical formulae the meaning behind the phenomena, to reach to the very sensorium of God. For such scientists, the Books of Daniel and of the Revelation were as much data as were Halley's tabulations of his comet.

In fact, Edwards' exposition of the chiliastic theory in his revival preaching must be viewed as an outcropping in New England of a radical vein which the conservative and reactionary of Christendom had for centuries endeavored to keep submerged. As Paul Tillich points out, by Augustine's identification of the millennium with the triumph of the church, history was represented as reaching its last period in the reign of the hierarchy, and no radical criticism was any longer possible or permissible. But the doctrine of the "third stage" could not be stamped out, and wherever there was a revolt of the people it gave direction and meaning to rebellion. Among the Anabaptists, for instance, and among the Puritan sectaries of the English Civil Wars, chiliasm was a mighty engine of revolution. "In all these movements," Tillich says, "the future is the decisive mode of time." Something is expected, for which the past and the present are preparations, and the chiliast invariably sees the victory as about to be won, justice about to triumph on earth, either through the immediate intervention of God or (more usually) through revolutionary action under God's direction.

In this light, I believe, we must interpret Edwards' preaching of the millennium; and, once seen in this perspective, his real significance begins at last to emerge. The first founders of New England, Winthrop and Endicott, Cotton and Dudley, were not social radicals. They disliked bishops, and so came to America and set up Zion; though they had no hierarchy, they established an order, and they did not want radical criticism of it. Hence in their doctrine of the covenant they presented God as bringing things right in a proper and gradual fashion, and so could encounter utopianism with the charge of enthusiasm. They looked upon the outburst of millenarianism among the sects in Cromwellian England, and they shuddered. When New England preachers expounded prophecies of the millennium, they made clear that the reign of Christ was not to begin for many centuries to come, so that for the present we must be visible saints and submit to church discipline. Yet for a hundred years New England had been, as everybody agreed, declining in spirit, while at the same time, especially after about 1715 or 1720, waxing prosperous. It was natural that as the preachers denounced worldliness and threatened divine judgment, they should talk of disaster and conflagration, and even invoke the Day of Judgment; but most of them, especially the free and catholic wing, were extremely chary of suggesting that the reformation they were demanding should become a thousand-year administration of social justice.

Edwards brought this hidden and hitherto deliberately suppressed doctrine into the light of day, and he not only shocked Chauncy's intellect, he raised the specter of a revolutionary slogan. Why Edwards advanced it, we may begin to make out as we review his denunciations of the age, and note particularly what he perceived the Arminian spirit became when translated into the ethics of traders and land speculators. Edwards' exposition of the millennial expectation, therefore, on the eve of the Great Awakening, was not a return to atavistic myth; it was the proclamation of a radical thesis, for which there was the scientific authority of Sir Isaac Newton as well as of Scripture, and which alone, as he saw the plight of American culture, was powerful enough to check the depredations of the river gods.

We are here, of course, upon treacherous ground. Not only is chiliasm nowadays an unfashionable notion—at least in its Biblical form!—but Edwards is traditionally cast in American history as the conservative and reactionary. He is pictured as in opposition, on the one hand, to the liberal Chauncy and the enlightened Gay, and on the other to the rising democracy which, in the person of Timothy Root, refused to worship a wig. In the very months when Edwards was trying to whip his congregation into submission, and in the prevision of defeat was forming in his mind the stately cadences of the *Farewell Sermon*, certain that on the Day of Judgment all recalcitrant people would meet their ministers before the bar, "without any hopes of relief or remedy, or getting any good by their means"—at that very time in Boston the latest and most advanced apostle of the free and catholic spirit, Jonathan Mayhew, was telling his people, amid quotations from Mr. Locke, that to attempt to dragoon men into religious orthodoxy was like trying to dragoon them into becoming poets or mathematicians. "A blow with a club may fracture a man's skull; but I suppose he will not think and reason the more clearly for that; though he may possibly believe the more *orthodoxly*, according to the opinions of some." By "some," he meant Edwards, and perhaps, he added, such persons act very prudently, "for their doctrines are generally such as are more readily embraced by a man after his brains are knocked out, than while he continues in his senses, and of a sound mind." In 1765, a year before his death, Mayhew was to become New England's spokesman against the Stamp Act; Chauncy was to become a patriotic agitator, and he goes down in history (as do most of the free and catholic connection) a liberal in theology, an advocate of the rights of man, and a champion of Americanism in all its phases. To call Edwards, the rejected autocrat of Northampton, the radical as against these liberals, may well appear a wanton distortion of history.

However, one or two considerations are frequently overlooked by historians and eulogists. When Mayhew was ordained at the West Church, on June 17, 1747, he was the first openly avowed Arminian to ascend a New England pulpit; of the free and catholic group, only Ebenezer Gay had the courage to preach his ordination sermon, although Chauncy, who envied Mayhew's free speaking, was his friend. During the Awakening, Mayhew had watched from the safety of the Harvard Yard, whence he emerged in 1744 filled with a deep conviction that reason must determine whether even revelation itself bears the proper credentials, and with a white hatred for all enthusiasts. "These enlightened Ideots make inspiration, and the Spirit of truth and wisdom, the vehicle of nonsense and contradictions."

Edwards had heard the reverberations of Mayhew's artillery by the time he delivered the *Farewell Sermon:* if Arminian principles prevail in Northampton, "as they very lately have done in another large town I could name, formerly greatly noted for religion," the result will be spiritual ruin. This was Edwards' last public defiance of the metropolis; but from his observatory in Stockbridge, he could study, as he had studied spiders, the writhings of the free and catholic sect as Mayhew embarrassed them by blurting out what was in their own minds. In 1757 he ventured to write from Stockbridge to the now venerable Professor Wigglesworth, the preceptor of Mayhew, who linked the New England of the French and Indian War with the New England Edwards had first addressed in 1731—a period that now seemed as remote as that of Winthrop. Although, he said, "I can't assign any particular acquaintance as my warrant for troubling you with these lines," he still called upon the cautious Wigglesworth, as the one "set for the instruction of our youth in divinity in the principal seminary of learning," where pernicious principles were most likely to spread, to speak out. Edwards had heard that Wigglesworth was not in good health, but still, in a just war, men are called to great fatigues, "and to very great ventures even of life itself."

Wigglesworth's reply is a shuffling evasion: he sent Edwards one of his lectures in which he manfully defended the canon of the Old Testament, but as for publishing against Mayhew and similar heretics, that would be only "to encourage hungry printers." Let disputation be kept at a comfortable distance in England; if we in New England write against each other, "Upon so interesting a subject, I greatly fear that the debate will be managed with so much acrimony and warmth on one side, and perhaps with such an intermixture of threat and sarcasm on the other, as would be a great disservice to the interests of religion." Besides, were such a controversy begun, neither he nor Edwards would live to see the end of it; you and I, the Professor dared to say to Jonathan Edwards, aim at the same end, "though we may not have the same sentiments about the means to compass it."

Thus Edwards made a last effort to call the liberals' bluff, to force them to live up to their formal profession, or else openly to go all the way with Mayhew and renounce it, as had long been evident they should. Wigglesworth declined the challenge, not in the name of intellectual honesty, but of prudence, which has so often been the standard of enlightened Boston and Harvard. Edwards had now to acknowledge, "I live one side, far out of the way," but it was axiomatic to him "that Christians may be evidently called, in adverse providences, to engage in very irksome and laborious services, and to run considerable ventures in the cause of their Lord."

When Mayhew ultimately defied Lord Bute, and Chauncy Lord North, they were not called to an irksome or laborious venture. In Boston they spoke for the same interest that was represented in the Valley by Whittelseys, Williamses, and Hawleys, for the self-reliant entrepreneurs of New England, who would, when the time came, resist the exactions of the British Parliament in the name of the rights of man, but whose conception of America was no more radical than of a land that should enjoy the rights of Englishmen without English interference. It takes no extension of historical imagination to conceive that had the lot of Chauncy or Mayhew been cast in England, as ministers in Bristol or Lichfield, they would not have been one jot different from what they were in America. By no stretch of imagination can Edwards be supposed anything but the child of the American backcountry, of the Connecticut Valley; he spoke not for cosmopolitanism but for deliberate provincialism, and he was the essence of the old Puritanism which took deep root in the soil and among the stones of New England. It was a spirit that knew no way of compromising with Mammon, least of all with the merchants it had fostered. Edwards' denunciation of businessmen was not just a convention of the pulpit—he meant every word of it; and so the men of business, mobilizing the populace, destroyed him, and only one of them, Joseph Hawley the younger, had the decency to repent.

Edwards' philosophy of history is utterly opposed to what finally became that of Marx, for to Edwards redemption is not to be achieved in history or among objective goods; his career is a flat refutation of what Marxists usually tell as history. He spoke out of an ancient Christian standard which in a commercial society had become as antique as the Druidical. Though he tried to impose it by the majesty of the wig and of Col. Stoddard, those he most outraged were not the Timothy Roots but Israel and Ephraim Williams. His chiliasm was offensive to them, not because it was intellectually or scientifically untenable, but because it was a judgment upon their transactions. They were not angered by abstract condemnations of Arminianism; they became Edwards' sworn foes because his attack upon the Arminian notion of free will arraigned their practice of free enterprise. They and he belonged to entirely separate and irreconcilable universes.

Chauncy, we noted, explained that new creatures, if any such there be, must not assume that by their newness they are enabled to unravel the knots of school divinity, which are the monopoly of the educated. Even when he preached the social contract, he said it in no way signifies "that men cloathed with honor and power should be brought down to a level with vulgar people." Edwards constantly preached (as the "Notes" discover) that persons of "mean capacities" may see what reason requires a long discourse to explain; because grace is sensible, unlettered people may well have the simple idea in perfection when the gentry know it not. Because the heart is the subject of sensible knowledge, simple souls may apprehend more of divinity than Harvard graduates. Edwards admitted that this is a trial for the learned, but still it is a fact: God intermingles stumbling blocks in his providence, "in pouring out of his Spirit chiefly on the common people, and bestowing his greatest and highest favors upon them, admitting them nearer to himself than the great, the honorable, the rich, and the learned." Spiritual knowledge is a taste or a relish that discerns "without being at the trouble of a train of reasoning," and therefore is always accessible to the democracy. For the mass of men, unread in historical monographs, "the evidence they can have from history, cannot be sufficient," but usually, the more men study history, the more they acquire doubts.

Thus, while Edwards wore a wig, his theology contains a democratic implication that was an affront to men like Chauncy. Just as out of his works can be gathered an indictment of the Age of Reason, so also there can be collected a prophetical identification of America with the judgment of righteousness that is, I suggest, a patriotism as deep as Chauncy's. It is not unlikely, Edwards wrote in the flood of the Awakening, that this extraordinary event is the dawning of the really great work, "and there are many things that make it probable that this work will begin in America." The old world slew Christ; the new world, though it does not escape the brotherhood of sin and though its victory shall come in accordance with the dialectic of history, is nevertheless the hope of the world, if there is hope anywhere. In America alone is the spirit of God fully poured forth upon the common people, in plain New England churches. "Whereas till of late, the world was supplied with its silver and gold and earthly treasures from the old continent, now it is supplied chiefly from the new, so the course of things in spiritual respects will be in like manner turned." And if it be that the millennium is to commence anywhere in America, "I think if we consider the circumstances of the settlement of New England, it must needs appear the most likely of all American colonies, to be the place where this work shall principally take its rise."

Chauncy would fight the King of England, once his rights were threatened, but on no such lofty grounds. He fought for tangible ends, for freedom from taxation and for habeas corpus; he was courageous and devoted, but he and his colleagues would have been disconcerted at the suggestion that America, led by New England, was to start a thousand years of heaven on earth. They wanted freedom of the will, and an opportunity to assert (as Chauncy finally did, after immense secret precautions) that all men shall be spared from judgment. Edwards' vision of America as the standard-bearer of Christ's kingdom was not what they had in mind, and assuredly not his further vision of the glorious extension of the kingdom, "that then many of the Negroes and Indians will be divines, and that excellent books will be published in Africa, in Ethiopia, in Tartary, and other now the most barbarous countries." The liberal and Arminian patriots did not contemplate quite so universal a democracy when they endorsed the Declaration of Independence.

After the millennium and the last apostasy, Edwards predicted, will come final judgment. Then will be enacted the scene portrayed in the *Farewell Sermon*, and right shall be done, and there shall be no more argument or dispute about it. The last trumpet shall be "blown in a more literal sense, with a mighty sound that shakes the earth." Sinners of all varieties shall be arraigned: "demure hypocrites, those who have the fairest and best outside, and open profane drunkards, whoremasters, heretics, Deists, and all cruel persecutors, and all that have died or shall die in sin amongst us." The church shall be seen "flocking together in the air to the place where Christ shall have fixed his throne"; but the wicked shall hear the sentence, "every syllable of it will be more terrible than a stream of lightning through their hearts." They shall be left upon the earth, which then, "some way or other," shall be set on fire.

As the scientific doctrine of nature took shape, there was a great expenditure of ingenuity, especially among the English, to prove that even in a world of inviolable law, an end of it could be contrived. Thomas Burnet and Newton's successor at Cambridge, William Whiston, wrote popular tracts to demonstrate that either by an irruption of fires from the center of the globe, or by the near approach of a comet, the prophecies of the Bible could be made good. Edwards was too pure a scientist to resort to such makeshifts. When he preached on history, he told of a beginning and an end, but he did not commit God to any specific agency of combustion. The end shall be by fire "some way or other." The important point was that persecutors of the church—by whom he meant opponents of the Awakening—shall dwell in everlasting fire, "and shall suffer torment far beyond all that their utmost wit and malice could inflict on the saints."

"Edwards' system," said Dr. Holmes, whom I take pleasure in quoting for the last time, "seems, in the light of to-day, to the last degree barbaric, mechanical, materialistic, pessimistic." No civilized man in our day, any more than in Dr. Holmes', can say otherwise if he dwells only on the doctrinal positions. But the deeper consideration, the intellect behind the doctrines, is not so easily dismissed. Edwards did indeed present to the public a scene of judgment and fire; he further demonstrated that those who have not the moral ability to avoid the flames will necessarily suffer unending torments. But the defeated and exiled Edwards, who preached to Houssatunnucks the epic of the Fall, the Redemption, and the Judgment in an even more simplified version, also wrote on the last page of his last great dissertation, on the reason why God created a world that must be given to flames, that there never will come a moment when it can be said that justice is done. He preached that all saints, white, black, or red, shall flock through the air to the throne of Christ, but he said in his final sentence that there will never be a time when it can be said that this infinite good has actually been bestowed.

Again, it must not be lost sight of that, on the surface level of the narrative, Edwards' version of history, past and future, is crude, not to say primitive. It is literal to the point of pedantry. The problem—which in one sense is the problem of this entire study—is what he really meant by it. Does the sculptor of a medieval Last Judgment intend no more than the disproportions of his figures or his foreshortened perspectives? The Edwards who wrote the *History of Redemption* is the same Edwards who comprehended Newton and read deeply into Locke. Hence I believe it not fantastic to suggest —assuming that my reading of him hitherto has been accurate —that in this dramatization of history he was working, nowhere else having such an opportunity so to work, as an artist.

Here he was forcing the Lockean sensationalism as far as possible away from a blank naturalistic passivity toward a creative destiny. He was making the nature of man—a creature of experience—a participant in a cosmic design which is not static, which is not merely an object of contemplation, but a design in time, requiring for its consummation struggle and anxiety, triumph and repeated failure. But his vision was of nothing so simple as a kind of "emergent evolution," because for him the pattern of history, even though implicated in time, is not of time. Even the millennium requires a judgment. There is God in history, but Edwards' version of history is not God. History to him is full, if not of contradictions, then at least of ambiguities and hesitations, which are not resolved in history; instead, the meaning of history is found in their resolutions. For the description—though not necessarily for any chronological specification—the traditional imagery of the millennium and an ultimate conflagration would serve. But he was not beguiled by mythology. There is no date within historical time for the Last Judgment. That is something incommensurate with time. It will come, but not in the sense in which the sun will rise tomorrow. As an event, it is eternal.

Edwards' meaning, as also his part in American history, cannot be defined without a grasp of this paradox. Beginning and ending are terms in a philosophy of history, not in matter-of-factness, and neither can be designated as finite dates in chronology. Edwards' journals frequently explored and tested a meditation he seldom allowed to reach print; if all the world were annihilated, he wrote (ringing changes on Locke's concept of identity as consisting in idea), and a new world were freshly created, though it were to exist in every particular in the same manner as this world, it would not be the same. Therefore, because there is continuity, which is time, "it is certain with me that the world exists anew every moment; that the existence of things every moment ceases and is every moment renewed." The abiding assurance is that "we every moment see the same proof of a God as we should have seen if we had seen Him create the world at first." The Holmesian comment shows itself incapable of appreciating Edwards' point which, even in the goriest passages of the sermons, is an exploration of intelligible meanings, of the dramatic perception, and not a surrender to materialism and pessimism. Truth is in the seeing, not in the thing.

The clerical aristocrat who opposed the river gods in the name of a sensational and emotional apprehension of beauty, who proclaimed it more likely to be perceived by the common man than by the learned and prosperous, was the same man who preached a final judgment that does not arrive in time, but is every moment renewed. It docs not, in scientific fact, belong to history at all, but must be told for the sake of the artistic coherence of the historical conception; therefore, it is a judgment upon history, because history requires it, because history is helpless without it. In that sense—if it can be made sensible in the psychological meaning of the word—it is pronounced anew every moment, and is declared as much at this moment as it shall be in any hypothetical future.

A Note on the Sources

For the general reader, an adequate selection from Edwards' writing is available in Clarence H. Faust and Thomas H. Johnson, *Jonathan Edwards* (The American Writers Series), 1935. The most readable as well as the most reliable biography is Ola Elizabeth Winslow, *Jonathan Edwards*, 1940. Both these volumes contain extensive bibliographies, which may be taken to furnish the bibliography for this work and so need not here be repeated.

Edwards' *Works* were edited by S. Austin, Worcester, 1808, and reprinted in four volumes, New York, 1844 and 1847; I have used this edition. There is also an edition by Sereno E. Dwight, 1829-1830. The major segment of the yet unpublished manuscript is the journal called "Miscellanies" now in Yale University Library; two volumes of extracts from this manuscript were published in Edinburgh: *Miscellaneous Observations on Important Theological Subjects*, 1793, and *Remarks on Important Theological Controversies*, 1796. I have published the entry most pertinent to the rhetorical theory as "Jonathan Edwards on the Sense of the Heart," *The Harvard Theological Review*, XLI, 123-145. A shorter but cognate manuscript I edited under Edwards' own title, *Images or Shadows of Divine Things*, New Haven, 1948. Other writings not included in the collected works are as follows: *Charity and its Fruits*, ed. Tyron Edwards, 1851; *Selections from the Unpublished Writings of Jonathan Edwards*, ed. Alexander B. Grosart, Edinburgh, 1865; *Observations Concerning the Scripture Œconomy of the Trinity*, ed. Egbert C. Smyth, 1880; *An Unpublished Essay of Edwards on the Trinity*, ed. George P. Fisher, 1903. Invaluable for the student of Edwards is Thomas H. Johnson, *The Printed Writings of Jonathan Edwards*, Princeton, 1940. I have published three sermons that exhibit social conditions in Northampton as "Jonathan Edwards' Sociology of the Great Awakening," *The New England Quarterly*, XXI, 50-78. See also, Stanley Williams, "Six Letters of Jonathan Edwards to Joseph Bellamy," *Ibid.*, I, 226-242.

Sereno E. Dwight, *The Life of President Edwards*, 1830, is essential for its detail and for its quotations from letters and manuscripts. A neglected classic of American biography is Samuel Hopkins, *The Life and Character of the Late Reverend Mr. Jonathan Edwards*, Boston, 1765.

As every student of colonial America must be, I am immensely indebted to Clifford K. Shipton for his continuation of *Sibley's Harvard Graduates*. I have been helped by Rufus Suter, "The Conception of Morality in the Philosophy of Jonathan Edwards," *Journal of Religion*, XIV, 265-272, and by his unpublished dissertation in the Harvard College Library; I am further indebted to the unpublished dissertation of Thomas H. Johnson, as well as to his "Jonathan Edwards and the 'Young Folks' Bible'," *The New England Quarterly*, V, 37-54, and "Jonathan Edwards' Background of Reading," *Publications of the Colonial Society of Massachusetts*, XXVIII, 1932-222.

For Edwards' grandfather, see my "Solomon Stoddard, 1643-1729," *The Harvard Theological Review*, XXIV, 277-320. For Colman, see Clayton Hardin Chapman, *The Life and Influence of the Rev. Benjamin Colman*, unpublished dissertation at Boston University School of Theology, of which an *Abstract* is printed, 1948. For Locke I have used the standard edition of Fraser; for Newton I have relied upon the translation and edition of Florian Cajori, *Mathematical Principles*, Berkeley, California, 1934. Colin Maclaurin, *An Account of Sir Isaac Newton's Philosophical Discoveries*, was published in 1748. On the seventeenth-century intellectual background and on technologia I have written at rather too great length in *The New England Mind*, 1939.

In conformity with the policy of this series, the text has not been burdened with footnotes; however, for the assistance of students who may wish to verify my references, a fully annotated copy is deposited in the Harvard College Library.

Index

Index